THE
POWER
OF TWELVE

•

A NEW APPROACH TO
PERSONAL EMPOWERMENT

•

Anne Brewer

Sun star
PUBLISHING LTD.

THE POWER OF TWELVE
A NEW APPROACH TO PERSONAL EMPOWERMENT
by *Anne Brewer*

Sunstar Publishing, Ltd.
204 South 20th Street
Fairfield, Iowa 52556

Graphic Design: Sharon A. Dunn

LCCN: 98-061429
ISBN: 1-887472-70-3

Printed in the U.S.A.

Readers interested in obtaining further information on the
subject matter of this book are invited to correspond with:
The Secretary, Sunstar Publishing, Ltd.
204 South 20th Street, Fairfield, Iowa 52556

For more Sunstar Books, please visit our website:
www.sunstarpub.com

Sunstar
PUBLISHING LTD.

TABLE OF
CONTENTS

CHAPTER ONE • APRIL 1996

CHAPTER TWO • MAY 1996

CHAPTER THREE • JUNE 1996

CHAPTER FOUR • JULY 1996

• • • • • • • • • • • •

• • • • • • • • • • • •

INTRODUCTION

People around the world have become intrigued, inspired, and sometimes even shocked when they hear my story. I have always had a reputation as a successful businesswoman. I spent seventeen years in corporate America, attaining a vice-president position at Sprint, before leaving and starting my own marketing consulting company. As a self-employed consultant for the past six years, I have worked with Fortune 500 companies such as Hallmark, Sprint, JC Penney, McDonald's and Pizza Hut, earning a reputation as an independent female who possesses a strong business savvy.

However, my life as a marketing consultant dramatically changed when three non-physical entities from another dimension entered my life. In April 1996, I received a phone call from a local Kansas City psychic I had briefly met at a party. This woman asked me to visit as my presence had been requested by the non-physical beings with whom she communicated. However, the psychic did not know what the entities wished to share as they refused to provide information until I was present. As might be expected, my curiosity was piqued by this unusual solicitation, so I agreed to a meeting.

This was the advent of a new life for me. During my initial meeting with the psychic, I was introduced to several non-physical beings from another dimension whose voices she channeled in order for us to communicate. These non-physical beings would communicate with me daily over the next year. Their mission was to impart a how-to process on expanding human potential and consciousness, called DNA Recoding. I was familiar with the concept of increasing the energy of two strands of DNA to the equivalent of twelve strands, since this theme sometimes appeared in the metaphysical literature I had been reading for the past ten years. I had read books that contained channeled conversations from non-physical entities like the Pleiadians and Kryon, and I had heard popular lecturers such as Gregg Braden and Drunvalo Melchizedek discuss topics alluding to expanding human potential. Based on this exposure, I had learned that twelve strands are necessary to take human beings to their next stage of self-actualization and awareness. However, none of the purveyors of this information had actually explained how to achieve the twelve-strand energy. Their data simply indicated twelve-strand energy was needed to expand human potential and provide the ability to ascend, i.e., move *consciously* to a much higher level of life experience, unlike birth where we lose our consciousness and have to rebuild it anew each time.

I have always been somewhat of a human potential movement junkie, searching for any information or healing technique that would expand my horizons and create the superwoman I knew I could be if only I knew how. After learning that human beings might not be operating at peak potential based on our genetic blueprint, I was very anxious to uncover the path that would lead me to increased self-empowerment, greater knowledge, better health, more wealth, the perfect mate, and general overall well-being. I guess I wanted to maximize physical life in every aspect of my experience. Plus, I wanted to feel more like a spiritual being having a joyful physical experience instead of a physical being attempting to incorporate spirituality into everyday life. The information I had read thus far created my exuberance for gaining twelve strands of DNA because it indicated the attainment of an improved existence. Ironically, from a scientific perspective, I probably would not recognize a strand of DNA if I saw one, and I certainly had no concept of its biological composition. Fortunately, the first time I spoke to a large group about DNA Recoding, the speaker prior to me covered DNA in his topic and showed several slides. Although I was grateful for the overview, I realized my interest in this process would never have been sustained on a scientific basis. As an art major in college, I found the material entirely too dry to hold my interest.

Despite my scientific ignorance of DNA, I had been focused on my quest to uncover a process for attaining twelve DNA strands, reading books that I purchased in metaphysical book-stores and affirming for the path to greater consciousness to reveal itself. Twelve had been my lucky number when I was a little girl, and I always placed my money on the number twelve at carnival games. Plus, there are a lot of significant twelves. There are twelve months of the year, twelve hours in a day and twelve hours in a night, twelve signs of the zodiac, twelve apostles. In addition, I was born on the twelfth day of the twelfth month of the year. Although I did not discover until later why I had been tapped to receive this information, I was thrilled to participate in the DNA Recoding experience offered to me by my non-physical friends on that propitious day in April 1996, and I held no fear about permitting invisible entities to use me in their experiment.

From the beginning, I diligently recorded the changes I encountered as I experienced the various stages of DNA Recoding. The intent of my journal was twofold: both for me to remember upon reflection what had transpired after I reached my enlightened destination and to inform others what they might experience, should they choose the same process. Because I am not a scientist, I can only share the information in an experiential way based on the changes that occurred in my life as the result of the twelve-strand energy. My book is an account of my personal journey that uncovered my self-empowerment via DNA Recoding. It is also a "recipe" for DNA Recoding, a defined approach for those interested in pursuing a specific methodology.

In the beginning of this process, I did not fully realize I was the sole creator of my life experiences. I viewed my non-physical friends as the ones who were orchestrating my life and managing the DNA Recoding since they seemed so much wiser than I. I have since gained such understanding and empowerment that I realize I am the one orchestrating my life from a physical and non-physical perspective. If I am to represent the results of a process that enhances human functionality, I can only do that as a self-empowered individual. My life is a process of creation, set forth by my intention to live every day in health, wealth, and happiness. I believe that Divine Creator energy resides in all of us, and our creation power grows significantly once we learn how to use it. The quality of the outcomes we experience from life are contingent on our understanding of ourselves as a creator and our retrieval of that power.

The original *Power of Twelve* was written in 1996 and 1997, and it was published in 1998. It became apparent in 1999 that I needed to rewrite the book for many reasons. Since the initial publication, I continued to learn more and more about the power that occurs from altering our genetic blueprint, since the power expands over time. I learned how to bypass some of the difficulties I encountered during my initial exposure to DNA Recoding, difficulties that caused concern in the original book among those less foolhardy than I. I also learned some methods for simplifying as well as expediting the process. By working with others, I learned that some of the guidelines I was given by my guides in 1996 did not fit everyone and needed to be modified. Most importantly, I had only experienced three phases in the DNA Recoding process by 1997 when, in fact, there are five phases associated with this particular method. Needless to say, we are only able to recognize unfinished business when we have the capacity to notice that something is missing. It took until 1999 for me to realize there were more stages to DNA Recoding than I had initially published. Although I did not relish the thought of rewriting *The Power of Twelve*, I also felt a responsibility to ensure the information I shared was accurately aligned with my experience in order to maintain the integrity of the work.

In addition to my increased knowledge about DNA Recoding, I have also been able to reconcile my feelings of discomfort about the story of human creation that was told to me by my non-physical teachers. Initially, I did not believe them since their version of our origin did not exactly coincide with the Judeo-Christian interpretations of the Bible. Much of the creation story revolved around the concept of genetic manipulation, a technique that might be acceptable in scientific laboratories on animals, but it is not well-received in the context of human development. As a self-employed marketing consultant to Fortune 500 firms, suburban resident, and mother of a teenager who strongly desired to appear normal in his community, I did not want to be identified with information that conflicted with the common interpretation of Genesis. In fact, this new creation story contradicted the Darwinian theory of evolution which had already caused an uproar in the 1850s. Nonetheless, since DNA recoding was responsible for bringing so many positive results into my life, I wanted to share the process. To accommodate the situation, I eliminated much of the creation story information from the original book and focused on the recoding method.

Prior to rewriting *The Power of Twelve*, I encountered two authors who assisted in alleviating my discomfort with the idea of human creation via genetic manipulation. The first author, Zecharia Sitchin, wrote a series of books called *The Earth Chronicles*. In one of the chronicles, *The 12th Planet*, he analyzed Sumerian, Babylonian, Akkadian, Assyrian, and Hittite artifacts recovered from archeological digs that validated the same story of creation given to me by my non-physical communicators. In his book, Sitchin introduced a comprehensive set of facts derived from epic tales, public records, astrological charts, decorative murals, and so forth, that leave the reader little doubt that an evolved group of heavenly beings resided on Earth prior to human development. According to the Babylonian creation epic which was based on Sumerian information and repeated in similar versions by later civilizations, these heavenly beings were members of an advanced civilization that was intimately involved in the development of the two-strand DNA body we currently occupy. Sitchin's scholarly approach of presenting ancient scriptures, artwork, and celestial maps made me feel almost foolish for doubting the veracity of the information brought by my non-physical team. After all, it was actually recorded in the recovered artifacts!

After encountering Sitchin's material, I learned of another author operating in the same venue, specifically William Bramley, who had written *The Gods of Eden*. Although Bramley's book does not offer the archaeological evidence that Sitchin's work does, he portrays an impressive account of the history of secret societies and the source of their ceremonies and symbolism. He tracks the involvement of the originators of these secret societies and how they have impacted institutions in government, religion, education, and finance to the detriment of the freedom of mankind. The book was a good accompaniment to Sitchin's work because it traced elements of our heritage to the source, namely an advanced group of beings who had developed powerful rituals based on their higher level of awareness and the technology they possessed. They used their rules and rituals to ensure humans remained subjugated to a perception of limitation, passing them down to the general population via designated rulers who came from mankind's gene pool but were given certain privileges based on association with the gods.

I grew more and more convinced there might be another plausible version of the Biblical creation story since the evidence both of these scholars presented was so compelling. I have become increasingly willing to share the creation information my invisible teachers provided. Although people have grown visibly angry and left my seminars upon hearing some of this information, I decided it was necessary to include more details in the Power of Twelve about the creators of the two-strand being. I believe this information enhances the reader's understanding about how the DNA Recoding process works as well as why certain advanced civilizations are interested in helping us.

Based on my business background, my approach to DNA Recoding is similar to following a recipe. Much like a business plan, I have outlined a step-by-step process that anyone can follow at their own pace without taking expensive seminars. According to my personal experience, DNA Recoding is an empowering and approachable process that allows human beings to function at higher skill levels, exponentially increase their psychic abilities, release debilitating emotions of fear and guilt, improve their health, and quicken manifestations. DNA Recoding is not a scientific study of evolution. It is a method of expanding human potential.

I attribute the expanded consciousness and self-empowerment that I experience today to the DNA Recoding process. I tap into the twelve strands of DNA energy which enter my physical body from my energy body through my endocrine system. These extra strands allow me access to twelve rather than two levels of information, resulting in an expanded state of knowledge. I make decisions that are based on a much broader perspective, and they are rarely based in fear and guilt since both of these emotions have been eliminated from my energy field, thus giving me a greater sense of freedom. I have an increased capacity for giving and receiving love. I act more often as a creator rather than a passive recipient or reactor. I feel a much stronger sense of purpose. And I tend to live in the present rather than focusing on the past or brooding about the future.

Among my many personal manifestations, I attained the courage to leave a love relationship that was not working and found and married my perfect partner in the course of three months. I also generated enough income within one year to buy my five-thousand square foot house back from my previous lover, and I paid off my entire mortgage the following year. I also was able to conquer several health problems due to my increased energy and the complete balancing of the endocrine system that is required in order to recode.

Based on my newly-found powers, I have created a thriving metaphysical practice, InterLink, which offers a fresh yet practical approach to removing blockages to the joy and peace that all of us want in our lives. I address broad areas of human experience, including balance, well-being, love, relationships, purpose, manifestation, and spirituality. In addition to this book, I published a second book entitled *Breaking Free to Health, Wealth, and Happiness, 100's of Powerful Ways to Release Limiting Beliefs*, in September 1999. I continue to act as president of my marketing consulting company although I foresee a complete transition to my healing work in the near future based on increasing demand and the high level of personal satisfaction it brings me. As I discovered through DNA Recoding, life is the ultimate experience of creation. You can expand your capabilities and experience exactly what you want. Or you can settle for less and miss a thrilling and satisfying experience. Which do you choose?

There are many paths available to each of us for reaching greater awareness. This is the path I have chosen for myself and, since it has significantly improved my life, it is the path I have opted to share with others. I have a soul destiny contract to experience DNA Recoding, bringing this particular method of retrieving twelve strands of DNA to others who desire it. For those who resonate with this process, please join me on this journey. For those who do not, I share my story and hope that you learn something that might be helpful to you in your own process.

The transition to a new level of consciousness is nearly upon us. We live in third dimensional bodies and reside in the fourth dimension which is the realm of length, breadth, depth, and time for all animate beings, e.g., humans, plants, animals, and insects. We are currently transitioning to the fifth dimension which is the realm of length, breadth, depth, time, and spirituality, a realm of deepened spirituality through love. As we move closer and closer to the new Light, I open my arms to embrace it rather than fight to retain the familiarity of a way of life that never brought me much joy, peace, or contentment. Join me as our energy frequency expands to encompass us in new physical, mental, emotional, and spiritual aspects. We will all recognize each other as we move toward the Light, a family of beings that originated from the single source of the Divine Creator.

Love and peace on your journey,
Anne Brewer

THE
CREATION STORY,
OUR BEGINNING

DNA Recoding is a process that enables a human being who has two strands of DNA to acquire twelve strands of DNA energy. The following information provides background on how we acquired our two-strand blueprint and why twelve strands of DNA are essential to our next stage of evolution. The information is based on the premise that members of advanced civilizations in other dimensions or solar systems live in a galactic human form which contains more DNA than us, and which therefore has more capabilities. Due to the fire in the great library in Alexandria during the era of Mark Anthony and Cleopatra, we have lost access to much of the information that would delineate our heritage and the advanced race of beings that populated our planet prior to our creation. Otherwise, this would be common knowledge.

Fortunately, there are enough stone remains from the Sumerian, Babylonian, Assyrian, Hittite, and Akkadian societies to outline the creation story. Sumeria emerged around 3800 BC, and it was the first full-blown, sophisticated society that offered written records in the form of stone tablets, decorative murals, cylinder seals, and more. Similar creation stories were repeated in later civilizations like Babylonia, utilizing different names for the characters but referencing the same chronology of events. According to these creation stories unearthed via archaeological digs, an advanced group of beings populated Earth approximately 450,000 years ago, *prior* to the creation of the human being as we currently know it. This advanced group of beings had physical bodies similar to ours, except they contained twelve strands of DNA.

The additional strands enabled these beings to live in their creation energy, manifesting what they desired and eliminating what they did not desire, rather than experiencing a less than optimal life experience due to the negative emotions such as fear and guilt that have tended to motivate us. These beings were extremely telepathic, lived long life spans that made them appear immortal, and were familiar with sophisticated technology. According to the story told to me by my non-physical visitors in 1996 as well as the stories that I eventually learned were on ancient Mesopotamian artifacts, this advanced race "created" the *Homo sapiens* form that we occupy today. This was accomplished through genetic manipulation by merging their genes with the genes of an ape-like primate called the *Homo erectus* that was evolving on Earth approximately 300,000 years ago. According to Sitchin in *The 12th Planet*, genetic tampering from a non-Earth source starts to explain why very common Earth elements like copper and nickel are scarcely present in our biological make-up while very rare elements in our environment like molybdenum are present and play a critical role in enzymatic reactions essential to life.

As might be expected, the two-strand *Homo sapiens* perceived the twelve-strand beings as gods due to their increased capabilities and advanced technology. This was reinforced by the fact that the "gods" lived in the heavens, visiting Earth via "fiery rockets" that landed at specifically designated sites in Mesopotamia, sites that have been indicated on recovered route maps and explored through archeological digs. The gods had access to a great deal of information, ultimately teaching mankind about farming, bringing completely developed grains like barley, hemp, and spelt to Earth that spontaneously appeared in their current form around 11000 BC without any history of development. The gods shared methods for domesticating animals to serve mankind as beasts of burden and food sources. They showed mankind how to build buildings based on advanced engineering techniques, using materials developed through brick making and smelting processes. From one point of view, human beings were created with a limited capacity based on a two-strand DNA blueprint. From another viewpoint, the *Homo erectus* gained millions of years in evolutionary progress based on a genetically manipulated intervention that led to greater capacity much faster.

Although this may sound far-fetched, there is much archeological, geological, and biological evidence to support the theory, and many scientists have devoted their careers to unraveling the mystery. Evolution simply cannot account for the sudden appearance of *Homo sapiens* which occurred 300,000 years ago, virtually overnight according to evolutionary standards, without a shred of evidence of earlier stages of evolvement that would indicate a gradual change in the abilities of the *Homo erectus*. The advanced Australopithecus, the first being to be considered "manlike," existed about 2,000,000 years ago. One million years passed before the next being, the *Homo erectus*, emerged. Then the first primitive man, Neanderthal, surfaced 100,000 years ago. One million years had passed between the Australopithecus and the Neanderthal, yet the stone tools used by Neanderthal man were indistinguishable from the stone tools used by its ancestor. Then, around 3000 BC, *Homo sapiens* appeared as if from nowhere, looking very similar to us. At that point, man was making specialized tools and weapons from wood and bone, using skins for clothing rather than walking around like a naked ape, living in organized societies called clans, and creating cave drawings that indicated a level of sensitivity beyond that of an instinctual animal. Based on the time intervals established from previous hominid species, mankind as we know it should not have appeared for another two to three million years. Evolution simply cannot account for the rapid appearance of *Homo sapiens*, especially when there are no earlier stages to indicate gradual changes among the *Homo erectus*.

Based on our current ability to genetically manipulate and clone animals in test laboratories, the possibility of the *Homo sapiens* being artificially created is not beyond the realm of possibility. Since we have traveled to the moon and sent explorer rockets into the far reaches of our solar system, it also very plausible that beings from a technologically advanced society could "fly." It is critical to appreciate that, unless we had attained a grasp of the fundamentals of genetic engineering, space flight, and the nature of our solar system, as we have only recently acquired them, we would dismiss reference to these items in the

Sumerian artifacts as allegorical rather than real or, in complete ignorance, we would worship these beings as gods.

Imagine how a person living in the year 1000 AD might feel if able to time travel and encounter a modern city with its skyscrapers, airplanes and hospital operating rooms where people's hearts are replaced. Based on this person's ignorance about modern society, he or she might feel they have arrived in a place where the gods had descended from heaven. It is interesting to note there is no word for god in the Sumerian vocabulary. Based on Sitchin's work, the word the Sumerians used was DIN.GIR which means "the righteous ones of the bright pointed objects" or "the pure ones of the blazing rockets." Plus, numerous graphic depictions of the gods show wings as a decorative attachment to their clothing rather than an angel-like attachment to their body. These "wings" were accompanied by helmets, earphones, goggles, and energy packs strapped across the back. All of a sudden, the supernatural abilities of the gods as they traveled from heaven to Earth in rocket ships and conceive babies via artificial insemination starts to sound exactly like us.

What was the origin of this advanced race of beings? We discover the source when piecing together the ancient creation stories that were recovered from the Sumerian and subsequent ancient civilization's artifacts, stories that have been thoroughly analyzed by Sitchin and a host of other scholars he references. Apparently, there is a planet called Nibiru that orbits in a pronounced elliptical path, circling close to the sun and extending far beyond Pluto in our solar system. While our orbit around the sun takes a year, this planet takes 3,600 years to make a complete revolution. Therefore, every 3,600 years, this planet is close enough to Earth to enable interplanetary travel which is exactly what happened. In fact, according to the creation epics that Sitchin has explored and the corresponding story told to me by my non-physical recoding team, a large planet was responsible for creating Earth and the Asteroid Belt by slamming into a much larger planet called Tiamet many years ago. This planet was referenced as Marduk in the Babylonian Epic of Creation since Marduk was the winner of supremacy among the gods by the year 2000 BC, and all references to the planet's original name of Nibiru were stricken from the records. My sources referred to the planet as Nibiru.

My recoding guides referred to our predecessors and creators as the Nibiruans based on the name of their planet. Sitchin called them the Nefilim, a name referenced in our Bible. According to Sitchin, he was studying the portion of Genesis that describes God's resolve to destroy mankind by the great flood, a time when the "sons of the deities" who married the daughters of man were upon the Earth. The Hebrew original named them "Nefilim" which Sitchin's teacher translated as "giants." But Sitchin objected, asking if the more accurate translation was "those who were cast down" within the context of those who descended to Earth. Sitchin was reprimanded and told to accept the traditional interpretation. Fortunately, his persistence at rejecting the current translation led to his theory about the origins of the *Homo sapiens*, called Adam in the Bible. Ironically, I did not become privy to his theory until after I had heard, and essentially rejected, the same far-fetched tale from my spiritual guides.

Neil Freer wrote an interesting book called *Breaking the Godspell* in which he also upholds Sitchin's theories of past Earth residency and periodic visits from an advanced race. Freer feels our attempt to view evolution chronologically interferes with our ability to see the truth. He refers to Ooparts or "out of place artifacts" that have baffled the scientific community because they do not support our chronological expectations of an evolving civilization. However, the Ooparts start to make sense if we incorporate the view that an advanced civilization was present approximately 450,000 years ago that existed in concert with the evolving hominid species on this planet. Unfortunately, since the library in Alexandria housing multitudes of ancient texts was burned, a huge number of records about our heritage have been lost from review. We are dependent on the ancient texts that have been recovered from a few ancient civilizations that existed between approximately 4000 and 2000 BC to piece together the information.

Sitchin offers a convincing theory about Ooparts based on the presence of an advanced population whose remains co-mingle with that of primitive man. He also describes how mankind's march to civilization passed through three distinct stages in recent years, all separated by 3,600 years. These stages are represented by surges in knowledge, followed by a general stagnation until the next surge 3,600 years later. The Mesolithic period occurred circa 11000 BC and was characterized by big surges in agricultural knowledge and the practice of animal domestication. This was followed by the pottery phase in circa 7400 BC when beautiful, sophisticated ceramic pieces fired in kilns emerged. Following another 3,600-year interval, we suddenly experience a full-blown Sumerian civilization around 3800 BC. Apparently, the Nibiruans, or Nefilim according to Sitchin, periodically reviewed mankind's progress and decided what they might introduce to Earth society since they could assemble on Earth or on nearby satellites each time their planet neared the area.

Relying on the creation epics told via ancient artifacts, we discover the Nibiruans waited for Earth conditions to become suitable for dwelling following the Tiamet aftermath when Earth and the Asteroid Belt were formed. In order to separate the Nibiruans who continued to reside on Nibiru from the Nibiruans who moved to Earth and populated it as the ruling class, I will call those on Earth the Nefilim just as Sitchin has. The Nefilim initially landed 450,000 years ago during an ice age that left very few areas habitable due to the existence of large ice sheets and glaciers. They settled in the Mesopotamia area near the Nile river basin, mainly due to the availability of land and water for farming and the wealth of fossil fuels needed for their technology. As more land emerged around 430,000 BC, they moved inland. Based on the recorded data, the Nefilim consisted of descendants of Anu, who was the ruler of Nibiru at the time, and the Anunnaki, who were the working class. When I initially visited the psychic in 1996 who introduced me to my non-physical friends, she channeled an entity who called himself Devin. Later, he told us he was the prior ruler of Nibiru, Anu, who was involved in creating our two-strand DNA composite. He was concerned about sharing his true identity because he did not wish to overwhelm me by his stature. However, his subterfuge was lost on me because I did not encounter his identity until 1997 when I read *The 12th Planet*.

Anu had entrusted his son Enlil to rule Earth. However, he had two other children, Enki and Ninhursag, who played key roles in the unfolding of our creation and our resulting survival. Although Enlil had been assigned to rule Earth as the eldest son, Enki was the first to arrive on Earth, and he spent many years building dams, creating fertile river valleys for crops, and building homes. Enlil and Ninhursag arrived later when living conditions were more favorable. Similar to how royalty is structured today, the members of the immediate royal family and their extended family made the rules and the general population, called the Anunnaki, implemented them. Given the incredibly long life spans of this civilization, the rulers stayed the same for what seemed like eons.

Earth's natural resources seemed to be a major draw for the Nibiruans, particularly gold, since they constructed cargo ships that were filled from ore extracted from the mines in Africa and sailed them to Mesopotamia. Per my sources, the atmosphere around Nibiru was eroding, and particles of gold dust were utilized to maintain healthy conditions. The value of gold has persisted to this day where jewelers charge an exorbitant amount of money for a relatively common commodity. The Anunnaki were responsible for mining, and they conducted this onerous task for forty "shars" or 144,000 years. This early drilling has been substantiated via carbon testing where mines were found in Africa dating as far back as 100,000 BC, an interesting fact given that the primitive man of that time did not possess the drilling tools needed for this type of mining operation. After 144,000 years, the Anunnaki mutinied and refused to continue their role as laborers due to the unpleasantness of the task.

Apparently, Anu agreed with the Anunnaki's feelings about the difficulty of their manual toil because he instructed his son, Enki, and his daughter, Ninhursag, who was chief medical officer on Earth, to create a primitive worker. In casting around for a solution, it occurred to the brother and sister team that Earth offered a docile, herd-like creature in the form of the *Homo erectus*, who might be able to be fashioned for their needs. Its current form was useless as a docile worker because it was too wild to follow orders, unable to grasp and use the tools necessary for mining, and unable to understand orders. After many genetic experiments that produced a host of bizarre results, all described in the epic tales, Enki and Ninhursag were able to create a viable worker.

The brother/sister team mixed the genes of the *Homo erectus* with those of the Nibiruans to produce a hybrid, much as we would cross-fertilize a mare with a donkey to create a mule. The fertilized egg was placed in the womb of a volunteer, Enki's wife, and the first acceptable model was produced. They called this hybrid a "lulu" which meant "primitive" or "primitive worker." The lulu had enough intelligence to take orders, yet did not possess the capacity to replicate the lifestyle of the "gods." This was accomplished by including twelve strands of DNA in the physical make-up but de-activating or de-coiling ten of the strands to reduce capabilities. When analyzing DNA, scientists reference the "junk" DNA present in our genetic blueprint because there appears to be more than we use. Given the operating efficiency of organisms, I find it difficult to believe an animate being has leftover junk in their system. Every cell, organ, mineral, enzyme, and so forth perform a very specific purpose, and any disruption to that purpose causes disease. Theoretically, our junk DNA may very well be the material needed for the additional ten strands that have been de-activated.

The initial primitive worker or lulu created by Enki and Ninhursag could not propagate since, like all hybrids, it only had one set of hereditary chromosomes and two are needed for reproduction. Nibiruan females were designated as birth goddesses, and their role was to receive artificial insemination and bear the offspring. However, like the Anunnaki, the birth goddesses tired of their role as producers of the work force, and after a while they rebelled at being treated like baby-making machines.

Enki and Ninhursag returned to the drawing board and developed a model that could propagate, calling it the Adapa, or Adam from the Bible. The Adapa is the *Homo sapiens* prototype that we know because it is us! By this time, Enki had become exceptionally fond of his creation, and often played the role of mankind's protagonist in the ancient epics. On the other hand, Enlil grew increasingly hardened to his slave race since the Nibiruans were beginning to become sexually involved with mankind's offspring, and a weakening of the Nibiruan racial strain as well as an upgrading of mankind's racial strain was occurring. Enlil was determined to eliminate the problem, creating many years of strategically induced sickness, pestilence, drought, and starvation to reduce the population of mankind.

Approximately 13,000 years ago, Enki seized an opportunity created by the approaching orbit of Nibiru and the unstable ice caps caused by the warming trend on Earth as it moved out of the last ice age. Knowing the gravity pull of Nibiru would cause a disturbance on the Earth that would dislodge the slushy ice caps, he forbade the Nefilim to forewarn mankind of the impending disaster. His goal was to eliminate the new race, a race that was dangerously close to becoming one of them. However, Enki could not resist sharing the information with his servant and friend, known as Noah in the Biblical version of the Deluge, and he taught his servant how to build an ark (the word literally translates as submarine which makes more sense given the severity of the flood) and stock reserves. Several days prior to the tidal waves that destroyed the planet, all of the Nefilim entered their rocket ships and orbited around the Earth until the water had receded. Upon disembarking and discovering that Enki had disobeyed him, Enlil was furious. However, he was also a practical man, and based on the level of devastation he surveyed, Enlil realized he could not rebuild the civilization without the help of manual workers.

This was a turning point in mankind's development, called the Mesolithic Era, since mankind was taught agriculture and animal domestication in order to develop a food and labor source. Sophisticated grains like spelt and barley appeared instantaneously whereas mankind had been hunter-gatherers prior to this development. Cows began grazing in fields and being used as a source of milk and beef, reducing the need to hunt for food. From an archaeological perspective, many have been puzzled by this rapid emergence of sophisticated techniques given the primitive ability of mankind just prior to this era.

Some say the Nefilim tampered with our DNA strands eons ago because they wished to use mankind for their own purposes, thereby limiting our abilities. However, we would be millions of years behind on the evolutionary tree without the creativity of the

Nefilim. Nibiru is due to return soon on its 3,600-year orbit, and some say the scientists have already viewed its approach but are hesitant to share the information due to the fear that might result. Based on all I have learned, I feel it is inevitable the Nefilim will return. However, I intend for them to greet me as a peer rather than as a member of a slave race. I believe DNA Recoding grants us our freedom because it enables us to have access to the same level of information the Nefilim used.

For many years, I had a recurring dream about traveling to a distant city and either losing my purse or having it stolen. I was unable to return home because I had no money or credit cards and, in my dream, no one would assist me. I felt like Steve Martin trying to get home but barely making progress in *Trains, Planes, and Automobiles*. Finally, I realized what my dream meant. I was relying on external items like money to give me the power to obtain what I wanted. Instead, I needed to utilize my internal resources, my self-empowerment, to achieve my goals. It was time for me to leave my "purse" behind, knowing I could reach my destination by relying on me and only me. DNA Recoding is a process that allows us to tap into a level of cosmic energy that will always provide us with what we need, whether we are carrying a purse or standing completely naked.

As a final note, I would like to address the motivations beyond the Nibiruan involvement. When I initially learned about DNA Recoding, I was informed that I needed to make a formal request to the "Sirian/Pleiadian" council in order to be approved for the process and begin it. At the time, I did not much care who was spearheading the operation since I was focused on my great fortune of obtaining access to DNA Recoding. Later, I wondered if I had unwittingly allowed some extraterrestrial group to infiltrate my energy under the guise of improving my state of being. However, as you will learn as you read the book, many fortunate conditions occurred which validated the love and support I was receiving.

I assumed the Pleiadians were involved because their cohorts on Planet Nibiru had originally altered the DNA of the evolving *Homo erectus* on this planet, and I felt the planetary councils would expect them to be involved. However, I later learned that the Sirians and Pleiadians are tied to our progress since they reside in our solar system. According to Val Valerian in *Matrix IV*, scientists determined in 1990 that our solar system is energetically tied to the Sirian system. Apparently, we rotate around the galaxy in a spiral corkscrew path that is connected to our Sirian counterparts. I am sure we will discover one day that we are equally tied to the Pleiadian system in some way. Given that energy is interrelated and we live in a cosmic soup of interlocking blueprints and matrices, I believe the Sirians and Pleiadians are confined in terms of their own progress until we move up the evolutionary scale. We are like a giant rubber band, continually snapping them back when they try to move forward since we share the same energy soup. I would like to believe the Sirians and Pleiadians are motivated by love, wanting to help their fellow galactic humans. Whatever the motivation, I am simply grateful they are contributing time and energy to helping us move closer to our Divine aspect of pure positive perfection.

A BRIEF
DEFINITION OF
DNA RECODING

DNA Recoding is a process that allows us to evolve from two-to twelve-strand beings by deactivating implants that prevent us from receiving the energy of twelve DNA strands. The reconnection of this circuitry enables us to have access to twelve levels of spiritual, emotional, physical, and mental awareness and information instead of the two levels available from two strands of DNA. Access to twelve levels results in expanded consciousness for human beings which manifests in characteristics such as:
- Operating at full evolutionary potential;
- Increasing psychic abilities;
- Releasing debilitating emotions of fear and guilt;
- Quickening skills for manifesting;
- Improved health by balancing the endocrine system;
- Living in path and purpose; and
- Positioning ourselves for ascension.

Some of you have asked to move to the next stage of consciousness, whether you call it DNA Recoding or activations, ascension, enlightenment, and so forth. Anyone who has asked for spiritual growth will, of course, move forward to the next stage. However, please understand that the method of DNA Recoding described in this book involves working with new spirit guides called genetic engineers to activate the de-coiled DNA programs in our system. According to my non-physical recoding advisors, energy implants were put in place to de-magnetize the twelve strands of DNA that actually reside in our system, thereby preventing them from aligning. Removal of these energy implants has to occur in order for our twelve strands to recoil and fuse, even in energetic form.

When we regain twelve strands of DNA, those twelve strands are initially attained energetically through our astral body since our physical body is currently too dense to accept the extremely high energy frequency of ten additional strands. The astral body is our bridge between our physical and spiritual existence. Those who have had a near-death experience are separating from their physical body with their astral body compelled to walk toward the white light they describe seeing. However, the astral body is still connected to the physical body via an energy cord and, given the inappropriate timeliness of the individual's passing, the cord is not severed in order to allow him to move into the astral planes. The astral body, when truly severed from the physical body at death, enables a soul to move into the astral planes and reside there until the next incarnation. Just like in a near-death experience, the astral body can travel, while you sleep, to other dimensions, yet allow your essence to remain connected to your physical body in order for work to be conducted on your DNA implants.

Some people are disappointed to discover that this DNA Recoding process does not change their physical DNA. However, I am a firm believer that we must alter our energy blueprint before we can effectively change anything in our physical experience. I have worked with many people who have blocks and barriers at the soul level from previous lifetimes. These programs cause them to have physical symptoms in this lifetime. For example, someone dying a prolonged, painful death of syphilis in a prior lifetime may encounter sexual organ problems, e.g., cysts, cancer, infections, in this lifetime since the trauma from the previous lifetime sits in the soul memory. Modern medicine treats the symptom by prescribing medicine or surgery, yet often these problems are recurring. When repatterning work is conducted to remove the old blueprint, often these physical problems disappear. This is the premise behind energetic DNA, that is, you must first incorporate the new program at the energetic level in order for it to manifest itself on a physical level, whether it occurs in this lifetime or future lifetimes when we have attained the critical mass needed to shift to a new pattern.

According to my guides, we would not care to reside in our body if it housed twelve strands of DNA because it would be too painful. It would give us more amps than we are designed to handle. Integrating the twelve strands into our astral body is the first step toward enjoying expanded consciousness because it establishes a higher frequency. The second step involves "plugging" the twelve strands of DNA into our endocrine system. Thus, we have access to the power of the twelve-strand energy without even needing to carry it in our body!

ANU
SPEAKS

Since Anu was the ruler on Nibiru when the Homo sapiens *was formulated and he was an active participant in my initial contact with DNA Recoding, I asked a trance channeler to share her voice and allow Anu to share his personal thoughts with you. The following message was channeled by "N," the name I use to refer to the psychic who contacted me in April 1996 and the psychic who introduced me via Anu to the notion of recoding.*

Greetings brothers and sisters of the Light. It is time for you to embrace a wonderful gift that is now yours. It is the opportunity to gain your full power through the realignment and fusion of your twelve strands of DNA. It is with great joy that I come to serve you by sharing the knowledge with you of this endeavor that you are now ready to embrace. I will give you a brief background on how this came to be.

I am of your parent race, the Pleiadians, and I am the one who was ruling the planet Nibiru, a planet of the Pleiades, when your two-strand DNA body was created. Nibiru is a planet with a wide elliptical orbit that travels the galaxy to protect human colonies on many planets. Initially, when Nibiru entered your solar system, it collided with a planet called Tiamet. Due to the collision, Tiamet shattered and one part became the Earth and the other part the Asteroid Belt.

Through millions of years, with the Sirians and your planetary hierarchy, we seeded Terra with various life forms and made it the beautiful planet that you see today. Ultimately, we decided to colonize it. We came 450,000 of your years ago to mine gold. During that time, we created a two-strand DNA vehicle for a particular group of souls. Our objective was to expedite growth among these souls since they had come into your Earth plane and gotten trapped reincarnating into animals. These were beautiful souls who had made this choice but could not seem to move beyond it, and we were given the task of creating a body that would give them the opportunity to evolve to galactic human status. Naturally, we also saw an opportunity to utilize these souls as they evolved, employing them in the mines that were established on Earth at the time to extract gold for use on Nibiru. My son, Enki, and my daughter, Ninhursag, created the two-strand vehicle for this group.

Although my children created a two-strand being, they also included the additional ten strands carried by the Pleiadian (Nibiruan) race. This was done by artificially inseminating the Pleiadian women with sperm from the original Earth soul group. Two of the strands were coiled to create the necessary DNA helix to create the new being. Obviously, two strands were needed since this was the minimum number needed to create any animate being. The remaining ten strands were de-coiled with implants. You may wonder why twelve strands were placed in the vehicle of these souls rather than confining it to two strands. Twelve strands were implanted in order to infuse the promise of the ultimate potential of this new soul group.

We, as the parent race, watched over this evolving being. Initially, the being was very limited as we used it to work the mines. It exhibited a herd behavior but could not propagate. Eventually, my children Enki and Ninhursag, felt compelled to upgrade the being in the form of Adamis, the story of your creation. This is the version of the vehicle you inhabit. We have been with you through this journey of all these thousands of years, sending beings from other places such as the Office of the Christos to expedite your growth. They would keep the Christ consciousness anchored as this two-strand soul group continued to evolve.

Now, you are the result of many eons of evolution, and you are at the place where you are ready to own your full power. I, Anu, have come to share this knowledge with you and to let you know you are ready for that power. I am karmically connected because of my children and myself. I wish to serve you and be here with you as you regain this power that is rightfully yours. I am heading up the Nibiruan Council, working with the Galactic

Federation, the different councils of the Federation, and your Planetary Hierarchies to fulfill this wonderful endeavor. I wish you all the best in going through this process, and I am with you. I love you as any parent would love their children.

Go in peace and in the Light,
Anu

JOYSIAH
SPEAKS

*I met Joysiah somewhat later in the DNA Recoding process.
He was introduced to me as the chief genetic engineer for DNA
Recoding, and his soul origination is Sirian from the Sirian star
system. Again, I asked the trance channeler who introduced me to
these entities to share her voice and enable Joysiah to speak to you.*

I am Joysiah, a consultant of the Galactic Federation to the Nibiruan Council. I am the Chief Genetic Engineer in charge of the DNA recoding process for human beings. It is with great pleasure that I come to serve you in this endeavor. DNA Recoding is a wonderful right that you have earned, the ability to own your full power and be able to funnel it into your soul contract and complete your work while you are on Earth. This will give you the great joy, prosperity and happiness for which you long.

I would like to begin by giving some information about how this has occurred. When the Harmonic Convergence of 1987 came to be, we knew that we had moved forward in great leaps as far as being able to put this plan into practice. We knew, though, that it would take some time before the souls who had come together for that clearing would be able to clear enough density from their emotional and physical bodies so they would not experience discomfort during DNA recoding. On March 21, 1996, on your Spring Equinox, you were cleared for recoding. Now, there are those who we would not hold back who were recoded before this time, but there were very small groups of them. The mass plan was put into place on March 21 when enough of you were considered clear enough from all of the healing modalities you had employed like acupuncture, massage, Reiki, attunement, breath work, repatterning, and so forth, to begin recoding. At that time, we knew the percentage of success was so great that we could not fail because you had willingly worked on clearing your bodies through the different modalities of healing that you had learned and experienced and brought forward from past lives.

We knew that we needed to begin with those who originated from other planets and star systems, the starseeds, because of their special forms of coding that would enable them to release and clear much easier than the denser humans of that original Earth soul group for which the physical bodies were created in the first place. Therefore, we needed to get the starseeds who currently resided on Earth in third dimensional form to recode first because they would give us a great leap forward in establishing this new higher frequency for the planet. We knew there would be others of the Earth soul group who would be able to recode, but it would take them longer. We needed to initially work with the ones who could move the quickest. Eventually, some of those among the general population will desire to experience DNA recoding, for there are humans of this Earth soul group who need to ground the twelve-strand DNA frequency in the Earth plane.

There is a saying in your Bible that says that knowledge must go out to all people in all parts of the world and then the end would come. This must be fulfilled, and this is the knowledge of recoding. The end is the end of the era of darkness and the beginning of an era where the veil has been dissolved and there will be no separation of dimensions. Recoding is the process through which a human with a two-strand DNA vehicle is able to realign and recapture the twelve strands. This is done through the astral body and filters down into the physical body through the endocrine system. It is not done directly on the physical body because you would not wish to stay in it. You would leave it because it would be too difficult. As much clearing as you have done to your physical vehicle, it is still too dense to hold twelve strands of DNA. Only a spirit body in your dimension can hold twelve strands at this time.

In order to recode, you must have the DNA implants removed that are demagnetizing or de-coiling your twelve strands. You must give us permission to work on your astral body for us to accomplish this task. If you are a starseed, we have communications with your original soul group, and it is decided which way to go. We also counsel with your superconscious self so you are always involved, even if it is on a subconscious level. We actually work on your astral body during your sleep state. The work filters down and is felt by the physical body just as the emotion of joy is felt in the physical body in the form of lightness and elation.

Through the fusion of the twelve strands, you will be able to do things with your mind that will effect your environment such as drawing energy from the universe more effectively, for example, drawing energy through your hands for healing. These abilities will be felt as greater power, a release of fear, a release of guilt, which is all in the mind (or mental body). The power comes through the mind and is felt in the body as joy because there is no longer the implants of fear and guilt, and you feel much lighter because of the clearing of these implants. Yet, you are still in a third dimensional body. As the days unfold you will feel yourself shifting and changing because you have completed DNA recoding, and you will become more fully seeded into new abilities and new feelings. There are no words adequate to describe this feeling. It is otherworldly.

With great love and respect,
Joysiah

CHAPTER ONE
APRIL • 1996

MEETING MY NEW GUIDES

April 17, 1996, was a turning point for me. The information I received that day markedly altered my life from a physical, emotional, mental, and spiritual perspective. April 17 is the day I learned about DNA Recoding, a process that would enable me to function at a higher level of awareness, increase my psychic abilities, release debilitating emotions of fear and guilt, and quicken my manifesting skills. All of these characteristics led to my ability to create a life of health, wealth, and happiness beyond my wildest expectations. Within two years after completing DNA Recoding, I had attained the courage to leave a love relationship that was not working, found and married my perfect partner, generated enough income to buy my house back from my previous lover, and paid off my entire mortgage.

My story began when I was contacted by a local psychic whom I barely knew. I had met her at several parties, but I had never held a personal conversation with her. We had met through a mutual friend, but we were not friends, nor even casual acquaintances. She had recently begun trance channeling, a method of obtaining information from non-physical beings who use the channeler's voice to communicate. For several months, she had been channeling an entity who called himself "Devin." Devin called the psychic by her first initial, "N," which is what I came to call her. N claimed Devin was interested in speaking with me, and he refused to share the objective of his communication until I was present.

Naturally, I was extremely curious about Devin's request since I barely knew N and certainly did not recognize the name Devin. In fact, all but one of my grandparents was still alive so I did not even have family members who had died and wanted to speak to me from the "other side." N and I set a date for me to hear Devin's agenda, and I went to her office on Friday, April 17, in the afternoon. Since we were both intrigued by what Devin had to say, we did not spend much time exchanging pleasantries. We dimmed the lights, shut the blinds, and settled back for a channeling session that would dramatically change my life.

N put herself in a relaxed state and, almost immediately, Devin came through and introduced himself. He was extremely jovial, almost boisterous with his quick wit and booming voice. And the energy was definitely masculine. Although I had experienced channeling several times in the past, I was not very comfortable with it and felt chills on the back of my neck, just like when I was a child and listened to ghost stories at slumber parties. I felt nervous in Devin's presence, sensing his power and feeling his energy surge through the room. Although I did not know N very well, I felt a definitive shift in her personality to accommodate this other being. I certainly did not feel like she was trying to fool me with some silly parlor trick.

Devin was only present a few moments before he said there was another entity who wished to come forward to speak to me. He claimed this new entrant was a dear friend of mine from long ago. I watched as N's body and overall demeanor shifted when Devin departed, and her bearing took on a new disposition as another entity entered it. Again, I associated a strong masculine essence with the second non-physical entity.

A different voice emerged as the newcomer introduced himself. Whereas N had been almost rambunctious while holding Devin's energy, she shifted to a much calmer, gentler, loving attitude. This second entity claimed he was a close friend of mine who had shared many prior experiences with me, both physical and etheric. He said he was extremely pleased to be with me at this time, and I felt the intensity of his pleasure as he communicated it. It was strange to feel the love and closeness exuding from this entity of whom I had no conscious recall.

I apologized for failing to recognize him or remember our past together and asked what I should call him. He said there was no word that came close to his real name, but I could use the name

Laramus since the tones formed by those syllables closely represented his energy. Laramus said he had "checked in" with me several times during my current lifetime, but he had not been very involved to date. I understood the concept of spirit guides, and I was very familiar with the energy of the four guides who assisted me in my daily endeavors. However, I had never sensed the presence of this entity called Laramus. Laramus said he would now be available on a regular basis as my evolution had proceeded to the point where it was necessary for us to reconnect. He called himself my "genetic engineer."

I immediately realized Laramus was the "new guide" referenced in the Kryon material. Lee Carroll channels an energy named Kryon, and I had read several of the Kryon books. Kryon had discussed our spiritual evolution, and he had said we would be moving to a new state of being in the near future. This new state of being has been referenced by many ancient societies, among them the Hopi, Mayans, Sioux, and Cherokee, as well as noted psychics like Nostradamus and Edgar Cayce. Based on past predictions, the shift to a new stage of consciousness would occur by the year 2012, the year that the Mayan calendar ends. Kryon speaks about the shift and the spiritual awareness needed to properly experience it, an awareness created by a twelve-strand DNA energy. He says when we are ready to move into the new consciousness we should request the "Kryon implant," and our request would be acknowledged. At that time, we would be assigned new spiritual counselors as we move forward in our quest for enhanced awareness.

I had read enough about the shift to the new level of consciousness and the need for twelve DNA strands. However, in all of my reading, I had never encountered a method of obtaining the twelve strands. Today, more and more healing practitioners are conducting "DNA activations" in response to the need for the additional strands to expand awareness. However, it was less common in 1996. At the time I visited N and met Devin and Laramus, I had already requested the Kryon implant but was disappointed because of the lack of events in my life that might indicate I was moving into an enhanced consciousness. I knew I needed twelve strands of DNA, but I did not know how to obtain them.

At this point in our discussion, Laramus asked if I was ready to accept the soul contract I had come to Earth to fulfill. He said I would need to accept my soul contract in preparation for receiving my twelve DNA strands. Obviously, I was floored by this statement. I had never discussed DNA with N, much less anyone else, since I did not want people to think I had lost my senses. How did Laramus know I strongly desired the twelve strand energy as an initiator of a better life, both in my current physical state as well as my future transition to spirit? I felt elated, yet trapped. I was unfamiliar with my soul contract and was unsure if I wanted to accept anything from a non-physical entity who might not be as friendly as he sounded. Yet, I had asked for guidance in obtaining twelve DNA strands, and I felt the universe had sent Laramus to provide the answers.

In an attempt to stall for time, I told Laramus I was unfamiliar with the specifics of my soul contract, if any such thing existed. I said I always felt my purpose involved helping others remove blocks and barriers to living a balanced life, but I was unaware of any specific soul contract. In fact, I was in the process of establishing a seminar business that would teach people some basic spiritual principles to support them in their search for joy and peace, a condition I had not fully discovered myself but was hoping to attain.

Laramus said he knew I was unconsciously familiar with my soul contract, and, unfortunately, he could not enlighten me at the time since I was not "ready" to receive the information. Again, Laramus asked if I would accept my soul contract. Intuitively I knew I could accept this contract because I was a positive being who desired a better future for this planet. This gave me some assurance that my soul would only have committed to work that aligned with my higher power and Divine Truth. I also knew I was a member of several soul societies that were part of the Galactic Federation, an organization that was committed to improving the evolutionary cycle of this and other galaxies by moving souls toward spiritual enlightenment. I assumed, and fervently hoped, that if I agreed to this soul contract, I would be agreeing to something that enhanced the greater good of all.

Nonetheless, being trained in corporate business for fifteen years, I began negotiating with Laramus. I asked if, by accepting my soul contract, I would be forced to radically change my life. Would I need to relinquish my loved ones for some spiritual quest or leave a flourishing marketing consulting business for a less comfortable lifestyle, devoting myself to some unknown and, perhaps, zealous cause? Laramus assured me that we lived in a free choice/free will zone, and I would always have choices in my life. He said there would be change, but I would never have more change than I desired to handle since I was the orchestrater of my experiences and was free to create as much or little change as desired. Laramus said the choices I might need to make would come when I was ready, and although some of them might not be gentle, I would feel the need for change. As I have come to understand, when we accept full responsibility for the outcomes in our life, we must credit ourselves with both our successes and failures. This encompasses all physical manifestations as well as our emotional, mental, and spiritual well-being.

Last of all, Laramus said those who remained in my life were meant to be there and those who left were meant to proceed to something else since everyone and everything operated in Divine Order. I knew acceptance of my soul contract would not have an impact on my relationship with my son, Drew, since there was an innate synergy that existed between the two of us. But, something in the manner in which Laramus imparted this information made me wonder how much of an impact my soul contract acceptance would have on my relationship with my partner, Jerry.

Jerry and I were already beginning to experience difficulties. As my spiritual growth expanded, it seemed to distance us more and more. We had known each other for twelve years. In fact, I had met him when he was married, working for him over a period of two years in New Jersey prior to our corporation deciding to relocate me to Kansas City. We had established a strong friendship from the beginning, keeping in touch during the years following our working relationship when I resided in Kansas. Jerry divorced his wife in 1993 and came to Kansas City on business. During that trip, we met for dinner and a relationship kindled since I had recently also experienced a divorce.

Subsequently, we discovered our strong attraction was due to the fact that we were divine soul complements, which essentially meant our souls balanced each other like the Chinese yin and yang elements. We had many past lives together, and we thought we were meant to walk a spiritual path together in this one. In fact, we had jointly purchased a house and intended to marry but had delayed the wedding.

Jerry was having difficulty with my focus on metaphysics since he was accustomed to interfacing with me as a businesswoman. He greatly preferred his traditional way of thinking to my alternative concepts, despite the fact his mainstream methods were no longer bringing him satisfaction. We loved each other, but we were constantly struggling with our diverging philosophies. As I have come to realize, logic has nothing to do with love. I was hanging onto a stagnant relationship out of love, a love that felt strong but was not creating the partnership I truly desired. I wondered what my options for a partner were, given the divine soul complement status of our relationship. Was he my one and only partner? If accepting my contract pushed me further down my spiritual path, would it split me from the only one who was meant to be with me?

I registered the fact that my current instability with Jerry would probably increase based on this new turn of events. However, the temptation dangling before me was too much to refuse. I weighed moving into an evolved state of consciousness with the stress of an unfulfilling relationship, and I opted for evolution. Then, I made one last effort to ensure stability in my life as I moved into this new world. I requested that the choices I would need to make in the future be made easy, that my transition be gentle, and that this being named Laramus who professed to know me very well would never pull the rug out from under me as I made my way down my somewhat undefined path. When Laramus reassured me that the transition would be as easy as possible and change would occur according to my needs, I agreed to accept my soul contract.

I asked Laramus when I would receive my twelve strands of DNA. I did not know if it was an overnight process, a lifelong endeavor, or something in between. Laramus said it was necessary to formally ask for the twelve strands to begin the process, a method he called "DNA Recoding." I was surprised since I had been requesting twelve DNA strands for the better part of a year, ever since I had read the Kryon material. However, Laramus explained that there were many forms of DNA Recoding, and this one required very specific wording. Apparently, a soul must unequivocally accept its soul contract in order to recode since there is hesitation to place increased power in the hands of someone who may not be fully committed to the light.

Laramus directed me to transcribe his words because he said I would need to give them to others at a later date. He proceeded to give me the exact terminology for my formal recoding request which is included in the *Summary of the DNA Recoding Process, Phase One*, on page 193. The request specifically addressed the Sirian/Pleiadian Council. At the time, I was so ignorant of the celestial civilizations that have been assisting us that I used the nationality spelling of "Syrian" rather than the star system spelling of "Sirian." I was told the Sirians and Pleiadians represented civilizations that were helping Earth move to the next level of consciousness, hence the Sirian/Pleiadian Council. Once again, I prayed to the Divine Creator that I was making a choice for my highest good. I had visions of extraterrestrials absconding with my body parts because I had unwittingly given them permission. Obviously, this was not the case since the beauty and the power derived from DNA Recoding has benefited many people since that afternoon in 1996 when I first learned about it.

After I recorded Laramus' words, I asked him if I could go ahead and read the request for DNA Recoding in order to begin. He invited me to do so. I re-read what I had written and was told to wait while the Sirian/Pleiadian Council reviewed the request, since this was the Council that was orchestrating the big event. The information was energetically sent before the Sirian/Pleiadian Council and a review of my soul records ensued. The approval process took several moments, during which time I patiently awaited my outcome. Laramus communicated with great pleasure the approval of my request. I was surprised when tears sprang to my eyes since I had not felt emotionally attached to the approval. However, at a subconscious level, the recoding approval touched a sensitive nerve as I felt relief from waiting for this moment for eons of past lifetimes on Earth. I thanked Laramus for his assistance.

I was touched by the passing of this key event, having requested the return of my twelve strands many times over the past year. I felt I was *regaining* capabilities rather than *acquiring* new ones. I did not feel as if I was on the brink of a new experience. I had a profound knowledge that I had relinquished this power upon my first Earth incarnation, and I was returning to a part of me I had lost. I yearned for the return of what had once been an integral part of me since I was convinced these abilities would assist me in fulfilling my planetary destiny. Laramus said he would now be close to me at all times, and that I could consider him my personal genetic engineer who would help me through DNA Recoding. At that point, Laramus said good-bye and told me we would be communicating directly in the near future.

Again, N underwent a transition as the gentle energy I associated with Laramus was replaced with the boisterous temperament of Devin. Since I had received so little personal information from Laramus, I asked Devin if I would be teaching recoding to other individuals. After all, Laramus had told me to record the formal request to give to others. At this stage in my spiritual growth, I was still asking channeled entities for direction rather than relying on my internal learning. I perceived any entity in non-physical form to have access to higher levels of information than I could as a mere mortal. This is a habit that would change as a result of the Creator power I retrieved while recoding. Devin said to be patient, that the reason I had been given the formal terminology for requesting DNA Recoding was that I would be sharing it with others. Devin continued, "Don't you need to experience what you teach? Haven't you just experienced something? Why do you think we gave this to you?" At this point, Devin abruptly concluded the session by withdrawing from N's energy field.

N returned from her deep trance. I was filled with excitement and asked what she thought. Apparently, when N channeled, she was so far removed from her own consciousness that she could not hear what transpired. I was disappointed because I wanted confirmation of what I had heard through someone else's ears. I relayed to her what had been communicated, and she, too, became excited by the information since she was also familiar with the Kryon material. She said Devin had shared similar information about DNA Recoding with her the previous month, but she had not been given the formal request, and she certainly did not know I was interested in it. I shared the information that had been communicated with her, and we agreed to remain in touch. I left feeling slightly dazed by all of this news. However, I also strongly resonated with it. Deep in my heart, I felt the appropriateness of the path that had been presented to me. I was excited by the prospects that awaited me as a more fully conscious being.

MY REQUEST FOR DNA RECODING CONFIRMATION IS ANSWERED

I waited impatiently for several days for a new feeling ... something ... anything ... to be different, to prove that I was actually, finally, in the process of receiving my twelve strands. But I felt like the same person. I was disappointed. After all of the excitement earlier in the week, I wanted to feel like I was transitioning into a new experience. I hoped my guides would communicate with me during my dream state, something they frequently did, to confirm I had actually begun DNA Recoding.

Apparently, my guides took my request very seriously. I awoke suddenly in the middle of the night because my body was vigorously vibrating. I was not experiencing any pain, but it felt like a jackhammer was beating on my back. I was not frightened because I intuitively knew this had something to do with my request for confirmation. However, just to be sure, I called out to Laramus to intervene if this riveting energy was not for my higher good. When I called his name, it came out in a staccato tone, as if someone or something was hammering my body. I laughed at how ridiculous I must look and sound, but I immediately plunged into a deep sleep that I could not seem to resist.

In the morning, I awoke and asked my guides to communicate with me, explaining what had transpired. I had recently begun automatic writing so I could access information from my guides by sitting down at my computer and listening to the words they put in my head. However, I wanted a simpler and more immediate approach to communication. As I lay there with my eyes open, I saw a bolt of white light come toward my body. My entire body was physically jolted as the ball of light entered my body. The jolt was more startling and energizing than uncomfortable. I didn't know what it was, but I knew someone was trying to give me something.

Later, I realized that Laramus was simply answering my request to feel something different. He sent me the ball of light to prove his presence and to show me the immediacy with which my requests would be answered as I moved from the denser, slower manifestation of a two-strand being to the lighter, faster manifestation of a twelve-strand being. The energetic transmission was enough to satisfy my request for a signal that something new and different was happening to me. Next time, I thought, I would ask for a less dramatic signal!

HEART HEALING IN PREPARATION FOR DNA RECODING

I set up an appointment to visit Bobbie, my friend and intuitive counselor, to share my recent entry into DNA Recoding. She listened to my story with interest, imploring me to experience recoding at a reasonable pace versus my typical impatience which sometimes drives me faster and harder than my body can withstand. As usual, I asked Bobbie to psychically scan my body for any distressed or repressed energy since her healing methods were very effective at balancing me. Plus, I seemed to attract discordant energies on a regular basis. All of us have an electromagnetic field that surrounds our body. If we open ourselves too fully, we sometimes attract energy that does not benefit us. Since I had not yet learned how to manage my power to thwart unwelcome energies, and I had not studied any clearing techniques, I was not always successful at keeping unwelcome energies out of my auric field. Bobbie helped keep my energy clean in support of my efforts to maintain optimum health.

In scanning, Bobbie noticed a ball of light in the middle of my abdomen. She felt it was a positive energy, but she could not view it because it was enclosed in a metal sheathing, much like a missile casing. There were energetic spider-like webs branching out from the sheathing, extending down to my ankles and up to my forehead. Bobbie told me I would need to request that the sheathing be removed before she could help me since it was not responding to her therapy. I complied by telling my guides that I was interested in having the sheathing removed so they knew my intention and could support it.

Bobbie began doing the energy work for which she was noted, and I focused my attention on bringing forward my guides and my superconscious to assist. As she worked, I felt the presence of a deep purple light inside me. The light eventually shifted to a bright orange as I saw two wood nymphs with fluttering wings square off, back to back, and then walk in opposite directions to stand on either side of me. After several moments, Bobbie asked me what I had experienced, and I described it to her.

She then told me what she had seen. She had encountered difficulty removing the sheathing and had asked for assistance. Several beings came forward, working hard to remove the metal casing. The light turned into a bright orange. At that point, Bobbie realized that the light behind the metal was my true essence which I had kept hidden for eons. She felt I would be too vulnerable with it immediately entirely exposed, and she wondered what to do. As she pondered, two winged wood nymphs emerged and stationed themselves on either side of me. They told her they were there to protect me whenever it was unwise for my true essence to be fully revealed. She also watched as they wove a golden net around me, replacing the metal sheathing with a scintillating golden web that was studded with jewels. She commented on the beauty of the structure although she was unsure of its purpose. Later, I would discover just how important this golden web really was.

Bobbie then noticed my abdomen because it began, energetically, to protrude to the point of appearing pregnant. Just as she began to worry how much larger I would "grow" or if I would burst like an overfilled balloon, an unusual looking entity emerged from my womb that was bright orange in color. Thankfully, although unbeknown to me at the time, my abdomen returned to its normal shape. Bobbie asked the unusual looking entity if it was a positive being who was interested in my highest good. Fortunately, she received a positive confirmation. She also asked the origin of this being and its purpose. The being said I had visited "a world on the edge of our universe" many hundreds of thousands of years ago where I had encountered it. As agreed between us, I was carrying a "seed" that housed this being in my abdomen until such time as I would know to let it free. Hence, the need for my earlier subconscious request to my spirit guides. The being said it would remain with me for a while, helping me to achieve my spiritual goals, and then leave to offer its assistance to others on Earth who were helping to expand human consciousness.

As Bobbie relayed the information to me, I was somewhat appalled. The thought of some "thing" living in a seed inside me, whether energetically or physically, was distasteful. I was squeamish about such things. When I learned in grade school health class that minuscule microorganisms called mites lived in our eyelashes and eyebrows, I went around washing my eyes for days. I got the same squeamish feeling when I heard about this orange being who had taken up residence in my space.

However, I was also impressed at the matching visions that Bobbie and I had received since I had not begun to tap my telepathic side. The ability to visualize the same thing simultaneously was a new experience for me, specifically the same orange color and the twin wood nymphs. Bobbie referred several times to the being as "it," and then laughed, saying: "It dislikes being addressed in that manner." Although "it" claimed there were no names close to its language, it asked to be called Raphael since the energy was similar to that of Archangel Raphael's realm. It was here on Earth to bring the Raphaelite attribute of Divine Love to those who needed it. Had Raphael been birthed sooner, he would not have been able to be effective in our energy field since there had been more darkness/hate than light/love in the past. However, the Earth had sufficiently increased its love frequency for Raphael to emerge and be helpful.

Bobbie commented as our session ended about how calm I had outwardly remained upon hearing this information. She said the person she knew several years ago would probably have been very upset to hear she had "birthed" a strange looking being from her belly. I concurred, unable to explain why I had taken this event in stride, unaware of the more arduous experiences I would have with non-physical entities in the future. Later, I would understand the extent of the healing energy Raphael brought me as I opened my rejuvenated heart energy, infused with Raphael's Divine Love, to my eternal lover, my future life partner. My heart energy had been closed for the majority of my this lifetime based on a series of past life betrayals that had turned me bitter toward relationships. Raphael worked with me to resurrect the heart energy I had relinquished due to the painful emotions I had experienced, preparing me for the open heart I would require to connect with the man who was meant to be with me forever.

INCREASING MY TELEPATHIC POWER

I was beginning to understand how DNA Recoding enabled an individual to tap into his or her psychic ability by opening blocked telepathic channels. These telepathic channels have been blocked in most of us based on societal training that honors the left rather than the right, or intuitive, side of our brains. Most of us are born with receptivity to being psychic but quickly lose that attitude as we learn to assess the world through five rather than six senses. If we cannot touch it, see it, smell it, hear it, or taste it, then it does not compute. In fact, children are often reprimanded for being imaginative or fanciful, especially as they grow older. Over multiple lifetimes, our cellular memory holds the perception that we cannot be psychic so we do not even try. Some human beings have developed their intuitive power regardless of society's conditioning. But, for most of us, it is very difficult as adults to train our linear minds to re-open the intuitive channels that would enable us to be psychic.

Fortunately, DNA Recoding reconnects us with a telepathic hook-up. Although I had become increasingly reliant on my intuitive side and practiced automatic writing, a form of quieting external thoughts and delving deeply into the void to hear and record telepathic transmissions via my computer keyboard, I never considered myself truly psychic and was excited by the prospect of becoming "all-seeing." I experienced my first strong psychic hit with Bobbie. The following week, I received another telepathic message that would be a precursor of many more.

The woman who assisted me in my consulting business had handled a two hundred piece mailing to my clients and prospects while I was on vacation. I regularly mailed a marketing piece to current and potential customers to stimulate memory of me and my business. The brochure had been developed by a creative free-lance artist so it was cute, fun, and very noticeable. But a month had passed, and I was surprised that none of my clients had remarked on the brochure. I also had not received any non-forwardable returns which were typical of my mailings since people changed firms.

I called several of my regular clients and asked if they had received my mailing. No one remembered it. Since everyone receives a large amount of direct mail, I was not terribly surprised. Yet, I felt these were my regular clients who would recognize my return address, and the piece was designed to be noticeable. Next, I called my assistant at home and asked her if she remembered when and under what circumstances she had taken the mail to the post office since no one could recall receiving it. She said she had mailed it when I was on vacation the previous month. As she responded, I clearly saw the boxes of mail in the trunk of a car. However, I was not accustomed to receiving telepathic transmissions, especially in visual form, and I dismissed the notion. The next morning, my assistant sheepishly entered my office and reluctantly informed me that she really thought she had mailed the letters when speaking to me yesterday. But, she had recently purchased a new car and realized my mailing was still in the trunk of her old car. Fortunately, the dealer still had the car parked on its lot, and we were able to retrieve the mailing.

I was amazed I had seen those envelopes so clearly and noted I would need to pay more attention to fleeting visuals because they were not as insignificant as I thought. I understood the implications of psychic power and why so few were afforded the ability to tap into this pool of information. If an individual was not balanced emotionally or felt a low level of responsibility toward others, this type of information could be used to weaken rather than strengthen. Ideally, telepathic powers should be expanded among those who will use that ability to increase their feelings of balance, heal others, or help evolve the planet to a higher level of consciousness.

LEARNING HOW TO RECOGNIZE TRUTH

N called to see how I was doing with DNA Recoding since she had also begun the process. Eagerly, I asked her to channel Devin for me to obtain a status report. I would occasionally attempt to gain information from Devin since I did not know what to expect of DNA Recoding because no one had ever experienced this particular process, and I was reluctant to trust the information I was receiving intuitively. I simply was not in the habit of prioritizing intuitive information over analytical information, even when substantiated by physical events.

N agreed to enter a trance, and Devin emerged. He began by saying he was very pleased with the progress I was making in DNA Recoding. I immediately began asking questions about some trends I was observing in my business, and some decisions I wished to have assistance in making. I felt these trends affected my experience with the DNA Recoding process, and I desired his insight. Devin repeatedly reiterated that I already knew the responses to those questions. He felt I was asking him superfluous questions that I knew how to answer. He said if I trusted the answers I was intuitively receiving, I would not feel the urge to query him or any other non-physical entity. He said my internal information was transmitted from the "purest" source since I had asked for DNA Recoding.

At the same time, I was frustrated when he put me off since I wanted information from a source who I perceived to have higher power. Now, I understand what he was trying to convey during a stage in my life when I was still looking for direction from beings I thought were more evolved than myself. When we align with Creator Truth, we are connected to the best information available. Devin was trying to tell me I would make proper choices based on the guidance of my superconscious, balanced with my experience on the physical plane which non-physical entities did not possess, and my own free choice – free will. I did not need to rely on the input of non-physical beings who sounded all-knowing to formulate my life or provide me with direction. I needed to listen with my ears but heed my heart, and I would find my own truth.

Devin used a wonderful analogy by comparing himself as well as my spirit guides to shepherds. He said it was their job to gently guide me to the pastures that offered the highest nutrition. It was up to me to decide if I wanted to remain with the flock and partake of the nourishment or stray to other pastures, some with less nutrition and some with more. However, it was the quality of my choices that determined how quickly I moved through DNA Recoding and entered expanded consciousness. He exited after saying there were many "old friends" around me that loved me very much and missed communicating with me. He said they were anxious for me to become an "open channel" in order to establish strong lines of communication so we could regularly connect. As always, I felt frustrated because I was unable to clearly see or hear them and was anxious for those abilities to return. I asked, "When will I be able to channel?" He responded, "When you are ready, dear one."

DISCOVERING MY OVERSOUL

I awoke suddenly out of a sound sleep at 3:00 AM. A loud voice had disturbed my slumber, and I was initially annoyed due to the abrupt and startling awakening. I knew it would take a long time to return to sleep. As I fumed, I realized that I had heard a name. Like recalling a dream, I reached into my subconscious memory and heard the name "Lahaina." It resounded in my ears as my guides told me that this was my eternal name.

Apparently, all of us have an eternal name that identifies the highest aspect of ourselves which some call an oversoul. In physical form, we incorporate a small element of ourselves. The superconscious or oversoul is the entire package. I understood this premise from reading books like Richard Bach's *One* or Jane Roberts' *Education of Oversoul Seven*. Our oversoul can be compared to the trunk of a tree. It is the core substance of all of our experiences. That was my Lahaina essence. Anne was simply a limb of the tree, an essential part of the tree's make-up but not the central piece. Our eternal or soul name is our identifier in the universe. It sounds a tone or vibration that celestial beings recognize when they hear it.

Initially, I felt confused about hearing the name Lahaina. It occurred to me this was the name of a town on the island of Maui that I had recently visited during my trip with Jerry to Hawaii. I wondered whether I was receiving my soul name or reliving the trip in a dream. Jerry and I had gone to Maui to get married in the Fall, but when we arrived the feelings of our spiritual incompatibility surfaced so strongly that we postponed the wedding. We knew we were going to be living together anyway since we were co-owners of a house so we enjoyed a vacation rather than a honeymoon. Looking back, I understand that part of that trip to Hawaii was to establish knowledge about the area called Lahaina because it was an integral part of who I was. The name connected me to a past Polynesian lifetime with my soon-to-be-encountered true life partner. It would be one of the important clues that brought us together. The name, Lahaina, also eventually identified my existence on the Nibiruan Council which I would soon discover.

A LESSON IN PERSONAL EMPOWERMENT

I received an unanticipated call from my HMO informing me I had "questionable" lab results from a recent Pap smear, and I would need to make a follow-up appointment for a colposcopy and a possible biopsy. Initially, I was startled by the information as I did not see dis-ease as part of my life lesson. I had dealt with medical problems during the first forty years of my life and had overcome many of them. I had virtually eliminated Western medicine from my regimen since most of what I had experienced through surgeries, prescriptions and invasive testing simply created more problems than it cured. I was very happy maintaining good health through my diet and monthly round of visits to alternative health practitioners for craniosacral therapy, acupuncture, Chinese herbals, deep tissue massage, and chiropractic adjustments. In fact, I had wrestled with myself about getting a Pap smear, preferring alternative procedures which were more maintenance-oriented than reactive to health problems. Typical of Western medicine, I had begun one procedure only to find I had to return for another.

I could not reconcile that I might need to devote energy to health problems at this juncture in my life. I felt poised to recover a long lost power, and now I was faced with potential medical concerns. I also felt I had been promised smooth sailing by my guides, and I was taking the necessary precautions in respect to my diet, supplements, and regular use of alternative healing modalities. Didn't my guides and the DNA Recoding team need me to be strong and capable rather than distracted by health problems? Didn't they want me to be focused on uncovering the steps of DNA Recoding in order to accomplish my path and purpose? I was upset and confused by the situation which usually meant I was receiving a lesson. But what was it?

Several hours passed as I continued to digest what I had been told. In the meantime, I went ahead and made my appointment for my colposcopy. I did not react as I might have in the past when told that there were no appointments available for a week. In prior years, having allowed doctors to hold the ultimate authority over my body, I would have experienced extreme frustration waiting an entire week to obtain more information about questionable results, results that might affect the quality of my life or my mortality. I realized I no longer believed that physicians had the ultimate answer. I was not sitting on pins and needles waiting to see the doctor, and I was even somewhat hesitant to proceed with the techniques a traditional HMO had to offer. Rather, I believed that many sources might have the answers to my latest health challenge, including myself!

I also wondered how serious this questionable situation might be since the HMO had already waited sixty days before contacting me on a lab report that typically took fourteen days. All of a sudden it hit me! This notification was tied to a time period in my life when I was being challenged to take back my power. I had always succumbed to the power of the physician, allowing them to make decisions about my body based on their typically non-spiritual perspective. As I pondered this new concept, I suddenly got the sense that my spirit guides were laughing and heard them chide me for judging my ability to hear their communications clearly. They said, "Where do you think you got the notion of coming up against an old archetype, the patriarch, as a challenge to your power?" As I began to get the joke, albeit not entirely funny, I joined in their laughter.

I realized that I could no longer live in fear of a strong authority figure in our society, the doctor. I needed to find answers that resonated with me, and those answers might not be acceptable in the traditional world of medicine. I also believed, at my gut level, that I was being tested on my faith in the DNA Recoding process. During the last channeling session, Devin said I had to hold an internal knowing of what was right for me rather than seeking answers from external sources. He also said my guides would grant me any assistance I needed to make this journey easier. So, I mentally projected the request to Devin to assist me in ensuring good health, now and in the future. I knew I was making a profound, life-changing shift in regard to my attitudes about my health and, hence, my power.

LEARNING ABOUT THE PLANET NIBIRU

I enjoyed my weekly appointments with Bobbie. This was someone who could tune in spiritually, emotionally, and etherically to me and assist me with my growth. It would be interesting to hear what my good friend and spiritual advisor telepathically received in regard to my recent health challenges. I explained my current dilemma to Bobbie. She asked me to lie down, and she scanned my body for any energy obstructions. She told me that she did not understand it, but she "saw" a great deal of radiation material in my liver. She asked where I might have contracted it, and I recalled information Devin had provided during one of his channelings about the unusual amount of radiation on the planet of Nibiru. I had not recorded this information because I became uncomfortable when any reference to extraterrestials was made. I felt I could experience the DNA Recoding process and disregard anything that pushed my comfort zone. I even omitted much of the material I received about Nibiru from the first *Power of Twelve*.

As I referenced in the introduction, I have come a long way toward embracing the possibility of other civilizations populating Earth prior to our existence after reading Zecharia Sitchin's work. I did not discover Sitchin until after nearly completing my DNA Recoding or, perhaps, I would have been more receptive to Devin's information. Sitchin's scholarly approach to analyzing remains from ancient civilizations like Sumeria and Babylonia gave credence to Devin's story since it essentially validated everything Devin told me. Devin said there was a planet named Nibiru that orbited in an elliptical path around our sun over the course of 3,600 years. The planet was initially responsible for forming Earth and the Asteroid Belt because it was pulled off course by other planets which caused it to run into an existing planet called Tiamet. Tiamet split and Earth and the Asteroid Belt resulted.

As Earth's atmosphere evolved and became increasingly inhabitable following the Ice Age, Nibiruans began to populate Earth. The initial landings occurred around 450,000 BC, according to the Sumerian and Babylonian records. Nibiruans were interested in Earth because of the vast amount of gold ore that lay below the surface. They needed the gold to act as a buffer for their planet since radiation was becoming an increasing problem. Apparently, they used gold dust to create a protective field around the planet.

Initially, the Nibiruans used members of their own society to mine the gold, called the Anunnaki. However, after 144,000 years, the Anunnaki mutinied because they had tired of laboring underneath the Earth's surface for gold. Sitchin's work discusses recent carbon dating techniques that place mining in Southern Africa as early as 70,000 to 100,000 years ago. This is interesting, given the capacity of the primate living on Earth at the time who would not have been capable of developing adequate mining tools, much less actually mine. When the Anunnaki laid down their tools, the Nibiruans had need for a primitive worker to continue the task. They merged the genes of the primate predecessor of the human, the *Homo erectus*, with the genes of the Nibiruans, to mine gold for use on Nibiru.

I sheepishly repeated the information about the mining for gold on Earth to use on Nibiru as protection against radiation. I was reluctant to share such unusual information but felt it might be important. Bobbie asked my guides to give her further clarification on the situation. They told her that I, indeed, was astral traveling nightly to some heavily radiated area to conduct work with its inhabitants during my sleeping hours. Apparently, all of us use our astral body, one of our energy bodies, as a link between our physical and spiritual lives. At night, we often travel in our astral body to speak with our guides. Information gleaned from those discussions bubbles up through our intuitive side, and we use it in our everyday lives. The astral body stays attached to the physical body via an energetic cord. When we die, we simply allow our astral body to detach from our physical body by severing the cord, exiting the Earth realm and entering the astral realms to await our next incarnation.

I asked Bobbie if I was astral traveling to Nibiru. Since we are energetically traveling, there are no restrictions in terms of distance or time so it was possible I could visit a distant planet during the evening. Although my physical body was asleep in my bed, my energy body was able to sojourn elsewhere. Bobbie confirmed this hypothesis. She said she saw me working with a civilization that was trying to overcome the difficulties on their planet by utilizing my knowledge of the people, plants, animals, and minerals that existed on Earth. Obviously, I did not remember any of this upon waking since we experience Earth without all of the knowledge our superconscious holds. As I ultimately discovered, we are given many clues along the way to assist us in lifting the veil if we choose. DNA Recoding is a method for shedding light on who we are, a road back to discovering our true soul identity.

As Bobbie continued to search for information, she was told I often traveled to other worlds at night. Prior to DNA Recoding, I had traveled using my astral body. However, the lighter I became through DNA Recoding, the more I was able to travel in my etheric body which is the blueprint for the physical body. The etheric body holds our blueprint throughout our physical lifetime. Those who have experienced an amputation feel the existence of that etheric body or blueprint when their missing limb itches, a phenomenon called phantom limb, even when the physical appendage no longer exists. Because the etheric body is the blueprint for the physical body, anything that occurs in the etheric body eventually siphons into the physical body. Apparently, this was an in-between stage in which my DNA Recoding had progressed enough to allow my etheric body to travel, but it was not quite light enough to travel without picking up atmospheric influences. As the DNA Recoding progressed, I would be able to move back and forth without suffering any consequences.

I wondered if this intensified radiation had anything to do with the questionable Pap smear results I had received. Bobbie and I surmised that the radiation might cause errors in reading, even for radiation that was not actually present in my physical body but sat in my energy field. She called her friend, Kim, another intuitive counselor, and left a message asking her to assist us in this perplexing matter, and we concluded our session.

SUMMARY

APRIL DNA RECODING LESSONS

- We must formally accept our soul contract in order to recode to ensure that only Positive work is conducted by those receiving power from twelve DNA strands.
- In order to recode via this particular process, we must formally request DNA Recoding from the Sirian/Pleiadian Council and receive approval. The terminology for that request is included in *Appendix A: Summary of the DNA Recoding Process*, which begins on page 193.
- DNA Recoding enables us to be more telepathic, clearing the psychic channels that have been unused, which results in increased clairaudience and clairvoyance.
- DNA Recoding requires us to rely on our internal barometer, taking our power back from authority figures, friends and family members who we allow to feed off our energy, and non-physical beings. Since we will be receiving enhanced abilities with DNA Recoding, we need to feel confident
and trust our internal information rather than relying on external sources.

CHAPTER TWO
MAY • 1996

MY SOUL ORIGINATION

I received a call from Bobbie's friend, Kim, in response to our question regarding the radiation in my energy system. She had received Bobbie's message and was contacting me to share information on cleansing it from my body. Kim was a gifted psychic who performed energy clearings that greatly healed those who worked with her. She had actually undergone a similar experience while doing nightly interplanetary travel as a result of her work. Ironically, she had also received a suspicious Pap smear during the time when she was astral traveling and had avoided surgery by refusing to follow the physician's regime in lieu of her own remedies. She quickly improved her health condition based on herbal supplements that cleansed her system. I listened closely as she described the natural healing mechanisms she had used, including a particularly aggressive metal cleanse that she felt would eliminate any radiation particles from my physical system. I was greatly relieved after hearing Kim's story since it implied that self-empowering methods of healing were effective and might be the proper methods for me.

Kim also confirmed I was traveling to my "home planet" to conduct work with a community which was trying to rejuvenate the planet following the harsh effects of radiation. I asked her if home was the Pleiades, since I knew I had lived in the Pleiades star system prior to incarnating on Earth. I also knew I had resided in at least seven other planetary locations in addition to Earth and the Pleiades. Several years ago, I had been informed by an impressively accurate psychic that I originated on a planet ruled by a supremacy society that existed beyond our sun. I had left that planet based on disagreement with the operating philosophy. I had recently wondered if that supremacist society was Nibiru. I already had received information about Nibiru from Devin who certainly seemed arrogant when channeled through N. He appeared to possess the personality that would fit with the definition of supremacy, and I could understand that I might have rejected that arrogance as part of my past soul evolution. I also had been told by Devin that Nibiru was actually a satellite constructed by Pleiadians rather than a planet. This is why it demonstrated such a wide elliptical orbit because it surveyed the solar system as it passed from one end to the other. Although this satellite was called Nibiru and its residents were called Nibiruans, they came from Pleiadian stock.

I felt that I was beginning to put some pieces together. I might be a Nibiruan, a soul with Pleiadian roots, who had a past history with Devin. Perhaps that was why Devin insisted on contacting me personally to impart the DNA Recoding information. Yet, Laramus was the one to actually give me the information. I felt it was because I did not feel the same level of trust with Devin. At this point, I wondered what he had done in the past to make me unsure of his agenda.

Kim and I concluded our conversation with my head bursting with questions. She recommended that I record all of my questions and send them to her. She said she would obtain the answers when she performed a cleansing remotely on my energetic body later in the week. We would discuss the results after she completed the clearing.

DEFINING THE FIRST FOUR STAGES OF DNA RECODING

After my conversation with Kim, I attempted to piece together my role on the Nibiruan team. Devin, currently the leader of a group called the Nibiruan Council, had finally shared during a channeling session via N that he had been N's father on Nibiru. He said he was Anu, ruler of Nibiru during the time the two-strand DNA hybrid was created on Earth. He had initially kept his identity from us because he thought we would find it difficult to believe. However, his subterfuge was lost on me since I was unfamiliar with Sitchin's work and had never encountered the name Anu. Later, when I read *The 12th Planet*, I realized what a key player Anu was in our creation story.

We also discovered why Anu referred to my acquaintance as N. N stood for Ninhursag, who was Anu's daughter. She had come to Earth prior to the existence of mankind, and she held the role of chief medical officer according to the ancient Sumerian texts. She was trained as a geneticist, and she worked with her half-brother Enki, another child of Anu's, to create the two-strand DNA primitive worker to mine the gold on Earth when the Anunnaki refused to mine any longer. Ninhursag and Enki had been responsible for genetically altering the *Homo erectus* on Earth by creating a hybrid using Nibiruan DNA. These primitive workers were called a "lulu" in the Sumerian texts which stands for "primitive" as well as "who has been mixed."

N was told she was operating in two dimensions, one as N on the Earth plane where she was responsible for spearheading the DNA Recoding process, and the other as Ninhursag on the Nibiruan Council where she developed the overall strategy. Essentially, she was acting as the link between the Nibiruans and mankind to initiate DNA Recoding. I strongly suspected I was a family member of this team but had been unable to define the relationship. Plus, whenever I broached the subject with Anu, he evaded it.

Based on my conversation with Kim which, in my mind, confirmed my connection with Nibiru, I called N and asked her to channel Anu so I could ask some questions. She went into trance, and the ebullient Anu emerged. I asked Anu about his choice of me as a member of the team. In his maddening, cryptic fashion, he said, "Dear One, you chose the project. It did not choose you." He asked if I noticed how my "heart came alive" when I recorded my progress with DNA Recoding. He was right. I craved the time to work on it during a very busy schedule, running my marketing consulting business and traveling with a portable computer that would enable me to enter my notes in the late night hours in my hotel room. I loved every minute of it, and I would frequently awaken between 3:00 and 4:00 AM and feel the need to rush to the computer and record my observations.

I asked Anu if he could define my soul contract and who I was vis-à-vis the Nibiruan team. He told me that clues were being provided if I would heed them. I objected, feeling he had shared information with N and should do so with me. Again, I was not in a place of power, begging a non-physical entity to tell me something about myself when I could have hooked up through my superconscious to determine it. I was frustrated, but I still had not gotten the joke. When I felt confident enough to believe my intuitive self, I would be privy to the information. Anu said to remember we were all connected in this plan and to know I was part of his "family." He refused to go any further than that. Finally, I asked if I had any medical problems that would cause me worry. Anu said my medical problems were about releasing fear, just as I had suspected. If I held onto my fear, I would create problematic situations. If I released my fear, I had no worries.

I thanked Anu for his input and thought we were concluding. Several moments passed before he spoke again, asking that I be sure to share the formal DNA Recoding request Laramus had given me with any others who desired it. He said we must accept our soul contract prior to being recoded, a process that will ultimately render us more clairaudient and clairvoyant to information from higher dimensions. The reason we must accept our soul contract is to ensure we will wisely use our enhanced power derived from DNA Recoding rather than aligning it with self-gain.

Anu also said there was no reason to grant someone recoding who had not accepted their soul contract because they would not know what to do with it. The reason for accepting a contract was to align the soul with his or her purpose, placing it among a team of assigned entities whose role was to protect that novice. Apparently, once someone is approved for DNA Recoding, they attract attention both from lightworkers and from negative beings which are attracted to enhanced power. It was necessary for the person undergoing DNA Recoding to be protected as they expanded their psychic abilities and power.

Anu continued by saying there were nine segments of DNA Recoding. According to Anu, we would *not* be given information on the segments until we reached them, as they would have no meaning for us until then. Since N was on Segment Four, we were given information up through Segment Four. Later, we would discover that both N and I sequentially experienced the segments in order to help educate the genetic engineers since no third dimensional being had been taken through this particular process. Those who subsequently experienced recoding might not undergo a linear process. They might move among the various segments, clearing and completing them in a random rather than a progressive order. In other words, one might clear and complete Segment Three while still working on Segment One. Or, one might need to release polarity vows in Phase Three before even beginning Phase One.

Anu shared information on the first four segments. Segment One, Releasing Anger, represented the resolving of old issues *without* anger and *with* love, healing our physical system through this process. It would be necessary to communicate with anyone with whom we had unresolved anger. In some cases, we should actually call these people if we felt we could speak to them on a heart level. If we did not know their whereabouts or thought we might elicit more anger or defensiveness, our superconscious could "speak" to the superconscious of those involved through a visualization process of sending our messages via our soul energy to the recipient. Segment One's removal of anger ensured that the extreme density created by anger in the physical body would be removed prior to receiving the twelve-strand energy, since it was possible that discomfort would be encountered if the higher twelve-strand frequency interacted with the denser vibration of anger.

The second segment, Managing Anger, involved calmly confronting issues while remaining in a neutral place, rather than stuffing anger over new issues, thereby creating resentment. If anger is stuffed during DNA Recoding, we might feel discomfort since it would re-create a dense vibration that would not match the lighter twelve-strand vibration. As we experience recoding, we will discover a feeling of neutrality toward situations and greater levels of compassion. Anu said we would be tested repeatedly on our ability to remain "unstuffed," finding situations thrown in our path which would require us to confront openly and calmly instead of with rage.

The third segment, Clairaudience, was when the telepathic channel began to open. As the lower emotions are cleared from the system, we become lighter. This is the point where we begin to speak to, and receive messages directly from, our guides. It is important to avoid heavy electrical environments during this stage because it can cause static in the telepathic channel which interferes with our ability to hear our guides.

I have worked with some people who become frustrated in Segment Three because they feel they are unable to open their psychic channel. I call most of these folks my "Doubting Thomases" because their doubt restricts them from experiencing the psychic connection they are capable of having. When we doubt, we move into a left-brain activity that restricts the intuitive action on the right side. We cannot impose judgment on our intuition and expect it to flow. When I tell them how they keep shutting themselves down by consciously imposing a restriction, some are able to overcome their self-judgment. For those who cannot, I recommend they dowse using a pendulum to obtain answers until they feel comfortable with the psychic process. In rare cases, I have encountered people who have been killed so many times in past lives for their psychic ability that their subconscious will not allow the channel to reconnect based on a program of self-preservation. When someone has a soul blockage to channeling, that must be cleared with specific healing modalities.

The fourth segment, Clairvoyance, involves the opening of the third eye. At this point we may begin to see guides or other entities that visit or assist the physical world. It may begin with a sensing of dark forms, followed by lighter forms, moving to full range color visuals. Or, it might be experienced psychically through the third eye. It is necessary to move through any fear that arises out of this new ability due to the viewing of previously unseen entities because it could keep us from progressing through the segment.

Anu said to try to avoid heavy electrical environments like video arcades or amusement parks during Segment Three and Segment Four. The extreme amount of electricity flowing in conflicting directions can create a clog in our telepathic circuitry. This type of electrical flow can cause so much static that our guides cannot effectively communicate with us for some time thereafter. I asked if my frequent travel caused communication problems due to the electricity experienced during plane trips. Anu said that plane electricity flowed in a circular motion so it did not cause static compared to environments bombarded by electricity from different directions like casinos, electrical power plants, and video arcades.

I wondered how I was able to channel automatic writing at my computer or receive intuitive messages despite the fact I was not an "open" channel. Apparently, I needed to clear the last vestiges of anger from my system, something with which I had been working for the past two years, and then I would be ready to receive continuous communication at any time. The major emotional blockages needed to be removed prior to complete clairaudience or they might create physical discomfort. I determined two people with whom I had to clear residual anger and decided to take care of it that evening. Since I did not know how to find these people, I simply visualized them and requested my soul to visit their soul with the specific information I imparted.

I thanked Anu for his information and N returned. I told N about my continuing frustration with my lack of knowledge about my role as a member of Anu's team. I said my only clue was the name Lahaina which had been given to me in the middle of the night and probably meant I was recalling my trip to Maui. N's eyes opened wide in surprise when I mentioned the name Lahaina. She said Anu had given her the names of the members of the Nibiruan Council on April 2, and Lahaina was mentioned at that time. I was equally surprised since, obviously, Anu had withheld that information from me. As I came to respect, his agenda was based on a sincere desire for me to trust my intuitive self. I wondered if, like N and Ninhursag, I was Lahaina in both places, a non-physical member of the Nibiruan Council called Lahaina as well as a physical representative named Anne on this planet. I tried to envision the logistics of living simultaneously in two locations, a problem solved by my complete lack of recall of my oversoul's activities during my conscious waking state. I wondered if I would be able to hold dual awareness of multiple states of consciousness after recoding.

It took me a long time to accept my role as Lahaina, who, indeed, was both a non-incarnate member on the Nibiruan Council and an incarnate representative on Earth named Anne. I had difficulty viewing myself as a higher dimensional being who had a level of knowledge and power that Anne had never experienced. Yet, as the days passed and Lahaina became more and more a part of my life, I grew to accept who I was.

At some point, I apparently merged a part of Lahaina with Anne because Anu and Joysiah spontaneously began calling me Lahaina during the channeling sessions. Ultimately, I understood my purpose was to assist the non-physical Nibiruan Council members in understanding how third dimensional beings would experience this version of DNA Recoding. The members of the Nibiruan Council needed a person with a dual perspective, someone living among them and conferring as a member of the strategy and implementation team as well as someone reacting from a third dimensional viewpoint by actually experiencing recoding. Anne and Lahaina were one and the same!

A DOSE OF ADDITIONAL POWER

I made the decision to cancel my colposcopy appointment. I decided that, even if cancer cells were discovered in my body, I would not elect to have a hysterectomy or undergo the intense effects of chemotherapy. I also decided that my guides were simply testing my faith in terms of how strongly I believed in the power of the DNA Recoding experience. I decided to continue with Kim's recommended herbal cleanse for thirty days and rescheduled the copolscopy as a Pap smear, assuming the results would be fine. At this point, I was still hedging my bets, wanting to have the faith to believe that all was well physically yet desiring the stamp of approval from modern medicine. Nonetheless, this action was my first toward breaking a fear cycle I had allowed physicians to impose on me. I had been in and out of hospitals and doctors' offices since I was a small child, religiously following the physicians' directions. I felt good knowing that I could direct the process according to my needs, rather than allowing the perceived authority figures from my past to impose their medical agenda upon my recovery.

ESTABLISHING MYSELF AS A METAPHYSICIAN

I received a postcard from a nationally prominent metaphysical magazine regarding publication of an article I had submitted based on prompting from my friend, Bobbie, to share some of the my automatic writing with the rest of the world. The name of the article was *You and Your Image*, and it consisted of information that I received from my guides. I was elated that a noted publisher was interested in my work, continuing confirmation that I was receiving telepathic transmissions that resonated for others.

The note from the publisher said the magazine needed a short biography on me, as well as information about my telepathic source, to publish with the article. I was unsure how to describe my guides, then thought, why not let them describe themselves? This is the information they provided:

"We are a group of non-physical entities who is actively involved in recoding the starseeded interplanetary light-workers who live on Earth at this time. Our work will ensure a smoother transition for mankind when the planet shifts to the next stage of evolution by preparing our emissaries, the starseeds, to act as experienced facilitators for the five billion residents on this planet who will be given an opportunity to ascend."

Tears came to my eyes when I read the information I had received since it emphasized the profoundness of the work in which I had become involved and solidified my soul contract. Essentially, my guides were telling me that they were assisting me in imparting a method for increasing power via DNA Recoding to the older souls on Earth. These souls are called starseeds because they have lived in other celestial locations prior to incarnating on Earth. According to this information, we are perched on the edge of change, moving from our current state of consciousness to a new one. Starseeds hold soul contracts to help this planet evolve, and the first step in evolution involves increasing their vibration via additional DNA strands. Once we reach critical mass with enough starseeds holding the new energy, the entire population can shift into a new way of being without experiencing unnecessary fear. This way, everyone has the potential to ascend, that is, move to the next stage of consciousness in full awareness, recalling all soul experiences we have ever encountered.

LINKING VERSUS CHANNELING

I received the tape from Kim that described the session in which she conferred with my guides to determine where my radioactivity originated and how to clear it. She said my guides apologized for the amount of toxicity I was carrying due to the radiation I was picking up during my travels to my "home" planet. My originating civilization had apparently underestimated the vulnerability we have to radiation, having boosted their own immune systems eons ago due to the greater amount of radioactive material in their atmosphere as a result of warfare. In fact, Kim said the entire DNA Recoding process had been slowed based on this finding. Apparently, this was the type of information the Nibiruan Council needed from my third dimensional body since it was a reaction to work I was performing in conjunction with DNA Recoding. As others recoded, they might incur planetary travels which would place them in the same position. In fact, Kim said the Nibiruan Council was working to alter this response, re-setting "dimensional coding" to allow third dimensional beings to etherically travel to "interplanetary stations" without picking up radiation.

Next, Kim spoke of my origins. She said my soul was conceived on Nibiru from a Nibiruan female and a Sirian male. They had come together for the express purpose of creating my energy field to, in Kim's words, "create a new form to help save the beings from both my planet of origin and Earth." This was shocking information for me since I hardly viewed myself as a prophet and certainly had no desire to be a savior. But, the information seemed to fit with the higher aspect of myself called Lahaina who was communicating regularly with the Nibiruans on the Nibiruan Council and the Sirians on the Sirian/Pleiadian Council, the two key organizations supporting this method of DNA Recoding.

Kim also said I was called a "mutable" because my energy field was extremely adaptable to differing planetary systems. I was also called a "gatherer" which meant that, even though I had originated on Nibiru, I had resided in various other locations due to my "mutability." To name a few, I knew I had lived with the Jolanderanz who look like the underwater beings in the movie *The Abyss*. I had lived with the Pleiadians and even re-located to live with those almond-eye abductors called the Grays as part of a research experiment that was Pleiadian-based. I also knew I was a member of a Sirian group who had resided on Jupiter. This combination of "mutable" and "gatherer" lineage created an element of fragility in my energy field since my matrix was loosely constructed to enable interplanetary traveling and communication.

It occurred to me that perhaps my soul father was of a different form than the galactic human form to which I was accustomed. Perhaps he was similar to the Raphael energy I had carried in my womb for eons which I had recently released on Earth. I asked my guides to determine if this was the case, and I was told that the energy of Divine Love was similar, but the body form was different. As I learned, Earthlings originated from Hominoid form but there are many forms of Hominoids, some human in appearance and some not so human. It is like comparing a whale in the ocean to a woman. Both are mammals, yet both have different forms. My soul father's form, albeit Hominoid, might look different than I do now. As a gatherer, I had enjoyed many aspects of physical and non-physical experience. It was time for me to understand our souls existed beyond human form, and I needed to love myself in any form, regardless of how unpalatable it felt based on Earth standards. This notion brought new meaning to the concept of self-acceptance.

Kim also provided a piece of information that explained the multi-dimensionality of Lahaina in which she could live simultaneous soul experiences. She said based on the flexibility of being a mutable, I had the ability to "break off" a part of my energy and co-exist in multiple dimensions simultaneously. It would be "easy" for me to live as Anne on this planet while acting as Lahaina in another dimension. In fact, it was very feasible that Lahaina was acting as the orchestrater and overseer of Anne. It was taking time for me to process, understand, and accept this concept. My ego kept interfering because I did not like to think that Anne was relatively unimportant, an underling to the more powerful superwoman side of myself called Lahaina. Eventually, I reconciled my egotistical reaction, realizing that our oversoul is comprised of every element of who we are, and that no element is more important than the other. As I accommodated this expanded view, a weight slipped from my shoulders as I realized I was not as remedial as I thought, based on my human efforts that were sometimes less than perfect. Somewhere out there existed an oversoul that was performing at a potential for which I was striving when, in fact, I was already there!

Next, Kim informed me that my people saw me as a "hero." This saddened me as I felt no ownership of this description. I wondered what I had done to deserve such standing, feeling weak compared to Lahaina's power. I have been without conscious knowledge of my abilities for so long, I had no memory of them. When I initially came to Earth on this "assignment" over 120,000 years ago, as I had been told, I am sure I envisioned a much shorter time line. I must have relinquished hope along the way, thinking I would never recover my abilities. Now that it was so close, I felt consumed by the desire to recode and gain broader consciousness.

Kim then gave some additional information on why we need to accept our soul contract before we can recode. A soul contract is a sacred agreement made between a soul and its galactic council that set the parameters for that soul's development prior to incarnating which, in my case, was the Nibiruan Council and the Sirian/Pleiadian Council. The process of recoding works in concert with realizing our soul contract. If we knew our contract before undergoing DNA Recoding, it would seem meaningless. We would not have the desire to manifest it because we would be unable to relate to it. We may not even perceive ourselves to be powerful enough to enact it. Once our vibration aligns with the same vibration that originally created the contract, we are able to perceive and accept it. In essence, we must somewhat blindly agree to something we do not presently have the capacity to understand, trusting that our soul knew what it was doing.

Having agreed to something beyond our comprehension, we are then awarded the return of our abilities to realize the intended outcomes of our soul contract.

Finally, Kim explained why I was having difficulty channeling, a step beyond my present telepathic capability of automatic writing. She said since the matrix of a mutable was loosely constructed for purposes of "shape shifting," it would be very uncomfortable to channel because I would have to hold my energy at a dense level for a long time period. Channeling relies heavily on the fifth chakra (throat), allowing the entity to enter one's body and use the throat energy to communicate. That process works contrary to the make-up of a mutable. Kim said I needed to learn a process called "linking" which would allow my guides to speak to me with great clarity. In fact, she said my guides felt I was ready for linking and had already selected an angel named Nephras to communicate with me.

Linking would utilize my telepathic set-up rather than my fifth chakra energy. Apparently, my telepathy was very well developed as a mutable and was constructed to have a broad range of frequencies, meaning I could interpret a wide variety of languages. Kim instructed me to link through my Alpha chakra, an eighth chakra that was situated above our seventh crown chakra, about a foot and a half above the head. She said the only reason I could not link today was because my Omega chakra (located eight inches below the root chakra in the mid-thigh region) and Alpha chakra were out of balance. I needed to tune them by holding one hand over the Alpha region and the other over the Omega region and circulate energy back and forth to bring them into balance. After I balanced, I would be able to receive energy through a universal telepathic channel that uses the eighth chakra.

Kim warned me to be patient. She said the information would flow slowly at first, and I might want to utilize a "yes" and "no" question format so I did not become frustrated. She also said I should rely on Nephras to assist me with linking. Nephras had contacted Kim when she was receiving the information on linking. She presented herself as a pregnant angel which surprised Kim. When Kim questioned her on her pregnancy, she said her role was to assist wounded souls by placing them in her womb and rebirthing them. Nephras' role profoundly touched Kim as she felt the healing energy move through Nephras to the soul in her belly. I was so excited by the information on linking and my angelic assistant that I could hardly wait to get started. I wanted to talk with Nephras as soon as possible.

LEARNING TO LINK

That same evening, my friend Pat came for a visit. I described the information I had received from Kim and asked her to assist me in linking. We lit some white candles, cleared the energy of the room, and asked our guides to come forward and assist in harmonizing my Alpha and Omega chakras. I placed my right hand over my Omega chakra and my left hand over my Alpha chakra and began to envision a clockwise circle of energy moving between the two areas. Pat envisioned the same to assist me in holding the energy.

After several moments, I needed to rest my arms. I had a pressing sensation behind my ears and a tingling in the bottom of my feet. In fact, the tingling continued to persist for several months which gave me the sense that I was continually "turned on." I requested Nephras make herself available in order to assist me. Immediately, I could sense her presence. Nephras would adeptly drop a concept into my head which I would then translate. The concepts were accompanied by supporting visuals.

Although Kim had said to use a "yes" and "no" format, I was eager to expand. In deference to Kim's advice, we began with easy questions rather than trying to explore the nature of the universe! Pat asked what she should do about her dog, Abby, a companion she had enjoyed for eighteen years who was in the process of dying. She said she had attended a dog show in Wichita the prior month and felt a strong bond to a Cocker Spaniel named Cici. The owner was keeping Cici until Pat decided if she wanted her, feeling that Cici and Pat were the perfect match. I immediately saw a type of dog communication system that allowed animals to speak with each other telepathically. Apparently, Abby had placed a dog version of a "classified," requesting a new body for her aging vehicle. I could see animals were different from us because their souls reside in a collective pool. Later, this was confirmed for me by the work of A.E. Powell, a noted early twentieth-century metaphysician. Animals can move in and out of their collective pool at will, not needing to wait until death to vacate their body. Cici had responded to Abby's call, offering her body as a vehicle.

I was laughing as I repeated this information, thinking it seemed silly, but Pat was pleased. She said she had sensed she needed to bring Cici home but had resisted. I told her Abby was waiting for Cici's arrival to ensure she had the vehicle before she left her aging body and would leave, that is die, shortly thereafter. Cici's soul would return to the collective animal pool. Based on the information I provided, Pat decided to drive to Wichita and get Cici. She then asked if she would need to put Abby to sleep or if her old friend would die of natural causes once Cici arrived. I hesitated answering because I knew Pat preferred her to die in her sleep, but I kept seeing one of those metal veterinarian cages in which they housed animals. I simply told her what I saw.

Pat asked me several more personal questions, warning me not to edit what was coming into my head since judgment would restrict the flow. We spent about an hour linking. I listened to Pat's questions, referred them to Nephras, and translated with ease. I was thrilled to finally experience a telepathic transmission that felt credible and did not require me to sit and write at a computer keyboard. As a final note, Pat asked if I would assist her with her DNA Recoding request based on the information I had shared about my new project with her. I closed my eyes, requested that Nephras assist us, and asked Pat if she agreed to accept her soul contract. She said "yes" without reservation, and I heard Nephras say that Pat's contract was to "sweetly heal" others, although not to underestimate the difficulties she might undergo when facing the dark forces. These forces were her illusion of the existence of darkness which attempted to hold her in its grasp through her emotions of fear and guilt. Pat would move with alacrity into her healing arts when she released her fear and guilt, thereby eliminating the energy she was feeding to darkness. Then, I saw a beautiful display of lights and heard clapping and cheering. Pat had been accepted for DNA Recoding. Pat thanked me for helping her come to a place of peace about her dog, Abby, and she went home.

Later, Pat went to Wichita to get Cici and await Abby's transition. She watched as Cici and Abby exchanged energy back and forth in preparation for Abby's transition. Literally, they would swap personalities which would have completely perplexed Pat had she not been forewarned of their plan. Pat's other dog, Alex, became very uncomfortable with the process, liking Cici when she held Abby's energy, but causing havoc in the house when Cici reverted back to her own energy. Eventually, Cici decided not to merge with Abby because she fell in love with Pat. She did not want to offer her body as a depository for the older dog, thus needing to leave Pat. She had also developed a similar eye disorder that Abby possessed so Pat decided to take Cici back to the breeder and graciously accept Abby's death.

It would take several years for me to gain confidence in my new psychic ability, but eventually I felt that I was receiving information that was not only accurate but extremely beneficial and healing to my clients. In fact, my psychic acumen continued to grow until I expanded beyond linking into full channeling, working within the confines of my body type, yet able to receive a full spectrum of information. As my confidence grew based on the positive results I saw people receiving, I established a business called InterLink which is devoted to assisting people remove blockages that stand in the way of expanding their consciousness and leading to health, wealth, and happiness. I am comfortable with this role since I feel it aligns perfectly with my soul contract. Finally, I was consciously and effortlessly channeling, maybe not in the way I thought I would, such as trance channeling, but in a way that was in alignment with my unique vibration.

THE CONCEPT OF COPIES

I touched base with N today. She was having difficulty because she was experiencing movement in and out of her physical body. Based on my astral traveling experiences, I queried her as to why this was causing problems. Unlike my exits which occurred in a sleep state when it would be less startling, her exits occurred when she was awake. Her guides had informed her that they had reached a stage in DNA Recoding when they needed to work on her for more than a few hours. Some of the work required several days so they needed to "borrow" her astral body to accomplish the recoding work. The astral body was needed because all DNA Recoding alterations were made in the astral body. The enhanced energy resulting from the astral changes is funneled into the physical body via the plug-in process described in Phase Two. In order for N to function without her own astral body, they left a "copy" in its place.

I eventually came to experience my own "copy," something everyone will undergo for short time periods in DNA Recoding. In dealing with my own copy, I grew to learn we needed to take responsibility for training our copies to our own standards. Copies were necessary because our astral bodies needed to undergo successive days of treatment by our genetic engineer as we became more involved in the intricacies of recoding. The guides simply could not complete all of their work during several hours of sleep each evening. However, copies tended to indulge rather than act disciplined. For example, my copy did not like to exercise, a routine I liked to maintain due to its stress and weight reduction benefits.

I have had many clients call me about copies. They were concerned they would not be able to control their lives with a copy in place. Mothers of young children would call and query me regarding the dependability of copies since they would never forgive themselves if something happened to their children during their DNA Recoding process. Based on this concern, I would like to emphasize that a copy would never be harmful to you or to your children. They may like to act frivolous since they enjoy being in physical form for a few days. They may allow your children to eat ice cream before dinner or forget to remind them to do their homework, but they are certainly not interested in undermining your life.

I conjectured on the incredible overload a linear thinker like myself would encounter if total recall of our astral body experiences was possible, especially since moving in and out occurred during waking hours for DNA Recoding. It would be like watching two movies at the same time, hearing and seeing two different story lines while living in a single physical body. I decided I was not prepared for this experience, and I was somewhat glad I did not have complete recall of my astral travels. However, I was told by my guides that all of us will eventually evolve to the point where we will be able to accommodate multiple simultaneous experiences without short circuiting our mind. We will live in simultaneous time, no longer viewing life in an orderly linear fashion. Instead, we will maintain multiple experiences in order to transcend past the illusion of chronological time which blocks us from our full knowing of every soul experience we have had.

ALTERING FREQUENCIES TO RECODE

I had entered a phase in my DNA Recoding where I was experiencing a great deal of sadness. I knew my relationship with Jerry was ending, but I was having a difficult time letting go. Ultimately, I released our union because we no longer resonated with the same agenda. Instead of being supportive of my emerging metaphysical talents, Jerry seemed threatened by them because he feared I would stop being the practical business-woman he had always known. We had been together many times, and we had planned to spend the rest of our lives together. However, it was simply not working. This was hard to accept due to the love I felt for him. However, I recognized that I was in a holding pattern in an attempt to preserve a dying relationship. I felt tremendous conflict. If I moved forward spiritually, I harmed the relationship, and if I moved forward in the relationship, I submerged my spirituality.

This decision was not easy. I often wanted to forget what I had recently learned and live the "old" way, although it was not satisfying. But I found the stress of disharmony and the lack of truth for my path taking its toll on me. I think I knew subconsciously when I accepted my soul contract that this was an inevitable outcome since Jerry and I had already encountered relationship difficulties. This is why I initially asked Laramus if Spirit could make transitions easy on me rather than "forcing" me to change.

I remembered him saying that the decisions would evolve naturally, and I would only facilitate change at the point at which I was ready. After all, we live in a free choice/free will zone and Spirit cannot subject us to anything unless we desire it. He omitted the part about the pain we might experience from a life change decision, no matter how "ready" we are to move to new territory.

After the first *The Power of Twelve* was distributed, I received a call from a woman who had purchased the book in a metaphysical bookstore. The owner of the store had read the book and was familiar with my break up with Jerry. She warned her customer not to experience DNA Recoding if she wanted to remain with her husband since it would sever the relationship. I was appalled when the woman repeated what the bookstore owner told her since I never meant to blame DNA Recoding for ending my relationship. Jerry and I were already having problems that had started before I began the process.

Plus, after working with a variety of people who recoded, both single and married, I find that DNA Recoding affects relationships in different ways. Those who are well established couples do not seem to be affected when one spouse recodes and the other does not. In fact, sometimes the non-recoder creates a balance for the one who is recoding, almost like a grounding wire prevents someone from getting shocked. Obviously, it is optimal when both parties recode in well-established relationships since the higher vibration enhances the interaction between the two partners. Those who were not in well-established relationships seemed to have the same problems facing them with or without recoding. As for Jerry and me, DNA Recoding acted as one more area that did not support compatibility. Fortunately, in a few cases, the poorly established relationships actually improved as a result of the DNA Recoding because one of the partners took it upon him or herself to enhance their spirituality which upgraded the energy of the couple's dynamics.

On top of my relationship problems with Jerry, I had been terribly ill, culminating in the hospital emergency room due to a virus located in my female organs that caused a 104° fever. Apparently the stress caused from the impending loss of my relationship and the reconciliation process with Spirit took its toll on me. Since my vibration had changed, it was uncomfortable for me live in conflict with the intent of my soul contract. I had to lower my resistance in order to feel peace. I felt I had no other choice but to follow Spirit. I allowed the illness to rid my body of an immense amount of toxic radiation and stuffed emotions. It was now up to me to expedite healing through natural mechanisms.

I decided to link in order to better understand the reason for the level of discomfort I had experienced. I was not yet ready to receive information on my relationship since I was not sure I would like what I heard. My guides gave me the following information:

"Dear one, you are going through a difficult time that you did not expect. You will survive quite nicely, although it does not seem like it. We have told you, yet you still do not quite believe it, that this purging of your system is the lesser of the discomfort you would have had to endure. Your earlier years were filled with high levels of negativity toward your feminine power which no longer mesh with your energy. You had to rid it from your system. Your prior emotional cleansing work has helped immensely because it cleared you in the area which held the most anger, your reproductive system. You have lived with this anger, not only from you but also from your mother who has felt limited as a female in a male-dominated world. She subconsciously knew she was carrying a daughter in her first trimester and transferred that anger to you, thinking you would not realize your full potential as she had been unable to do in her world of the 1930s and 1940s. You have sat with this energy in your own female organs, supplemented year after year with the gender imbalance of your society. Now, it is gone. You are truly cleansed and will have no more problems. Your residual discomfort will eventually stop. It is part of the balancing, and it is also a reaction due to a weakness inherent in this part of your body. We knew this was coming and apologize, but it was necessary. You would have manifested diseases that were far worse if you had not cleansed due to the discord of your new energy frequency with the old. This is why the first step toward DNA Recoding is the release of anger since it will cause discomfort due to the discord."

I was fascinated by this response. First of all, I knew my mother would truly be dismayed to learn that she had transferred any negative feelings to a baby she had waited four years to conceive. And yet, it was integral to her and the society which had thwarted her development as a powerful female in a male-dominated world. I began to fathom the extent of the difference in energy I would be experiencing as part of DNA Recoding. I was moving into an energy frequency that was more ethereal than physical, that resided in love and joy as opposed to fear and anger. I could envision how this energy would be discordant with any old, negative energy residing in my system. That continual tug on the old energy from the new energy would create a pressure system in the physical body that would have to release itself in dis-ease. This was why releasing anger was fundamental to moving forward ... otherwise the new energy would hurt rather than help all of its long awaited disciples who were emerging into the light! I considered my bout with pain a true success and the marking of a major hurdle overcome.

HOW REPATTERNING EXPEDITES DNA RECODING

I was honored to be able to assist another person, Julia, to begin DNA Recoding. Julia and I met at a Holographic Repatterning™ class, a technique that takes negative energy patterns and transforms them into positive patterns via energy healing modalities. It works with the energetic blueprint that surrounds our bodies, reprogramming information that entered our energetic bodies during past traumas. Before I assisted Julia with her DNA Recoding request, she suggested that she repattern me to gain more experience in our new healing technique.

Julia went through a six-step process that was designed to identify any negative frequencies by surfacing core issues. Julia used kinesiology to determine the accuracy of the fact-finding. Kinesiology is a method of finding the body's truth by imposing pressure on muscles and checking the strength of the resistance. If the body resonates with a "yes," the muscle remains strong under pressure. If the body resonates with a "no," the muscle cannot withstand the pressure. Chiropractors often use kinesiology to determine which bones are misaligned rather than

relying on X-rays that are more invasive and sometimes not sufficiently revealing. The chiropractor touches a particular bone and
applies pressure to the patient's arm or leg. If the appendage
wavers, the bone is out of alignment. If the appendage is firm,
the bone is in place.

Julia and I were led via a series of questions and kinesiology
to a past life issue for me that dealt with a lack of self-forgiveness.
I immediately knew what it was since I had dealt with the issue
in other healing sessions. I recalled a lifetime in Sedona, Arizona
when it existed as a crystal city, far before the formation of the
Sedona we know today. I always "saw" this crystal city hovering
above the red rocks when vacationing in Sedona, like a mirage
hanging over the entire area. I knew from past psychic readings
that I had been put in charge of the sacred codes for the ancient
society that existed in Sedona. My selection to this responsibility
had been based on the society's trust that I would make decisions
framed by the principles of love. I had faced a difficult time,
because I was put in the position of protecting the society's
destiny by keeping the codes from an invading civilization that
would increase their power by obtaining the codes. I had learned
about the upcoming invasion based on my mutable composition
that enabled me to communicate with others. This made me privy
to information no one else could access. In order to protect the
codes, I hid them somewhere under Sedona and "blew up" the
area, destroying the society that I had loved in an attempt to
circumvent an even greater disaster. Apparently, I still know
where these codes are and I am to discover them in this lifetime
when I gain consciousness regarding their meaning and whereabouts. In the meantime, I had experienced great pain over many
lifetimes due to the decision to destroy a society I loved.

The last time I visited Sedona, I sat overlooking Boynton
Canyon, crying as I repeatedly said, "I'm sorry." At the time, I was
unsure why I felt sorry. Yet, I was wracked by pain. Later I
learned through my guides about the decision I had made that
destroyed something so dear to me. When I told Julia about the
Sedona experience, I started sobbing again, recalling all of the
anguish I felt from this very distant lifetime.

As Julia waited patiently, I recovered from my emotional outburst and proceeded with the repatterning. I had to diffuse my lack of forgiveness by first experiencing my extreme judgment and breathing it out of my root chakra. My healing modality consisted of placing various tuning forks on my nine chakras, the traditional seven, plus my newly discovered Alpha and Omega points. I could see why I had difficulty resonating with channeling. When I had been privy to other worldly information in another lifetime, it led me to make the decision to destroy that society. I carried a fear of accessing ethereal information since it might drive me to equally painful decisions. I was finally cleared from that guilt and pain and was even more ready to link for Julia and others.

Then, it was Julia's turn. Julia's reading flowed easily and apparently brought her great comfort as she had several life change decisions to make. The beauty of her soul contract was also brought forth to her in a memorable way and fit nicely with her talents and interests. She kept exclaiming, "how perfect!" as I answered her questions. I was pleased with this response since we had not really spoken personally, and I had little point of context for interpretation. I was glad that I kept gaining experiences that built my confidence about my telepathic skills.

I had wondered why I had taken the Holographic Repatterning course at the time since I did not desire to become a professional repatterner, and now I was beginning to understand. When we recode, there is much baggage from past events that stands in the way of the new, lighter energy that is coming into us. The repatterning process or any clearing process can clear emotional scars from past lives, prenatal experiences, and our current life within minutes, eliminating the need for years of therapy to erase those patterns. As we approach the final days before our shift to a new level of consciousness, we do not have the luxury of time to experience lengthy therapeutic treatments. We also need to ensure that we have eliminated negative energy frequencies from our system that go beyond the sometimes superficial healing we undergo when dealing on a mental level. Holographic Repatterning had been offered to me as a clearing modality.

RELEASING TOXINS IN ORDER TO RECODE

I met with N in order to speak with Anu and obtain confirmation of what I had experienced to date with DNA Recoding. I knew I was currently in Segment Three, Clairaudience, but I felt the need for reassurance. The session began with Anu stating that there was "another" who was jumping with impatience to speak with me but that the "other" would have to wait until Anu had finished. I laughed and asked if it was Laramus. Anu said, "Yes, it is your old friend Laramus who awaits with great impatience." He asked if I would like to speak with Laramus first and I said, "no," I would hear what Anu had to say prior to communicating with Laramus. I figured that I should apply the first-come, first-served policy to non-physical beings since it was the way I liked to be treated myself.

Anu began by telling me he loved me and held me in his highest regard. He said he was proud of the way I had decided to move through the DNA Recoding process without fear, leaving doubts behind me as I held onto trust and faith through the emotional and physical events of the past few months. He acknowledged the difficult emotional lessons I had been learning during recent weeks in regard to my relationship, and he told me to continue to remain true to my path. He said I was surrounded by assisting guides at all times, and I was very well-protected.

I asked Anu about my recent intense viral infection which resulted in a visit to the hospital, and the nature of its purpose. He confirmed that the infection was the necessary elimination of toxins and negative energy in my system, assuring me it would not be repeated. He said DNA Recoding required the use of an entirely different vibration and, if it met with discordant energy, it would create discomfort. Anger had to be released prior to receiving the twelve-strand energy frequency, or there would be discomfort as the lighter energy encountered the denser energy of anger.

I asked Anu to give me a sense of how I had performed during my linking sessions when I had assisted my friends who had asked for DNA Recoding. He said I had done very well and just continue what I was doing. I asked if I should do some type of advertising to let others become aware of my assistance. He said I should wait to receive requests for information from interested parties through word-of-mouth at this time. He then referenced the nine segments of DNA Recoding which clued me into the extent of the process. If I was in Segment Three, then there were six more segments to complete. Anu said that some of those who were initially interested in DNA Recoding information would not move through the entire nine segments. Others would proceed through all nine segments. Many of the younger souls who had always incarnated in the Earth realm would show interest in DNA Recoding much later, after many of the older souls had attained the twelve-strand energy and grounded it on the planet. Anu said the younger souls might only make it through the initial few segments of DNA Recoding. However, he also said that each would attain the segments needed for their specific soul evolution at the time. In other words, the segments we attained would either match or exceed our soul contract.

I had suspected for some time that I had originally been part of Anu's Nibiruan family. I asked Anu if I held any relation to him. He confirmed that my soul creation was tied to members of his family, saying that I needed to speak to a genetic expert about my lineage if I wanted more information. I asked if that would be possible during this particular session and he said, "yes," after I spoke with Laramus.

Anu exited, and Laramus emerged. He said he was most anxious to speak with me since he knew my personal relationship was rocky. He requested that I "simmer" for a period of time. I guess he knew I had decided to share my concerns with my partner, Jerry, concluding through much grief and pain that it would be best for us to pursue separate paths. He said I had the right to exercise free will, and he respected my decision to communicate my feelings. But, he requested I wait a short time period before sharing my thoughts since Jerry's guides were actively working on a certain "barrier" that he needed to cross. If he chose to cross the barrier, we could complete our work together during this lifetime. If he did not, we would probably be more satisfied by parting ways. I told him I would wait a brief interval based on his loving input, but that I desired to resolve the situation shortly since it potentially involved changing my residence since Jerry owned half our house. He thanked me, reminding me that part of the lesson I was currently learning involved patience and tolerance.

I asked Laramus when I would be able to communicate with him directly as I could with Nephras while linking. He said I needed to proceed two more segments in DNA Recoding prior to being able to clearly hear him. I asked him to share the upcoming segments, and he said he could not provide that information in advance of experiencing them. I always tried to wheedle more information out of these non-physical beings, but they liked being mysterious which greatly frustrated me. Later, I would understand that they simply did not want to rob me of my own experience by predetermining or predicting my future. I also grew to appreciate their stance since we tend to create within the limitations of our perception, and I might have altered my experience, perhaps restricting it, had it been defined.

Next, I asked Laramus to shed light on the relationship between the Nibiruans and the Pleiadians, now knowing I had lived in both colonies but originated on Nibiru. I was confused about the connection, unsure if Nibiruans were Pleiadians or vice versa. Laramus said that Nibiru was an artificial planet made by the Pleiadians for use as a satellite that could explore the far reaches of our solar system. He compared Nibiruans and Pleiadians to Americans and Texans, explaining that they both were the same, but one was a subset of the other. He also said the Pleiadians had frequently cross-bred, but the original, pure Pleiadian strain that populated Nibiru was "Lyran" and produced eight to ten feet tall beings with blond hair and blue eyes. Out of curiosity, I asked him how many lifetimes I had incarnated since my soul's inception into physical form. He said I had lived 836 lifetimes, 362 on Earth and the remainder on eight different planets and a variety of lesser known stars. Knowing the Nibiruan year was equal to 3,600 of our Earth years, I assumed that the disproportionately high number of lives on Earth was probably due to our short life expectancy.

Laramus shared his love and left, allowing Joysiah to come forward. I had never spoken to Joysiah. He explained that he was the chief genetic engineer for the DNA Recoding project that was being spearheaded by the Syrian/Pleiadian and Nibiruan

Councils. Since I had questions regarding DNA Recoding, it had been determined that I should speak to a resident expert. I asked if I should be introducing my son, Drew, who was eleven, to DNA Recoding. Joysiah said not to worry about Drew since the children would be protected during the Earth's shift to a higher level of consciousness regardless of their spiritual progress. He said Drew would begin DNA Recoding at the appropriate time.

I knew Drew would need to eventually recode. He was an exceptionally spiritually gifted child as I had learned thorough channeled information I had received over the years and his own psychic performance. He was part of a soul group of twenty-three beings, some physical and some non-physical, who had a soul destiny contract of some kind with our planet. He also had thirty guides and teachers observing him, placed there for his higher good according to the input I was receiving. I knew he would be involved in work that would heal others. It was just a matter of time before Drew would be attracted to the DNA Recoding process.

Next, Dyjouniaa, the Keeper of the Records, emerged to answer some of my questions regarding my lineage. By now, I was accustomed to the many personalities and voices of N as she drew forth the energy of these non-physical beings. Again, I was being presented with the resident expert. I asked Dyjouniaa to tell me about the inception of my soul. He said my mother was one of Anu's daughters, and my father was a "great one," a leader among the Nibiruans. He said my father currently was an eleventh dimensional entity who would eventually like to speak to me. I did not know what an eleventh dimensional entity meant, but I knew Earth was supposed to be evolving to the fifth dimension so eleven sounded very progressed. My father currently acted as a "consultant" to the Nibiruan Council.

Dyjouniaa said my father was part Sirian and part Nibiruan/Pleiadian and my mother was part Sirian and part Nibiruan/Pleiadian, intentionally mating to produce my body type which would carry multiple codes. Dyjouniaa said matings were done with precision and care on Nibiru since DNA codes were very precious. Each individual was inseminated with certain combinations of codes in order to ensure the development of specific talents. I had been created with much forethought because my codes would allow me to communicate with many beings from different planets. In fact, he said I was frequently taken on space missions since I was the "communicator." He called me a special child who could decipher the codes like a computer. I wondered when in the recoding process I would be able to regain this incredible talent since Dyjouniaa said I retained this ability, capable of tuning into different people on different frequencies just like a TV had multiple channels. I certainly had no conscious awareness of this talent and could barely keep track of the details on my calendar. I asked Dyjouniaa if my father had looked like a human since I felt he carried the same energy as the Raphael being I had brought to this planet as a seedling. He said my father was human but had slightly different appendages than we know. My mind was bulging with all of this new information trying to visualize different possible styles of arms and legs, and I decided it was time to end the session.

SUMMARY

MAY DNA RECODING LESSONS

- The Nibiruan Council is a key player in the DNA Recoding process based on the past involvement of the Nibiruans in creating a two-strand DNA primitive worker. The primitive worker was a hybrid, using genes from an ape-like creature from Earth called the *Homo erectus* and cross-breeding it with the twelve strands of the Nibiruans or Pleiadians. Ninhursag and Enki were the two Nibiruans who were involved. Both Ninhursag and Enki are children of Anu, who currently heads the Nibiruan Council and was ruler of Nibiru when the genetic manipulation occurred. *Note:* This earlier two-strand version was very limited in its functions, that is, it could not propagate or mentally process information in a cognitive fashion, and was eventually replaced by Adamis who could propagate and is the predecessor of modern mankind. Both N and Anne agreed to incarnate on Earth in addition to their oversouls maintaining a presence on the Nibiruan Council to assist the Council in understanding the third dimensional thought process as well as to physically undergo recoding as a trial run.

- Joysiah is the chief genetic engineer of the DNA Recoding process, and he acts as a consultant to the Nibiruan Council. He and his team are responsible for actually reconnecting the twelve strands of DNA to our astral body.
- DNA Recoding is a process of trust. We must let go of our fears of the unknown, because fear causes discomfort when moving to a higher frequency and will actually hinder the process. Recoders have nothing to fear and everything to gain from experiencing the new DNA energy.
- The process of DNA Recoding works in concert with realizing one's soul contract. We may need to begin DNA Recoding without knowledge of our soul contract since we sometimes cannot align with the superconscious vibration that created that contract until we have experienced a lightening of our energy through the DNA Recoding process.
- Not everyone will complete DNA Recoding since some will not have the commitment to focus on clearing themselves of discordant energy and resistant behavior patterns, a necessary element of DNA Recoding in order to prepare for the higher vibration of the twelve-strand energy. DNA Recoding requires a total housecleaning of old issues and complete faith on the recoder's part that the outcome will be positive since things may potentially appear worse before they get better.
- Those who are recoding are surrounded by energetic protection in order to ensure they successfully complete DNA Recoding without any interference, should they desire.
- There are nine segments to DNA Recoding in Phase One. Later, Anne learned there were four more segments, again identifying them as she experienced them. Although N and Anne moved sequentially through the segments to support the learning process for the genetic engineers, DNA Recoding may not be sequential for everyone. Ultimately, all nine segments must be cleared and completed in order for one to plug into the twelve strands.

- The first four segments are Releasing Anger, Managing Anger, Clairaudience, and Clairvoyance as follows:
  - *Segment One, Releasing Anger* – Anger must be released to eliminate discordant energy in order to accommodate the higher vibration of the twelve-strand energy. The release of anger minimizes discomfort as the enhanced energy from DNA Recoding combines with the denser energy of the physical body. One should make peace with those who have caused anger in the past. This release can occur in person or at a soul level.
  - *Segment Two, Managing Anger* – If anger is stuffed during DNA Recoding, one will feel discomfort. Segment Two ensures that anger does not rebuild in the system after clearing it in Segment One, which would re-create a level of density that would cause discomfort. As one experiences DNA Recoding, one will discover a feeling of greater neutrality toward situations and a stronger sense of compassion. However, one should not expect to completely remove anger since anger is an aspect of the Earth experience that enables us to externally explode rather than internally implode and harm ourselves.
  - *Segment Three, Clairaudience* – The telepathic channel begins to open in Segment Three. As the lower emotion of anger is cleared from the electromagnetic system of our energy field, we become lighter. This is the point at which we will be able to hear directly from our spirit guides rather than getting the information via the dream state, intuition, or another individual who has psychic abilities.
  - *Segment Four, Clairvoyance* – Segment Four opens the third eye or telepathic channel so we will be able to see guides and other entities that are visiting the physical world. This is a gradual process since the third eye has atrophied through lack of use. Clairvoyance may begin with the sensing of dark forms followed by lighter forms and, finally, a full color range of vision. Or it may occur entirely in the third eye via psychic vision.

CHAPTER THREE
JUNE • 1996

SOME GLITCHES EXPERIENCED
DURING DNA RECODING

I called my friend Pat, the owner of Abby and Cici, to forewarn her of the difficulties I was experiencing due to lingering discordant energy in my body while experiencing DNA Recoding. I felt responsible to share this information with those who had made their formal request and begun DNA Recoding since I had been the informant of the process. Pat laughed when I called, claiming that the last several weeks of her life had been particularly interesting since many of her old issues had resurfaced. She thought she had resolved these issues, but apparently she had not cleared them at a deep enough level to satisfy her recoding team.

At first, Pat thought she was experiencing a backslide into poor habits. However, after consulting her spirit guides, she determined she was undergoing a final purging process. I confirmed her conclusion, explaining the necessity of releasing conflicting energies in order to make room for the new higher frequencies. We commiserated over how de-energizing it felt to repeat patterns we thought had been resolved. On the other hand, knowing we were going through a final release of negative energy patterns, we blessed our progress and resolved to endure.

In working with others, I have noticed a wide range of reactions in how people experience the new energy. Some glide effortlessly and easily through the process since they have conducted a large amount of clearing work prior to beginning the recoding process. In fact, I spoke to several clients who had completed DNA Recoding, including all three of the original phases, in a week or less! I have also worked with clients who ask where they are in DNA Recoding, and we discover that they are beginning the process at a later segment since the earlier segments have already been accommodated from previous healing work. Then there are others who cannot seem to complete and clear the first segment since they are not ready to release anger toward a particular individual. Or they move into the later segments where manifestation is a key part of the experience and struggle with self-empowerment which does not allow them to create. I have found that repatterning techniques that remove old behavior patterns at the soul level are extremely helpful for those who have difficulty releasing discordant habits. Instead of wallowing in a segment for months, they can clear the discordant energy in minutes. However, repatterning must be accompanied by a positive conscious or mental orientation to be effective, i.e., clearing someone of their anger toward an ex-spouse will not hold if they insist on continuing to build resistance by holding a grudge.

LEAVING JERRY

Jerry and I mutually decided to separate. Well, so much for "simmering" per Laramus' instructions. Apparently, Jerry did not cross the barrier his guides had presented to him because he was the one who broached the matter. I was contemplating bringing up the subject of separation, but Jerry had tripped in the parking lot at his office and broken his arm. He was having difficulty getting around, and I was hesitant to mention a major life change while he was in a vulnerable position. However, his own sense of the unlikelihood of our success must have motivated him, because he approached me one day while I was reading in a rather frantic fashion, claiming he was not comfortable pursuing our relationship any further since we had very different values and viewpoints. Instead of objecting, which I think he expected, I hurriedly concurred and asked what we should do about it since we co-owned our house.

This separation was very painful to me, yet I knew I had to honor my evolution and eliminate the restriction due to our mutual lack of understanding and communication. I felt anger and bitterness at Jerry for rejecting a spiritual way of thinking that would have kept us together. And I grieved losing my intended life mate, even though we were moving in conflicting spiritual directions. I applied myself to releasing the anger so it would not hinder my DNA Recoding, using repatterning techniques to resolve my feelings. It took me several weeks to release the anger despite my ardent attention to it.

Jerry said he would start looking for a house while we put our house on the market. However, I was not in the mood to move. Together, we had bought my dream house. It had five thousand square feet of open living space due to the contemporary design. The house was situated on an acre in the middle of town so I had a great deal of privacy from the neighbors, and there was a lap size swimming pool and Jacuzzi in the back yard. My windows displayed a park-like setting that was beautiful to behold especially when the pool was open.

I suggested to Jerry that I might want to keep the house. He looked surprised since it was very expensive. However, feeling somewhat guilty since he perceived he was abandoning me, he offered to give me a year to pay him for his half of the house. When we had purchased the house, he had enough money from the sale of his prior home to pay cash for his half of the house. I was paying a mortgage on my half. I found his offer extremely generous and quickly agreed to it. I was not only able to pay Jerry for his half of the house before the year had transpired, but I was also able to pay off my *entire* mortgage the following year. I have always attributed this incredible surge in personal wealth to the power I received from the additional twelve-strand DNA energy since it significantly increased my manifestation skills.

In an effort to understand my strong desire to choose DNA Recoding over my relationship, I queried my spirit guides. Based on what my guides shared, it seemed it required blind faith to reach my objective since I had no point of reference toward which I was navigating. I was told that I must trust my intuition and my soul's knowing that the ultimate result would be in my highest good. Here is what my guides shared with me:

"We feel your pain. It is very intense and heavy. You must take care not to make yourself ill with this feeling. Try to lighten it with laughter when possible. Sometimes lessons take you to painful places. We are holding as much of your energy as we can to lighten the load. You are on the threshold of all that you have longed for although we know it does not feel like it. You will experience such profound joy that you will look back on this pain and feel like it was utter nonsense. There is not a long path to the threshold. You are standing on it right now. Do not turn back by hanging onto old patterns. Move forward and those who wish to come with you, will indeed. We are asking you to be very brave by moving forward with blind trust. But you have no choice, do you? There is little to satisfy you where you are. You cannot find anything but the emptiness you have always found because the Earth experience encourages emptiness in its current prioritization of thinking over feeling. Jerry is not ready to change at this time, and he is also unwilling to support your changes. He has specifically opted to remain entrenched in habit patterns that cause more resistance than harmony. We have pushed on him so he would get serious because you selected him to be your life mate for this experience, but he prefers to stay where he is at this time. You are not to blame for his decision. We tried to assist him because he had a soul contract to accompany you. Now, you see how all souls do not move ahead just because they have agreed to a contract. Sometimes, on the conscious level, they simply cannot let go of old habits. We suggest that you understand this deeply because there will be those who will not choose to move forward in DNA Recoding. This is not your failure or theirs and should be met with complete acceptance. It is simply choice."

In addition to the above, my spirit guides told me they did not wish me to experience DNA Recoding alone. They felt I needed male energy to balance me during this process and to support me in my future work. They said the love frequency exponentially expanded the new energy we carry, magnifying it well beyond a single person's capacity by creating a dynamic interaction at the higher energy frequency. A love frequency would intensify the effect I had on others as I evolved through DNA Recoding, improving their chance of succeeding by raising the overall vibration. This would be true for everyone experiencing DNA Recoding, not just me.

My guides said they knew I was grieving the loss of a loved one. However, when I was ready, they would send me another mate. This time, my mate would be a recent walk-in. A walk-in is an entity who, through a contract with another soul, exchanges places. This is not a demonic possession since the contract has been negotiated between the two souls. In all cases, the work of the original soul has been completed on this plane and it is time for the soul to return to Spirit. Essentially, a walk-in uses the physical vehicle of a soul who has died but bequeathed their body to another. The walk-in lives with the experiences and memories that are held in the original soul's body while bringing their own database into the equation.

My guides were sending me a walk-in because my mate would need to be someone who could be comfortable with my spiritual goals and perfectly match my energy in order to support me. He needed to be able to move in concert with my current progress rather than me acting as mentor to him. Essentially, there was no need to train someone. And my mate needed to be a partner. This walk-in would rely on me to prod his memory, immediately moving into his own DNA Recoding and be in synchronicity with my own. My guides also desired for me to be with someone who perfectly matched my *energy* vibration so we could meld. We could focus on our spiritual mission, basking in the strong essence of love, rather than spending our time working through past lifetime issues. I was somewhat cheered by this information, feeling perhaps I had not failed a relationship as much as I simply needed to keep moving. I told my guides I would let them know when my heart was ready to receive a new life partner.

REVISITING THE GOLDEN WEB

Julia called to tell me she was separating from her husband, and she needed a place to live. This news confirmed my sense that my spiritual team would help me as I continued to move through DNA Recoding since I was currently wondering how I could afford to pay my mortgage and save money to pay Jerry. I offered to share my house with Julia so we could emotionally support each other during our transition, and she could financially support me in my goals. She was quick to accept my offer, and she decided to move in when Jerry moved out the following week. Typical of the type of support I was receiving from Spirit, Jerry had found and purchased a house in the ridiculously short time frame of three weeks, and he was already in the process of relocating.

Julia came over to determine how she would arrange her furniture in her new living space, and I asked her if she would spend some time repatterning me. I had used the kinesiology technique I had learned in Holographic Repatterning to determine if I resonated with a "romantic" love energy, wanting to ensure great success for my future promised relationship. I resonated with love, but did not resonate with "romance" since I had always primarily experienced life from a mental level. I was a thinker rather than a feeler, and my tendency to prioritize mind over heart would not support the type of relationship I envisioned having. Julia agreed to assist, enjoying opportunities to practice her new repatterning skills. She decided to repattern me on all multi-dimensional levels rather than limiting it to my Earth incarnations since I had told her I experienced Lahaina's existence in another dimension. I agreed, not realizing how complete a healing I would undergo during a very intense two-hour session.

Julia and I uncovered the discordant impact of a past life I had experienced which affected my ability to easily align with the feeling of love. It was a lifetime where I had traveled with a team of Pleiadian scientists to live among the Grays, those blue-gray entities with the almond-shaped eyes who, according to books like *Communion*, have abducted mankind and cattle for experimentation. I lived among the Grays for several lifetimes, as had Jerry, but had chosen to leave when their philosophies no longer aligned with mine. I was living in much pain in the lifetime that Julia discovered through her repatterning techniques, apparently resulting from DNA experiments to which I had personally subjected myself in support of scientific discovery.

Who knows why a soul agrees to uncomfortable experiences? On Earth, we certainly seem to need to have our issues repeatedly shoved in front of our face before we choose to address them. But I assume at some level we possess a sound rationale for enduring painful life lessons in support of our soul evolution.

In this case, I must have underestimated the pain I would endure from my decisions. During a past life regression I had done several years ago with Bobbie, I re-experienced my rapid exit from the Grays during the same lifetime that Julia had uncovered. Jerry, who had been a partner in that lifetime, was attempting to help me leave. Based on the pain I was experiencing and the independent spirit I still exercise, I grew tired of waiting for him to determine the best exit strategy.

In my intense desire to leave the planet, I had goofed by taking matters into my own hands, and I had blown my grid structure apart during my quick exit. Our grid structure houses our "hard drive" which essentially contains our soul programs. Our grid holds our past, present, and future soul records. It also connects us with all that is, via a matrix structure that extends from the electromagnetic field that surrounds us in all directions. By destroying my grid structure, I had altered my operating program. I saw myself explode into a mass of red lava during the regression I had done with Bobbie, but I did not know I had incurred permanent damage to my grid. I confirmed through later channeling sessions with Bobbie that I returned to the Pleiades after unintentionally blowing myself apart. I spent time in the Pleiades before coming to Earth over 120,000 years ago to experience life in my current guise and prepare for the day when Earth would be ready to move to its next stage of evolution.

While Julia was attempting to uncover the information required to complete my repatterning, she encountered information about another person who was involved with my rapid exit from the Grays. I heard my spirit guides say that this person was my future life partner. It seems that Jerry and my future mate were busy debating my most propitious exit, wanting to return me intact to the Pleiades. However, they could not come to agreement, and out of frustration, I left on my own initiative. This is probably why Jerry made a soul contract to assist me during my current transition since he had not been able to help me in that past life. How appropriate that he was to be replaced with the other player who had also desired to assist me.

Through a combination of the repatterning method and our combined growing telepathic skills, we determined I had severely damaged my grid structure in that explosion. Essentially, I was not aligned with my true self. In fact, I was still sporting the same grid injuries after all these years. In addition to the grid damage, I was carrying several negative emotional patterns that were interfering with my ability to resonate with romantic love. First of all, I had isolated myself with intense self-sufficiency, not allowing others to help me. This reflected my feeling of really needing someone to help after being blown to pieces in a hostile reality. Yet no one was there. Secondly, I carried an underlying fear of the future since I had lost my unique communication faculties, unable to relate as I had in the past. Julia said she could see my grid and that it was different than any she had seen before, a sparkling gold net interspersed with precious gemstones. It was interesting, and confirming, that Bobbie had seen the same gold net and jewels several months before.

Julia told me to lie down. She held her hand over my heart chakra to hold the energy as my guides repaired my grid. During this time, I envisioned the explosion I had witnessed during my earlier regression with Bobbie. I felt my vast neediness when no one was there, and my ensuing fear when considering facing the future being handicapped. While lying there, I realized the implications of damaging my grid. Apparently, I used my grid to communicate with the other planets. It linked me to thousands of different languages. The jewels were the minerals that resided on the planets and stars with which I was communicating, each one representing the universe from which it came. For example, quartz crystal was the mineral for Earth since it is a primary component of the planet. These minerals are like crystals in radios, transmitting the energy frequencies and the translation codes for the matching locations. No wonder I had developed a fear of the future. I knew I had lost my talent for communicating which had been carefully created during my soul inception on Nibiru many years before. I do not know what prevented me from mending my grid prior to this time. I only knew that I needed to be consciously aware of the infraction and request the repair.

Julia had been using kinesiology to obtain answers to some of her own questions during my grid repair. She was trying to determine if anyone had a similar grid to mine. She said my guides wanted me to know I was "special and unique." I asked Julia if my future partner would align with my energy, thinking that Jerry may not have matched. Julia checked and said our grid structure would totally align, and we would recognize each other immediately due to the complete synergy of our energy. I wondered what it would feel like to be so similar to another person since I had lived the majority of this life feeling alone and different, never understanding why I could not connect with others. It had taken many years for me to learn I was a starseed. Once I understood I was in the smaller percentage of old souls who had not originated here, it was easier to handle feeling different. But I had never overcome this feeling in my intimate relationships. Perhaps that time of isolation was finally ending for me in finding my life partner.

Julia completed the healing by having me do some deep breathing patterns as I cried and cried, releasing the pent up emotions carried for so many lifetimes. When we were done, I felt like a different person. I held no grief nor anger toward Jerry. This was an odd feeling since I had been regularly addressing these emotions over the last few weeks but could not seem to let go. After less than two hours of therapy, they were gone! I felt optimistic and positive. I felt one thousand pounds lighter, eagerly anticipating the future. I was amazed at the transition from depressed and miserable to joyous and energetic, bounding with life. I hugged Julia and thanked her for the immediate relief.

BECOMING A TEACHER INSTEAD OF A PUPIL

Bobbie called and asked me to utilize my new, ever-strengthening telepathic abilities to do a linking session for her. I was amazed since she had been my teacher for five years, yet she was asking me to examine something for her. I certainly did not feel equipped since she had always played the psychic role, but I decided it was time to put my doubts aside and move into the new arena of teacher rather than pupil. Bobbie had been dealing with a highly emotional issue that involved a man, and she needed an unbiased and objective interpretation. I told her I would gladly assist.

We explored Bobbie's problem which involved her need to separate from a man she had been dating. I wondered why this issue kept surfacing and grew concerned that everyone who recoded would experience this problem. However, I was reassured that I was attracting those who were undergoing similar problems since I was holding a vibration of separation. In other words, I was so focused on my own separation that the universe kept matching my energy with similar energy, namely those who were also going through separation. DNA Recoding would not stimulate a lot of divorces!

During my linking session exploring Bobbie's personal problem with her partner, I received some answers regarding her resistance to recoding. I had provided her with the formal request for DNA Recoding several months ago, but she had experienced hesitation about starting the process. Instead of viewing DNA Recoding as an opportunity to improve the Earth by expanding her abilities to heal others, Bobbie saw it as a potential severing of her Earth ties by aligning her more with Spirit than with the physical life that she loved. Indeed, Bobbie was my most "Earthy" friend. She, unlike my typical new age counterparts, preferred the physical to the non-physical and felt her life was rich due to the dense matter in which she operated. For the rest of us, we felt hindered by the density of the Earth plane and desired to move more freely like energy beings.

As further understanding of Bobbie's attitude, I telepathically viewed a past lifetime when she was a Goddess on Earth. I began to comprehend her hesitancy to recode. During this time period, she was completely unified with the Earth, a true Earth sprite. I watched as she danced across fields, naked, hair streaming behind her, living a life of joy and communion with the Earth energy. I also saw how she would have difficulty regaining that level of synergy with the Earth due to its current fear-based condition. Her past life as a Earth Goddess had been devoid of fear. She would be better able to recapture that feeling and improve the energy of the Earth by raising it to a higher frequency and removing fear, a process available to her through DNA Recoding. Ironically, she would become *more* grounded by raising her frequency instead of being *less* grounded on the Earth plane. This would be an important concept for all recoders to understand. We are not recoding to expedite our exit from the Earth. We are recoding to become more at one with the Earth energy and maximize our experience while we are here.

Based on the information I provided, Bobbie decided to read the DNA Recoding request. Her query soared energetically to the top of a mountain where a group of elders sporting white beards and long white robes stood by a ceremonial altar. They seemed amused when they determined the originator of the request, recognizing Bobbie immediately because she worked with them daily as an Earth representative of their non-physical team. In a breathtaking fashion, they sent approval of her request down the mountain by way of a soaring white dove. Later, in a channeling from Joysiah, it was explained that Bobbie, like many of the older souls, had assisted in evolving many civilizations from lower to higher energy frequencies in the past. It was a mission in which we apparently liked to enlist. However, Joysiah explained that Bobbie needed to formally request recoding because the Sirian/Pleiadian Council must be assured that each individual is asking for DNA Recoding of their own free will based in *this* life's experience.

Prior to making her request, I needed to call home to obtain the formal wording that I had left in my office. My son, Drew, was home, so I directed him to where I kept the formal request and asked him to read it to me over the telephone. I assumed that the request would not be honored for him since there was no conscious intent involved. After our session, it dawned on me that perhaps Drew had unknowingly gained approval due to his readiness for the process. I asked Bobbie what she thought, and she checked to determine if Drew had been given approval. Sure enough, Drew was our first male (and child) who had requested DNA Recoding and been approved for it. I hoped he would have an easy time of recoding because he was too young to have established any strong discordant behavior problems. I decided it was time to explain the DNA Recoding process to him when I returned home.

As it turned out, Drew acclimated to DNA Recoding very nicely since he was emerging into puberty and had no prior point of context for adult living. Essentially, he was able to make new rules that were unavailable to the rest of us when we were growing since he possessed the twelve-strand energy. There were periods during Drew's recoding when he consciously applied the brakes since he was simply not ready for a fast ride. There were other times when his genetic engineer slowed his progress because he felt Drew desired to move ahead to gain adult approval rather than for his own spiritual progress. We worry so much about our children and what they can handle. Yet they either seem to have an innate sense of where they need to be or else Spirit will assist them in finding balance.

I was also told to establish a formal ritual for reading the request for DNA Recoding so anyone casually reading the words would not worry about unintentionally starting the process. The ceremony that my guides and I developed is simple but involves lighting candles and drawing a bath. That way, no one can begin DNA Recoding like my son, Drew (although I believe there are never any mistakes). They will consciously initiate the request.

INFORMATION ON MY FUTURE MATE

Bobbie called and said she was conducting a channeling on love relationships, and would I like to attend? I agreed, holding the intent of asking some questions about my future partner since I was intensely curious. I also felt freed from Jerry, ready to plunge into the meaningful relationship mentioned by my guides. Bobbie had already begun channeling information about love when I arrived. I listened to her information for the other attendees, including N and Pat, some of which involved DNA Recoding in addition to relationship information. When Pat asked what segment she had completed thus far in recoding, Joysiah emerged to respond to her question. Pat was told she had finished Segments One and Two. I asked what segments I had completed and he said, "Segments One through Four." I was surprised since Segment Four is Clairvoyance and I had yet to "see" any entities. But Joysiah said I would soon be able to "peer into other dimensional levels while living in third dimensional reality."

Bearing in mind we were not given information on the segments until we had attained them, we were surprised when N was told she had reached Segment Five. N always seemed to precede me by one segment, give me some rudimentary information on it, and leave the rest to me. Through my continuing ability to hear my guides, I would record my experiences as well as other types of information that were pertinent to the particular aspect of DNA Recoding that I was experiencing. We asked if Joysiah could share information on Segment Five since one of us had entered it.

Joysiah explained that Segment Five, Integration, was an assimilation of the first four segments. Segment Five is critical because it builds the foundation for the final work. It is a segment some would elect not to complete due to the fact it requires complete acceptance of one's soul contract which *may* mean changes one is not ready to make in one's current life. This does not mean we have to *leave* the life we have created. We simply need to *amend* it. I was never required to alter my values or lifestyle or change the way I chose to make a living. I felt my relationship changes had been initiated far in advance of DNA Recoding.

The Integration phase provides the focus we need to fulfill our planetary contracts. In other words, we have removed discordant energy from anger, and we have opened up our intuitive side so we can experience synergy with the soul contracts that brought us here in the first place. Naturally, an integration of who we are and what we wish to attain would need to occur. During Segment Five, there were also some steps the genetic engineers needed to complete that could not be done in the first four segments based on the method used to reconnect the twelve strands. During Segment Five, the engineers were at the point where they could ensure that everything had been integrated. Joysiah said Segment Five was the most challenging part for them since it laid the building blocks for progressing through Segments Six through Nine.

Joysiah also informed us that some might think they were undergoing DNA Recoding since they might be experiencing physical symptoms associated with clearing blockages. He said this should not be confused with the actual DNA Recoding process, where the genetic engineers work on our astral body to recoil our ten additional DNA strands. Apparently, we already hold twelve, but ten are de-coiled. DNA Recoding involves removing implants that de-coil ten of the twelve strands and keep them separate. He also said Bobbie would speed through the different segments since she had been there before, although a few of the segments would take her for "a ride." We laughed, acknowledging the ride we were all encountering as the first individuals to hold the energy from this particular process on Earth. We felt joy in having formed a solid support network during this incredible experience.

It was finally my turn to ask about relationships. I asked Laramus, my genetic engineer, to come forward to speak with me. I wanted him to shed some light on my future life partner. Ever since the repatterning session I had experienced with Julia, I had felt complete closure regarding my relationship with Jerry. I was anxious to experience this profound love that had been promised to all recoders. I asked Laramus if my future mate would be himself, Laramus, entering from the other side to be with me? Over the past few months, I had developed a slight crush on my genetic engineer. After all, he was a part of my everyday life and acted like a partner and friend through his loving support.

Laramus said that, indeed, they were sending me someone who was currently in non-physical form although it would not be himself. He was flattered by my feelings, but he was there to help me from the other side. Ironically, I had met an intuitive artist, Phyllis, who had a tremendous talent for capturing the image of our spirit guides. I had employed her to draw several of my guides in the past, and I called her around this time to do a depiction of Laramus. I loved the physical rendition of Laramus and had it framed to hang on my office wall. When I eventually met my partner, or walk-in as we referred to him at this stage, I realized that Phyllis had actually drawn my walk-in. Although Laramus never admitted to moving from the non-physical to the physical side, I always felt Phyllis' picture confirmed that an essential aspect of my partner existed in Laramus and vice versa, whether or not they were one and the same.

I asked Laramus to give me information about my walk-in, but he said that type of information would solidify the walk-in's energy in spirit form because I would send thought patterns about his current configuration. My future mate was in the process of extracting himself from the non-physical world, and they did not want to hamper his progress. Nor did I, since I was interested in the experience of meeting another being with my identical grid structure! I moved to another tactic and asked for Earth information about the walk-in. When was he to arrive and how would I know him?

Laramus said I would connect with my walk-in during the late summer. But that was all of the information he could provide about the walk-in. Later, when Bobbie came out of trance, she said she saw a cute Scotch Terrier standing there the entire time Laramus was talking about my walk-in. I considered the possibility that he might be named Scott. We all decided we would faint if I met a man named Scott this summer who was walking a Terrier! While discussing my future mate with Laramus, I caught a glimpse of an individual who practiced a more traditional healing technique like chiropractic, but was not a traditional healer. This person used chiropractic therapy as a springboard for less mainstream types of healing. I confirmed this information with Bobbie. Now, I had some clues. I knew he was a healer, owned a dog, and would appear, according to Laramus' promised time frame, around August.

Next, I reminded Laramus I needed money to buy Jerry's share of my house. I also requested assistance selling the one hundred acres of farm land I owned in Missouri. I had originally purchased the land to build a spiritual training center, but the expense of maintaining the land while accumulating funds to build the meeting rooms seemed overwhelming in view of the money I owed Jerry. Laramus said a large sum of money was coming my way. I reminded him I did not want to earn it by working around the clock since I had been doing that since I started my business four years ago. He replied, "You have already specified that, haven't you, dear one?" I laughed since I frequently requested that my spirit guides assist me in my venture of winning the lottery. I asked if I would be winning Publisher's Clearing House as a means of solving my financial situation. Laramus said that "a lot of people are asking for that so I don't know if that is possible, but it will be something similar." He also said my land would be replaced by something more suitable to my dream rather than a large tract of undeveloped land an hour away from Kansas City. I told him I looked forward to paying my debt to Jerry and realizing my dream. I left Bobbie's house feeling uplifted by the experience and assured that my life was on an incredibly fast and exciting, if yet somewhat undefined, path.

INCREASING TELEPATHIC SKILLS

My mother had given my name to her neighbor in Florida, Kristin, because I wanted to practice my psychic ability on a complete stranger. Kristin and I scheduled a call in order to explore my emerging telepathic talents within the context of the unknown. The only information I had about Kristin was that she had a son with allergy problems, and she desired information on the source of the problem. Ironically, Kristin never mentioned her son's allergies during our conversation. My mother had never given me information about Kristin or her family other than Kristin was a kindred spirit in terms of her love of spirituality.

Kristin called me, and I spent some time talking with her about her passion for metaphysics. We compared books we had read. I asked her if she knew of her origins, assuming she was probably an older soul and, hence, a starseed who had lived in many different galaxies before Earth. Usually those who exhibited an intense passion for esoteric subject matter were starseeded souls. She said she was unaware of her origins but was ready to hear what I had to say. I checked her soul origination and that of her family members. Not too surprisingly, they were all starseeds. She and her son were originally from Sirius, and her husband and daughter were from the Pleiades. She did not seem distraught to discover she had not originated on Earth, and in fact said she had suspected as much.

She asked me to give her information on her daughter. I could see that Kristin's nine-year-old daughter, Marissa, was a walk-in, and the swap between her original daughter's soul and the walk-in's soul had occurred the prior year. Again, my vibration resonated with walk-in's based on my interest in finding my own, and I was drawing those to me who were dealing with similar situations. I did not know how to tell Kristin that the daughter with whom she was currently living was not her original daughter, so I asked her if she had noticed any recent changes in Marissa's behavior. She confirmed my suspicions by saying her typically cheerful, bright daughter had plunged into dark moods and fits of anger. I asked Kristin if she had ever heard the term "walk-in." I breathed a sigh of relief when I heard that she had read two books on walk-ins the previous year. I silently thanked Spirit for preparing Kristin for my information.

I took a deep breath and gave Kristin the news. Fortunately, she was relieved to hear about the walk-in, suspecting something such as I described due to Marissa's dramatic personality shift. She asked about her original daughter, and I could see her happily swinging from a crescent moon outside a beautiful castle, laughing and saying, "Hi mommy, I'm so happy here!" Wherever her soul had gone, she had found great peace in her new location. I also understood why the new Marissa was moody and angry. Apparently the original Marissa had contracted to experience the birth process on Earth as part of her soul development. She was supposed to switch with the new Marissa some time during the first year of her life. However, the original Marissa grew to love Kristin so much, she did not want to leave. She stayed on Earth for nine years until her guides cajoled her into fulfilling her commitment to the new being. In essence, the new being felt cheated of her Earth childhood experience. She did not consciously know why she was angry, but she knew she had missed something. Kristin could heal her by replaying elements of childhood, actually doing things like giving her a bath and washing her hair like a baby or feeding her. I told her to make little games of these events, perhaps having other babies around so her daughter felt like one of the crowd.

Several months after our session, Kristin called to thank me for the information I had shared since it had generated a healing for her daughter. Apparently, Marissa began having moments of regressing to babyhood, gurgling and babbling baby talk. Without the information I had provided, Kristin said she would have been alarmed and tried to stop it. However, based on her insight, she simply nurtured Marissa even more during those episodes, holding her in her lap and stroking her hair and cooing to her. Kristin quickly outgrew these age lapses based on her mother's approach.

As a footnote, I heard through my mother months later that Kristin had undergone her own healing as a result of our session. During our telephone conversation, I noted a deep grief in her heart and asked her if she had lost a child in the past. Kristin had, in fact, experienced a miscarriage a few years ago. I told her she needed to heal this wound, or it would never resolve itself. I gave her a technique for working through the pain which apparently she followed. In October, Kristin visited a famous psychic who had come to Florida. During her reading, the psychic confirmed the information I had given Kristin without any knowledge of our previous session. She also told Kristin that she saw a baby growing in Kristin's womb that would arrive in the near future. Unfortunately, as I later discovered, Kristin experienced a miscarriage with this fetus as well. However, we looked at the remaining soul issues surrounding this repeated experience and, eventually, Kristin came to peace with her miscarriages. Given the level of resonance Kristin had with the information I provided, I resolved to stop doubting my telepathic information and simply share what I saw when others asked.

TELLING OTHERS ABOUT DNA RECODING

Based on word of mouth, more and more people have called me to obtain information about DNA Recoding. In an effort to provide them with what they need and lessen the burden of running both a marketing consulting and metaphysical business, I asked N to ask Anu if he would be willing to conduct some public sessions. Anu agreed and said he would be happy to introduce the concept of DNA Recoding and give some background information. However, he told N to tell me that I should develop a written summary of what I knew about DNA Recoding to distribute during the first session.

Later, I asked Laramus, my genetic engineer, to help me compile information to distribute to the attendees. I was finally able to receive information from Laramus since I clearly heard him respond in the affirmative. The following summarizes the information he sent via telepathy and was the first of many transmissions that formulated the DNA Recoding process outlined in the appendix of this book.

INFORMATION ABOUT THE DNA RECODING PROCESS PER LARAMUS

DEFINITION OF DNA RECODING

DNA Recoding is a process available to mankind which enables you to move from a two-strand DNA system to a twelve-strand system. The twelve-strand system is already resident in the *Homo sapiens* form, consisting of two strands that form a double helix and ten strands that are de-magnetized. This is the "junk" DNA that your scientists reference because they are unable to determine its purpose. The reconnecting of your complete circuitry enables you to have access to full consciousness, including telepathic abilities, memory of past physical and non-physical existence, and knowledge of your Akashic (soul) records.

- "Recoding requires that we accept our soul contract. Otherwise, we would be giving powers to those who have not made a commitment to the light. We will provide as much information as possible regarding your soul contract. However, some information will not be shared since it would be meaningless until you achieve greater awareness and knowledge. This information will be given to you as you move through DNA Recoding.
- DNA Recoding is not a defined process. We are learning with you since third dimensional beings have never reduced their density and moved to a lighter frequency. This means we may make you uncomfortable at times, but we have no intention of harming you and will withdraw efforts immediately if you are experiencing any discomfort. We assure you that we will love and care for you and no harm will come to you. In fact, we promise you an outcome that will expand the meaning of your life.
- DNA Recoding will take commitment on your part. You will need to rid yourself of toxic energy, mostly in the form of anger or fear, from this life as well as past lives. This means you may feel worse before you feel better as

you process all of your clearing. But believe us when we say, you are on the brink of a great joy that you have awaited for many lifetimes on this planet.

- If you are a starseed, you are an old soul who has had many planetary experiences before incarnating on Earth. For you, DNA Recoding is a process of remembering what you agreed to forget when you came into a physical body on Earth. You are simply activating the codes already residing in your etheric body in the form of crystals. The only "new" information will be how to transform the human vehicle you are inhabiting to a higher state of consciousness, not what it will feel like.

- Not everyone will complete DNA Recoding. However, that possibility is extended to all of you, so make of it what you will. Bear in mind that whatever you do complete will be sufficient for your evolution since it will fit with your Divine Purpose.

- When you begin to recode, you extract yourself from the pool of mass consciousness of anger and fear that constructs reality for your planet. You are part of the recoder pool of consciousness, one based in love and joy. As you expand your consciousness and continue through the process, the recoder consciousness grows in strength, creating a new pool of consciousness for mankind to attain. For this reason, some of you may feel less inclined to maintain relationships with non-recoders since you no longer exist in the same pool of consciousness. Others will benefit from these relationships, both for yourself in terms of the grounding the non-recoder brings you and for your partner due to the enhanced energy you bring to the relationship. For those who wish to move to new relationships, we will assist you in attracting more appropriate partnerships since love magnifies the consciousness you are experiencing for the greatest good of all.

- Once you have undergone DNA Recoding, we ask that you remember where you came from and help those who live on this planet and have not recoded. Young souls have only existed on Earth, and they need your assistance to succeed at moving to the next stage of consciousness. Remember, for these souls, they have no point of context like yourselves to different vibratory states so they may not embrace this process as easily as you do based on fear of the unknown.

• No matter how overwhelming DNA Recoding may seem, life will be better beyond your expectations when you have completed the process. Stay with it, dear ones, for the time of your life."

DON'T TELL ME I'M A WALK-IN!

I am meeting more and more walk-ins or soul transfers who share their experiences with me. I had never heard of a walk-in until I met my friend Pat, who almost had a breakdown in 1971 when she walked-in due to the complete disconnection from the life her predecessor had led. Her husband abandoned her as a result of the dramatic shift in her personality, even ridiculing her in court during their divorce about her perception that she had had a soul shift. I was curious about walk-ins since I was meeting so many of them, including N who had walked in several years ago. However, I felt no connection with the phenomenon.

During dinner one evening, my son asked me if I was a walk-in. He had heard some of my friends discussing their soul exchange experiences and knew what it was. I immediately responded, "no." He persisted, asking me if I had ever checked via kinesiology to determine if I was a walk-in. I liked to encourage Drew to be responsible for his own information and told him to check for me if it was important to him. He used the kinesiology I had taught him and got a "yes," exclaiming, "Mom, you're a walk-in!" I looked at him with surprise and decided to check for myself, quickly confirming from my guides as I opened to the possibility that I was a walk-in who had swapped places with the original Anne at five years of age.

All of a sudden, it made so much sense. This is the age when my personality changed, according to the stories my parents shared. They claimed that I went from this placid, peaceful little girl to an angry, fearful child who slept on the floor of my parents' room because I was so afraid of dying. I remember envisioning a black nothingness that would descend and blot me out forever, feeling so engulfed by the void that I would move into my parents' bedroom for comfort. Now, it made sense to me. What walk-in wouldn't fear death after knowing that life is eternal, then being flash cut onto Earth where death was described as an ending? I was so nervous at the age of five that my mother took me to Florida for several weeks of relaxation, hoping her focus on me would encourage me to relax. It was a difficult time for me, and it took years to heal my fear of dying.

Later, I was told by a new mentor and teacher, Venessa, that I walked in at the age of five to ensure that I lived in a healthy body. Based on my energy type and my rather unique grid structure, I would most likely have endured birth defects had I attempted to inhabit a fetus. I needed the more mature body of a five year old to ensure a healthy vehicle. My soul path would have been hampered by birth defects, causing me to focus more on healing my physical limitations rather than attending to emotional and spiritual healing. This also explained why I felt little affinity to walking in since it had occurred at such a young age. The majority of Anne's life had been led by the walk-in, a third dimensional aspect of Lahaina, rather than the original occupant, Anne. I thanked my son for helping me incorporate this new piece of information although I was still stunned by the information.

THE COLLECTIVE
CONSCIOUSNESS OF RECODERS

Julia finally moved into the house, and we decided to end the day by doing a linking session with my interpreter guide, Nephras, and Julia's own guides and teachers. We wanted to explore the reasons for her marriage ending, a parting of two people who loved each other but were no longer compatible. I felt that Julia and I mirrored each other's lives since she was experiencing a similar situation to the one I had with Jerry. We spent some time examining the past lives Julia had with her husband, and we determined how this parting represented a major healing for her in this lifetime.

While examining the current situation and where she was heading, Nephras showed us an important element of DNA Recoding. Up until recently, Julia had resided in the mass consciousness of our society, strongly impacted by the same energy patterns that composed the collective unconscious of our reality. For example, she might resonate to a life of love and joy, but based on the pervasive fear and anger characteristic of our society, she was constantly bombarded with those elements and easily absorbed them into her system. A great deal of her energy had been directed toward maintaining love and joy to combat the drag created by society's negative consciousness. However, with DNA Recoding, she was freeing herself from the negativity of the mass consciousness, and she was connecting to a new, upgraded energy based on higher spiritual principles.

We were thrilled by the implications of this information since it required us to put a lot less energy into maintaining elusive frequencies like love and joy, freeing us to focus on pouring our energy into moving higher and higher. Nephras explained that currently, as we entered this new pool of consciousness, we felt the need to shed our old relationships with partners who no longer meshed with our energy. However, we were not intended to be alone. We were meant to enter relationships with males who were recoding as a means of exponentially growing the newly emerging consciousness. The energy of love was like pouring lighter fluid on charcoal. It acted as a catalyst to grow the recoder consciousness so much faster than could be done without the male/female energy. This information further confirmed what we had heard earlier and fed my growing confidence that I would soon meet my life partner, one connected on all spiritual, emotional, mental, and physical dimensions.

Nephras explained that it would weaken our new state of being, *during the process of DNA Recoding*, to be physically intimate with those who held lower frequencies. In particular, we would slow our evolution by making love with someone who was not recoding since we would interact with a lower energy vibration. Since Julia had been interested in pursuing a relationship with someone who was not going through DNA Recoding, she was told she needed to insulate her new vibration so she would not be buffeted between two different energies. If she decided to pursue her interest in this new male in her life, she was advised to surround herself with a sheathing of gold light prior to any physical contact. She was to place the gold light around her like a glove fits a hand. This would act as a filter, allowing the positive energy associated with love and the physical act of intercourse to penetrate while lessening the impact of her partner's lower energy frequency. However, Nephras warned Julia that her relationship with this particular man would probably be temporary because she would not be satisfied in the long term.

I realized that some would not undergo DNA Recoding because they would feel disloyal to partners who were uninterested in the same path. Sometimes, we believe we are supportive when we remain static so we will not rock the boat in the relationship. We forget that any upgrade in emotional, spiritual, or physical energy is always beneficial at some level, sometimes in support of maintaining the relationship and sometimes expediting its demise. Based on this logic, some may be interested in recoding but refuse to pursue it. Of course, we live in Divine Purpose so if someone chooses to forgo spiritual growth to uphold their relationship, that was the perfect path for them. Per Laramus, every soul would arrive at the perfect destination for their respective experiences. I knew I had to honor and respect how far one wished to go without judgment.

ARE WE ALL NIBIRUANS?

N came over to have her picture taken for a brochure she was creating about her channeling. She had decided to be in trance for the picture and did not wish to go to an unaware photographer who would not understand channeling. I had asked my ex-husband, Ed, who had photography experience, some very sophisticated camera equipment, and heightened spiritual awareness, to take her photograph. Ed was happy to assist, and he came over with our son, Drew, to take the pictures. We created the appropriate backdrops and lighting, used a fan to obtain a more etheric look, and N went into a trance.

Anu emerged during N's trance, asking if he had permission to open "this one's eyes" and read our energy. We said "yes," knowing he had to open N's eyes anyway for the picture and wanting the experience of sharing energy with him. He asked to

see the "young one," slowly rotating N's head without blinking
and looking directly into Drew's eyes. It was an eerie experience
because N's eyes were very out of focus, and she seemed to look
at us yet through us. As Anu aligned his head with Drew, he said,
"Ah, my grandson. You are our one child who is going through
DNA Recoding." He sounded as proud as Drew's current grandparents, just as if he had made the honor roll on his report card.

Drew's relationship as grandson to Anu was news to us,
although we suspected some tie due to his supposedly inadver-
tent plunge into DNA Recoding. Plus, he had chosen to incarnate
with me as his mother so he probably had foresight of his interaction with recoding at an intuitive level. Anu said, "Child, you
do not have a genetic engineer assigned to you." Naturally, we
were unaware of this situation since we were unsure if Drew was
actively recoding or simply playing with the process as a means
of adult acceptance. Anu asked if Drew would permit Joysiah to
be his genetic engineer. I was honored by this offer since Joysiah
was the head geneticist for the DNA Recoding project. Drew said
he would like to work with Joysiah although he was less
impressed than I was. Based on Anu's pronouncement of Drew
as his grandson, I wondered if all of us who were initially experiencing DNA Recoding originated from the same Nibiruan roots,
similar to some huge, sprawling Tennessee family.

Later that same day, a woman named Jeanne came to see me
for a reading since she had heard I was experimenting with my
new telepathic powers, and was involved with DNA Recoding.
Jeanne's session was fascinating. She had been a high priestess in
a prior lifetime, an oracle of her planet prior to its demise by
destructive invaders. She was in the process of birthing a Christ
consciousness being who would extend the energy to rejuvenate
her ailing planet. Prior to the birth of the evolved soul, the invaders,
knowing the light would overcome them with the advent of this
entity, trained a laser at her womb and aborted the fetus. Jeanne,
in her fury, redirected the laser at the invader's star and blew up
their home. Subsequent to the explosion, she felt great remorse
based on her violation of the principle of compassion. I knew what
that felt like after my own experience in the crystal city of Sedona.
She has lived with the guilt and shame from her action for eons,

playing roles on both sides as she has learned about the balance between light and dark and the importance of both for evolution.

I felt Jeanne's pain, and told her we needed to do a repatterning to remove the guilt since it would interfere with her DNA Recoding. As I examined her purpose, I saw that she would heal others by increasing the world's understanding of light and dark energy and how both interact to assist each other. This is very different from the perspective we hold where we evaluate light as "good" and dark as "bad." In fact, we need the darkness in order to recognize the light. I saw her writing a book about her life as an oracle and the ensuing lifetimes following that experience. The book would read like an adventure story, much like *The Celestine Prophecy*, and would eventually be made into a movie, one that would bring her much wealth.

I asked Jeanne to voice the formal DNA Recoding request. Her request was sent into a volcano and down into the center of the Earth. I told her what had happened, wondering why her request had gone "down" while everyone else's had gone "up." Jeanne clarified the situation by telling me that volcanoes had a special meaning for her which made it a highly appropriate setting for her request. She worked with Earth energy, and the volcano was a key element in the healing work that she did. Jeanne had mentioned that she was engaged during our session so I told her it might be propitious for her fiancé to undergo DNA Recoding. Otherwise, they risked having misaligned energies. Jeanne promised to share the DNA Recoding information with her future mate, Mark.

MORE INFORMATION ON MY FUTURE MATE

Kim, who was visiting from Colorado, and Bobbie came to see me. Kim was interested in DNA Recoding because Bobbie had felt a positive change in her own energy after completing her formal request. Kim thought she might obtain equal benefit, and she wanted to discuss it with me. However, I felt she had already begun retrieving the twelve-strand energy and strongly perceived that she did not need to follow the DNA Recoding process. I checked telepathically as well as via kinesiology, and I was told she did not need to formulate a formal request.

We sat and tried to understand how Kim had received approval without formally requesting it. I already logically hypothesized that all recoders did not need my particular wording since I could hardly be the gateway for everyone on Earth. The geographic and language barriers made that self-evident and, besides, my frail ego would never accept a role as planetary savior. The best we could determine was that those who had worked through their toxic emotional issues had a soul contract to ground twelve DNA strands on this planet, and held clear insight into their role in upgrading the Earth's energy pool at this time could recode as long as they clearly voiced their intent for their twelve strands. This was the case with Kim as well, as I would determine, as with my future teacher Venessa.

Later, I worked with many clients who were interested in DNA Recoding but felt they had already experienced some, if not all, of the process. They enjoyed reading this book because it framed their experiences, making them feel a little more sane about the changes they had felt. I confirmed, when working with them, that they had, indeed, already passed through either some or all of the DNA Recoding stages. Looking back, I think I was naïve to entertain the notion that the process I outlined might be a leading method. There are numerous ways to get from "A" to "Z" and, with clear intentions, we can usually succeed in our journey.

Since Kim was exceptionally gifted as a psychic, I asked her about my future partner. According to her input, he was already "visiting" the body he would assume in Kansas City, moving in and out of a physical and non-physical state in preparation for the final transition. I was surprised since I thought walk-ins swapped in a manner of moments, hence Pat's difficulty with her noticeable shift in personality. Kim said she had worked with two types of walk-ins. One type of walk-in was the instantaneous switch which sometimes occurred consciously and sometimes occurred unconsciously when a person had fainted or was under anesthesia. The other type of walk-in was a gradual transition over time which was less traumatic for each soul since it gave both the physical and non-physical being an opportunity to become acquainted with their new status.

A walk-in's memory was erased while in physical form, to be stimulated for recall at a later date. Otherwise, massive confusion would exist as this displaced soul tried to reconcile two very different realities. According to Kim, the swapping process would take my future mate two months to complete which placed the eagerly awaited meeting in the August time frame, a time frame I had already been told. I asked Kim if she knew why Bobbie had seen the walk-in with a Scotch Terrier. Kim said she knew he had a dog but was unsure if it was a Terrier. She also said he wore business casual clothes that leaned toward a preppy style, something along the lines of golf shirts, Dockers, and deck shoes. Although that style did not appeal to me, she said I would like it on my future mate. She also said he appeared to be a teacher of metaphysics, and he would be very supportive of my metaphysical work, unlike the lack of support I had experienced with Jerry. I marveled at the varying tidbits of information I was collecting along the way toward discovering him. We ran out of time because Kim and Bobbie had other appointments, but Kim promised to touch base in August to see if my future mate had arrived.

WINNING THE LOTTERY

I had my weekly appointment with Bobbie. When I arrived at her office, I was frustrated due to unsatisfactory outcomes regarding the money I would be winning. Julia and I had repatterned several items over the weekend that were standing in the way of my being emotionally receptive to winning, so I was very clear for receiving it. I have always had an easy time manifesting abundance. But this time I was interested in manifesting without working so hard. I was realizing that money had been the outcome of severe workaholism due to my association that hard work equaled money. I also had been programmed through mass conscious beliefs to fear the lack of money, learning to hoard it as a security blanket. At this point in my life, I view money as a form of energy our planet uses for sustenance. I intended to have enough money to make life comfortable without feeling the need to hoard it for the future. Essentially, I intended money to provide freedom.

I had purchased a lottery ticket on Saturday, and the win was so close I could smell and see the money. I was cleared from emotional blockages and resonated with the win. When I went to the supermarket to get the winning numbers on Sunday, I had not won. In addition to not winning the lottery, my financial solvency had frozen overnight. I had transferred money from my money market to my bank account since I had to make my first payment to Jerry toward his half of our house. When I went to the bank, someone had botched the entry and I had a two million rather than two thousand dollar hold on my account. I was so overdrawn that none of my money was available! I was leaving town the next day and could not even withdraw a dollar! I realized how quickly one could go from "provided for" to "penniless" in a computer-driven society. I asked Bobbie what she thought was happening.

Bobbie examined the situation telepathically and started laughing. She said I had won, but I had won in another dimension. Apparently, I had not specified that I wanted to win money on the *Earth* plane. Since I existed in more than one dimension, I had won elsewhere. I was not amused by the concept of living a life of luxury in another dimension. Bobbie also said the reason my funds froze in this reality was a direct result of winning elsewhere. The frozen funds acted as a balance – incredible abundance in one dimension versus total lack of abundance in the other. I remained less than amused since I had to obtain a cashier's check for Jerry's payment, and could not get into my account for twenty-four hours, by which time I would be in Baltimore. I would deal with the frozen state of my bank account, but I asked Bobbie what I should do on an energy level.

First, she said I should always specify what I want, including winning the lottery, for the Earth realm since there are many dimensions of soul experiences. Being a fast learner, I had already absorbed that concept, and I was in the process of mentally reformulating my request. Secondly, she said I had three groups outside the Earth realm with whom I was working, but I had never requested for the three groups to work with one another. She described one group as the fluid, watery creatures from the movie *The Abyss*. I knew these entities as the Jolanderanz since they had visited me the prior year during one of their brief scouting excursions to Earth. I was shocked when she said this because it was the second time someone had mentioned this movie to me when referring to the energy of the Jolanderanz. I had contacted a psychic when they first came to visit us because we thought the house might be haunted. That psychic told me we were housing a beautiful creature of the light, similar to the sea creatures who saved the people in *The Abyss*. In fact, within days of the first psychic's analogy to *The Abyss*, I was flipping through channels while I exercised in front of the television set on my treadmill and "happened" to see the movie. Actually, I was exercising at an unusual time since I had been on an early morning conference call and had decided to work out mid-day rather than skip the day. Just as I began my workout, these beautiful creatures presented themselves on the screen and I immediately knew who they were.

Jerry and I had both resided on a watery planet with these incredibly beautiful and loving beings for a period of time, and apparently they felt comfortable staying with us. We welcomed their presence after discovering they had taken up residence in our swimming pool, although initially their energy was disturbing physically since they are quite different than we are. We would awaken in the middle of the night because the handles of the dresser drawers would move due to their presence, humming as the metal vibrated against the wood, hence the belief the house might be haunted. Or, we would feel like we were swimming in champagne due to the fizzy bubbles they made in the pool. In fact, they eventually left after an unsuccessful mission, not able to communicate with us in the density of the Earth environment. Jerry and I both tried to communicate with them during their visit, but their energy was so different that we actually felt sick.

Bobbie said the second group of beings were small creatures, like a combination of a Spielberg's ET and wookie. I had no recall of these entities or their form, but assumed they were friends from my distant past. The third group had a shadowy Darth Vader-like presence that made them appear ominous. However, as they moved forward, she realized they were lightworkers of a deep shade of blue. I asked Bobbie to gather the three groups together in one place because I wanted to talk to them.

I could see them filing into an amphitheater, but they sat in three separate sections. I stood in the middle speaking loudly to them, proclaiming:

"You are not working together, yet you are all light beings. You have a tremendous opportunity to achieve your goals more quickly on Earth by assisting me in obtaining money. This money will be used to build a spiritual meeting place so we can hold seminars that will teach people methods for healing themselves. You do not work together to provide this when your combined energy would make it happen so much faster. If you want me to succeed more quickly in helping to heal the planet, then get your act together and combine forces!"

I was breathless as I concluded my passionate speech. I felt annoyed that lightworkers would operate under separate agendas, just as people on Earth had individual agendas which caused less to be accomplished. I wondered how we were supposed to evolve when entities from other planets, supposedly more advanced than ours, forgot to confer with each other in support of a common mission. However, as I was lecturing them, I saw three different colors emerge, one from each group. The colors came together in the middle of the amphitheater over my head and twisted together, much like hair is braided, and came down in a column around me.

They were working together! But, they were working together through me as the common denominator. Apparently, their energies were so different that they either could not or did not know how to team, and I was the communication link. It was much like the experience I had with the Jolanderanz the previous summer. As much as we tried to communicate, we were not very successful due to interpretation barriers. I was beginning to understand how being a mutable was important to others since they needed me to be the interpreter. I hoped to learn more about how I communicated with the various beings. In the meantime, I planned on winning the lottery with all of this additional support.

USING REPATTERNING TECHNIQUES TO ENABLE DNA RECODING TO OCCUR

Apparently, Jeanne took my advice about sharing DNA Recoding with her fiancé since I received a call from him requesting an appointment with me. His name was Mark, and he said he was interested in meeting to learn more about DNA Recoding. I was glad Jeanne was concerned about possible discordant vibrations if she recoded and Mark did not, especially since they were in a new relationship. It would be easier for them if they both held the same energy. I told Mark I could see him that evening.

When Mark arrived, I knew I needed to repattern his energy prior to his being able to make the DNA Recoding request. I had learned from my own experiences that it was critical for those interested in DNA Recoding to clear themselves of negative emotions and energy patterns to avoid unnecessary discomfort caused from these blockages. I asked my guides if they would approve anyone for DNA Recoding, even if they had the potential to encounter either pain or disease. I was told "no," since our safety was a primary concern for them. Mark fell in that category, needing a repatterning of discordant energy patterns that were preventing him at a subconscious level from embracing DNA Recoding. He could make the request, but his subconscious would not allow him to actually pursue it as a self-protective mechanism.

Mark and I spoke briefly about the repatterning it appeared that he needed prior to being approved for DNA Recoding. I asked him if he felt any negative energy in his body as I said the words "DNA Recoding," and he said he felt fear around his heart. As we moved through the repatterning process, I was told he needed to clear his fear of death. However, Mark insisted he did not have a fear of dying because he believed in reincarnation. I started over, attempting to find another issue to repattern but the fear of death kept surfacing. Finally, I determined we needed to link to his guides to uncover whatever past life was affecting the current fear pattern lodged in his heart, a pattern he did not feel was associated with death.

As I brought the information forward from his guides, the purpose of the repatterning became very clear. In a past life, Mark had lived a life in a society that operated by a group rather than an individual mind. He had originated from a society that honored the individual within the context of the whole, viewing each being as separate, but also understanding every individual was connected via a vast cosmic network. The life I examined was characterized by a group mentality. Mark had chosen to immerse himself in a society that was so interrelated that when one person was hurt, the entire society felt pain. The energy of the society was almost dysfunctional in its cohesiveness. I got the impression of a celestial Nazi Germany where everyone marched to the same drummer since living outside the group energy was not a viable option. Mark felt a tremendous fear of death in this society because he was unable to steer his own destiny. He knew he did not have free choice or free will, and his future was the future of the team, regardless of his individual feelings. If the group decided to plunge over a precipice, then everyone had to jump.

Once this past life surfaced, Mark could easily relate feelings he had in his current life to the fear in his heart even though they were not directly related to death. These fears surfaced when participating in group situations, because it constrained Mark's individuality which made him feel like he was dying. Due to this emotional discomfort, Mark went to great lengths to avoid groups, and he even worked independently as a computer consultant. With Mark's awareness of where the fear originated, we were able to work on his repatterning. I quickly moved through the healing modalities, enabling him to release the fear in his heart in preparation for DNA Recoding approval. When I linked with Nephras to bring Mark information about his soul contract, I was immediately taken to his life in the single minded society and shown why he had chosen that painful experience. At a soul level, he desired to experience the energy required to create interrelatedness. He selected an extreme example in order to optimize his learning, extracting what he needed to know. However, his subconscious had not forgotten the dysfunctional portion of the experience that entirely subjugated his individual needs to the needs of the whole.

Mark's future role was to teach a balanced form of interrelatedness to those on Earth. I could see this connective energy, a cross between the softness of a daisy chain and the vibrancy of an interwoven fabric of white glow sticks. It was very beautiful and held the promise of a loving integration for all of us who have resided in an individualistic, ego-related society. As Mark read his formal request for DNA Recoding approval, I saw the request go via the daisy chain. When approval was returned, it overlaid a blanket of glowing daisy chains over the single-minded organism Mark had once occupied, breaking the energy into individual yet interrelated beings.

MY FINALE WITH JERRY

I was accommodating my lifestyle to a female house mate. I had not shared living space with a female since college, and I had forgotten how much negotiation was required when two people used the kitchen or desired privacy for visitors. I wondered what would happen to Jerry. He was very spiritual yet resisted that input, insisting on following the path of familiarity rather than moving into the vibration needed for the rapidly increasing pace in our everyday lives. I understood Jerry's unwillingness to live life differently than in the past since it was very demanding from an emotional perspective. He was close to my parents' age, and that generation was accustomed to creating order in their lives. They resisted change rather than flowing with it. All of my friends who were recoding were experiencing a catharsis at some level as they cleaned up discordant patterns. The Earth was increasing its vibration, and we needed to be clear of toxic emotions and static habits in order to quicken our own vibration and align with the new pulse of the Earth. I clearly understood why our guides wanted to ensure we were as "clean" as possible prior to DNA Recoding. Otherwise, it would be like mounting a bike to coast down a hill but never taking our foot off the brake.

I desperately wanted to accept Jerry's decision to end the relationship, since it aligned with my own, but feelings of resentment would periodically surface. Sometimes, I could repattern them, as in my session with Julia, and other times they seemed to linger. I did not want negativity evoked through judgment to interfere with my DNA Recoding progress, so I visited Bobbie to see if she could help me. I felt very "human" as my new higher level vibration conflicted with the less evolved emotions coursing through my body, wondering if I would ever reach the state of joy and love that DNA Recoding promised.

Bobbie scanned my body and could see the lingering emotional attachment to Jerry that was lodged in my solar plexus. She explained that, although I had cleared much of the emotional pain through repatterning, I still held an attachment. Apparently, when we decide to love someone, that commitment remains present in the body's memory for a long time after we split. By doing energy work to erase the soul memory of the commitment, it allows the body to eventually get rid of the emotional ties, and the memories begin to fade. If we try to move forward without repatterning our soul memory, we are working against our subconscious. On the conscious level, we desire the relationship to be over. On the subconscious level, we have not let go. I had watched this phenomenon with divorced couples who, unfortunately, typically experienced the dichotomy of conscious and subconscious agendas during their divorce proceedings which simply prolongs the process.

I did not want my spiritual growth hindered by a subconscious desire to remain connected. Bobbie and I worked together to remove the roots that I had inside of me, wrapped around my energy and Jerry's, binding us together. I felt this tremendous energetic release as she helped me extract and unravel the roots, and freedom ran through me. After completing the work with Bobbie, I returned home and performed an energy ritual on the house, clearing Jerry's energy from our bedroom so I would not be immersed in his lingering presence. I felt much better afterwards and wondered if people who had once loved each other ever healed the damage from their break-up if they did not work on eliminating the internal energy that held their connection.

EVERYONE DOES NOT WANT US TO RECODE

I received a call from my friend Wendy. I had recently worked with her to assist her in obtaining DNA Recoding approval. Wendy's session was interesting because, like Mark's, it began with the need for repatterning before she could gain acceptance for DNA Recoding due to anger sitting in her system. I know her guides were protecting her from getting ill during the DNA Recoding process by ensuring that the incompatible energy of anger was removed prior to entering Segment Three. Segment Three is the first segment that intensifies the co-mingling of the higher with the lower energy. It requires us to be light enough to receive telepathic transmissions, and anger creates density.

I had forewarned Wendy about the discordant energy clean-ups that were required of those experiencing DNA Recoding. She understood and acknowledged the commitment to being responsible for her spiritual growth and stood firm in her request for DNA Recoding. However, she had called me in a panic because she was sitting in a pool of broken glassware and dinnerware trying to remain calm and understand the lesson she had just received. Her kitchen cabinets had detached from the wall and every piece of glassware, dinnerware, and crockery she owned had smashed to bits. She asked me what type of message she was getting, attempting to be non-reactive to the situation and focusing on what she needed to learn. Bearing in mind that Wendy was someone who had already endured two floods in her home in the past few years due to plumbing problems and had totaled her car when a storm window fell out of a third story window, I thought we should not chalk this latest incident up to poor cabinetry workmanship. I asked Nephras to shed some light on the situation.

Nephras showed me a strong energy that has been present with Wendy for many lifetimes. Wendy had first encountered this energy in Egypt when she played the role of priestess. Her feminine power was fundamental to supporting her spiritual work. However, a group of men in secular positions were trying to eliminate the priestess energy since it conflicted with their control over the general population. Often, there is a dark collective that works behind the scenes when issues of power emerge. They feed the frenzy of emotion around beliefs like male supremacy at a non-physical level, enjoying the havoc they play in people's lives by stimulating witch hunts and inquisitions. The ruling males held viewpoints that were fueled by a dark collective, believing they should make the rules for the population.

These men did not want the population practicing spiritual rituals that would empower them. The female priests were undermining their efforts because people would come to them for healing.

During her Egyptian life, Wendy was publicly humiliated in her role as Priestess by the men who ruled as a means of reducing the level of influence she had on the population. She was considered a threat to the agenda of the dark collective who desired a dominance of male over female power since it kept society in a constant state of imbalance. The dark collective had dogged her for multiple lifetimes, dulling her memory through everyday distractions which prevented her from fully focusing on regaining her Goddess energy. Despite this intruding force, Wendy had become a powerful woman in her current life, attaining a high-level job and large salary in a corporate setting before single-handedly starting a not-for-profit organization devoted to supporting girls who wished to enter the gender-biased fields of math and science that contained very few professional women.

Apparently, this dark collective knew how to muddle Wendy's thoughts and distract her, but it could not fully interfere because she operated with so much light energy that it created a protective field of love, light, and truth around her. However, at this stage, Wendy was about to reclaim her full potential, a potential that was so powerful it threatened the solidity of the rascals who provoked her.

Wendy had recently traveled to Greece to participate in a ceremony of the Goddess at the Oracle of Delphi. She was stimulated to take the trip because she felt the need to connect with powerful female energy, although she had no recall of her lifetime as a priestess. Her trip provided a regenerative ceremony for her since she it reconnected her with the priestess energy she had relinquished when humiliated in Egypt. Then, she had returned from her trip and began the DNA Recoding process. I could see that the dark collective who "monitored" Wendy was worried. They foresaw Wendy regaining the power they had assisted in removing from her long ago, and they were going to do anything to distract her. I saw them more as an irritant than a harmful menace, but knew that Wendy needed a clearing to permanently remove them. It appeared that a fire incident was next in their bag of tricks. I gave her Kim's number in Colorado because I was not yet capable of clearing this type of energy. I was scheduled for a soul clearing seminar in July which would teach me how to remove negative entities. I knew Kim held a lot of warrior energy and would not be daunted by the evil of the dark collective.

After I told Wendy she was being strongly distracted by a dark collective to prevent her from focusing on recovering her Goddess energy, she informed me that she and her daughter had just been preparing to re-enact a ceremony they had recently learned in Greece to honor the Goddess in their garden when her cabinets fell off the wall. I was hardly surprised. What better time to distract her than when she was in the process of generating more power? The collective would try anything to hamper her progress. I knew this was a lesson for all recoders, since recovering our power often draws the attention of those who do not want us to have it. We are so accustomed to living in fear and anger that we have become unable to recognize darkness in its daily presence. We need to develop an awareness of love and joy, realizing that it is our Divine right to experience it daily rather than living primarily in the dysfunctional and disabling energy of fear and anger. We also need to be savvy about maintaining a force field of love around us, realizing there are those who desire to stop us from unleashing our creator abilities if we enable them to enter our energy field. I gave Wendy some information about clearing herself and her daughter until she could contact Kim to permanently remove the dark collective from her presence.

LEVERAGING THE WRITTEN WORD

Publishing opportunities were really beginning to surface for me, providing channels for the DNA Recoding information to get disseminated. I received a call from another nationally recognized metaphysical publication which also wanted to publish my work. Again, I was grateful for the confirmation that my work was newsworthy since I was a novice at metaphysical writing and had to be considerably prompted by Bobbie to send samples of my work to some of the alternative publishers.

I immediately called N to tell her the good news. Naturally, I asked her if she had progressed to Segment Six because, if she had, then I would be able to get information on it. Typically, N would enter the next segment and give me a topic heading. Then I would link with Laramus to fully define the segment in written form. I kept a summary of DNA Recoding as it emerged for distribution to those calling me for information. Eventually, I asked my guides why N entered each segment first since I seemed to be the one who received the information for it. They said they were concerned that my lack of confidence in my telepathic ability would cause me to doubt the information. They had purposely sent the initial information via N in order to circumvent my self-doubt. I understood their concern since I was constantly questioning the veracity of the information. Yet the strong self-confidence of both N and the entity she channeled, Anu, made me feel more comfortable with the information I received.

N had, indeed, moved into Segment Six which was called "Owning Your Power." Subsequently, I learned from my guides that Segment Six and beyond provided the real power, and our guides were not going to assist us in retrieving that amount of power if we were not aligned with our soul contract. That was why Segment Five was designed to halt the process until a complete alignment occurred between DNA Recoding and our intent to fulfill our soul contract, i.e., live in the light.

I was somewhat uncomfortable with this information because it was my perspective that I was the driver of my experiences and could determine how I wanted to live my life. I had been very clear about my interest in DNA Recoding as a means to improve me which would, therefore, assist in upgrading the energy around me. However, I was not interested in giving up my life as a result of this process. The days of obtaining enlightenment on a distant mountain were over. I believed DNA Recoding would only be embraced if it could be integrated into our everyday lives, living by example rather than retreating from a desirable lifestyle in exchange for spiritual enlightenment. For myself, I had experienced even greater growth in my market research business as DNA Recoding lightened my energy. I assumed that DNA Recoding would bring us whatever we desired if we clearly stipulated our requests as long as those requests aligned with bringing more light to the planet.

Since both magazines wanted to publish the same articles, I called the editor of the first publication that had accepted my articles to determine if they expected to have exclusivity on my work. She happened to answer the phone instead of my call going to voice mail, as it had in the past. Given the opportunity, I informed her of our DNA Recoding work and what we were doing in Kansas City. She grew very excited. She said she had desired her twelve strands after reading the Kryon material which referenced the need to request the Kryon implant to void all Earthly karma in order to ascend. However, she was unsure how to proceed.

I told her I could help her if she was interested in DNA Recoding, thrilled by the prospect of expanding my work beyond Kansas City. I said I would fax her the write-up that Laramus had given me about DNA Recoding. After she reviewed the material, I told her to call me, and we would schedule a time to work with her guides for more information and send her DNA Recoding request to the Sirian/Pleiadian Council. She said she would be happy to support my ventures through her publication. I had been provided inroads into two metaphysical publications in a very short period of time. My guides were giving me a great deal of assistance to help me spread the information. All I had to do was focus and wait.

RECLAIMING TELEPATHY

Pat came over to work on her channeling ability. I was finding that most of the recoders who entered Segment Three (clairaudience) had difficulty opening their third eye to receive telepathic information. This was true for me until Kim advised me how to stimulate the alpha and omega chakras which were my transmitters for communication. Most who have resided in physical form through multiple reincarnations have allowed their pineal gland to decrease to the size of a pea when it used to be the size of a golf ball. Some of us have even intentionally shut down our telepathic channel out of self-preservation since access to that type of information has resulted in death in previous lifetimes. In addition to the poor resiliency due to lack of use, many have heaped a load of social conditioning and emotional baggage on top of their telepathic abilities. For Pat, she had been ridiculed by her ex-husband for claiming to have psychic abilities. Pat had learned to stuff her natural talent in order to protect herself.

Pat and I conducted a repatterning session in which she cleared her energy blocks regarding her psychic ability. When we had completed the repatterning, she was ready to channel, having cleared her pipeline and past life issues associated with blocking it. I told her we needed to practice and instructed her on how to focus on who she wanted to bring into her body. Silently, I was amused by myself for playing the role of expert when I had so recently learned to be telepathic myself. I told Pat we would be doing conscious channeling, not trance channeling, where she would be hearing a voice and would repeat the information in her own voice rather than allowing an entity to enter her body and use her voice.

Pat settled into a comfortable chair and identified a Native American energy she frequently imagined in her presence that wished to speak through her. She was excited to finally be able to speak directly to this energy. I asked a series of questions and felt she received some good information. However, some information did not seem to ring true. I remembered the first time I did automatic writing and how I had achieved an eighty percent accuracy rate. My mentor, Bobbie, told me at that time that the best we can hope for is a ninety-five percent accuracy rate. This is due to two factors: 1) Non-incarnate beings are attempting to communicate from non-physical to physical form which creates some margin of error as they attempt to merge their multi-dimensional thinking with our realm; and 2) The English language is very limiting with significantly fewer words than the ancient languages. For example, the word "love" might have several hundred words with varying nuances in ancient languages like Hebrew or Sanskrit, but English only has one. I determined that Pat had achieved a seventy-five percent accuracy rate which was very good for the first time. I had discovered for myself that the ease of hearing the information and deciphering it had quickly increased with time. I assured her the transmissions would begin to flow now that she was open, and that her accuracy would quickly improve as she grew in confidence. Recovering telepathic abilities through DNA Recoding is not an overnight process. Years of stifling this ability can be dramatically altered by DNA Recoding, but one must still undergo a healing and rejuvenation period. Plus, like any talent, continued practice improves the outcome.

SUMMARY

JUNE DNA RECODING LESSONS

- DNA recoding is initially intended for older souls who have lived in other planetary experiences in more advanced civilizations since it will be easiest for them to accomplish. These beings have already experienced an evolved state so DNA Recoding is a process of connecting energetically with what they agreed to temporarily forget when entering the Earth plane. In other words, the older souls would not be hindered by the fear of the unknown. Rather, they will be extremely motivated to recover abilities to which they were accustomed in prior lives.
- This version of DNA Recoding has not been performed on a human being until now. Although the genetic engineers do not wish to place any of us in discomfort, they may need to calibrate as they work on each individual since everyone has a different body make-up. Their goal is to minimize discomfort during the process.
- Although many think they are undergoing DNA Recoding, most are experiencing the physical symptoms associated with the *preparation* for DNA Recoding. Actual DNA Recoding consists of allowing the ten additional strands of DNA already present in our system to coil together in pairs rather than remain apart.
- Recoders are not meant to be alone. The love frequency exponentially expands the twelve-strand energy a recoder carries. However, those with spouses or life mates who are not recoding will be challenged to maintain status quo since recoder and non-recoder energy are not similar. It is recommended that both parties recode when possible. When one partner recodes, the parties will encounter a variety of possible outcomes. Some relationships will improve since the DNA Recoding energy will upgrade the dynamics of the two parties. Some relationships will

decline since the different vibrations of the two partners do not permit a common agenda. And some relationships will basically remain the same, as the person who is recoding is anchored during times of heightened change by the energy of the partner who chooses not to recode.

- Recoders exist in a separate collective consciousness, one consisting of a higher energy frequency of joy and love as opposed to the dominant mass consciousness frequencies of anger and guilt.

- Should a recoder desire to have sexual relations with a non-recoder during DNA Recoding, it is important to protect their energy field with a golden sheathing. Otherwise, it will take some time for the incompatible energy frequency of the non-recoder to completely leave the recoder's energy field, slowing the recoder's process.

- Every recoder is assigned a new guide in the form of a genetic engineer who heads up the team working on reconnecting the twelve DNA strands. It is important to hone your telepathic abilities in order to communicate with your genetic engineer during the DNA Recoding process.

- Recoding significantly enhances telepathic abilities, which is key to enabling the recoder to receive the information available from the twelve levels. This telepathic power should be used to support work around recoding and one's soul contract, or a recoder will probably not proceed through the remaining segments since their enhanced energy could, potentially, be misused.

- Segment Five is critical because it builds the foundation for the final four segments. It is a segment some will elect not to clear due to the fact that it requires incorporation of one's soul contract into one's life. Integrating one's soul contract may lead to changes in one's lifestyle should the current lifestyle be unsupportive of the contract. Some will not desire change in their life, even if that change is ultimately positive.

CHAPTER FOUR
JULY • 1996

MORE ABOUT SEGMENTS
ONE THROUGH FIVE

Anu and Joysiah made their debut at our first public channeling session. Of the forty people invited via word-of-mouth, twenty-five actually attended. The session began with N bringing forward Anu, followed briefly by a new entity named Antron, and, finally, Joysiah wrapped it up. As usual, N gave an incredible performance as the vastly different personalities of the various entities were projected through her. I had purchased a two-hour tape to record the session, and, as I expected, the session ended in exactly two hours.

Anu began by giving background information on the relationship between Nibiru and Earth. I could see that many listeners were disturbed by his information, as I had been. In fact, some became so angry that they never returned which is why I omitted this information in the first *Power of Twelve*. Anu spoke about the creation of the lulu, a primitive worker that was genetically produced by Anu's children, Enki and Ninhursag, by crossbreeding the *Homo erectus* with the Nibiruan/Pleiadian genes. Typical of hybrids, this initial version could not reproduce. Originally, the lulu was reproduced via the Pleiadian female wombs through artificial insemination. But Enki grew fond of his creation and decided to allow it to reproduce, thereby creating the later version known as Adam. Plus, the Pleiadian women tired of being the birth vehicles. The lulu was ultimately replaced by the presently enhanced *Homo sapiens* format we inhabit, called Adapa in the Sumerian texts and Adam in the Bible. Anu told how he, as leader of Nibiru, had requested his two children to use their genetic engineering knowledge to create a placid, hard-working being who would help in the gold mines on Earth to collect the ore the Nibiruans needed to shield their planet from radiation resulting from atomic fallout. This would enable the Nibiruan mine workers, or Anunnaki, to put a halt to the drudgery of mining.

Anu spoke of his current tie to Earth, aligned with us through his family who had created us for their personal use during earlier times. He said the Nibiruans had advanced the *Homo erectus'* evolution by millions of years. Now, he and his family were inter-ceding on our behalf once again, to assist us in evolving to the next stage of our evolution. Although Anu sounded very noble and obliging, I had a sense the Nibiruans had a personal interest in our evolution. Since we all live in the same solar system and all energy is interconnected, I would assume the Nibiruans cannot evolve without us. Anu said twelve strands were placed in the physical vehicle of the *Homo erectus* during its genetic develop-ment. Two strands were coiled into a working double helix. However, ten of the twelve strands were de-coiled to permit the Nibiruans to have superiority over the primitive workers. He gave many details of the names, dates, and events, answering questions from the group regarding the Nibiruans' role in the story of creation. A great deal of the information can be substantiated in Sitchin's book, *The 12ᵗʰ Planet*, and is summarized in "The Creation Story, Our Beginning" in the front of this book.

Anu assured everyone that God existed in the form of First Cause, an energy no one in the galaxy had reached in their own evolution. However, he advised the group that his grandson Marduk was currently leader of Nibiru and held a negative disposition toward Earth. Apparently, Marduk did not feel impulsed to free us from our two strands. He was the person responsible for establishing anger, fear, and guilt on this planet as control devices that would perma-nently enslave us, despite our technological advancement. No one could achieve expanded consciousness when operating under these distorted values. Marduk was due to return on Nibiru's 3,600 year orbital cycle to re-establish his influence on Earth, an event Anu was trying to circumvent by helping us attain freedom by expanding our consciousness through the twelve strands.

An entity named Antron briefly visited to tell us that thousands of beings were watching and protecting us at this time. They had waited years for this moment, and many throughout the universe were observing our initial meeting. He said the beings primarily involved were the Sirians and Pleiadians since those were the Planetary Councils most involved with Earth at this time. I felt a sense of adventure as I considered the implications of being among the first to experience DNA Recoding.

Finally, Joysiah spoke to the group. He initially entertained questions from the group regarding DNA Recoding, then reviewed the information I had recorded and distributed on the initial five segments, adding some information about the sixth segment. Joysiah said recoding was not exactly a sequential process since one might finish something from Segment Four, then return to Segment One for refinement. This was due to the fact that the codes for recoding are scattered throughout our body. During our sleep state, our genetic engineer works on our astral or spiritual body. These changes are ultimately integrated into the physical body just as a blueprint eventually results in a finished building. Sometimes, in the transition from astral body to physical body, something from a prior level is mis-aligned and needs realignment. This is why the genetic engineers need to continuously work up and down the various levels. Additionally, if fear is present, it can undo some of the work that has been done. Fear was a Marduk creation, designed to keep us from our source of power. It was very important throughout DNA Recoding to have strong faith and keep fear out of the body. This is particularly critical when Marduk returns to Earth, an impending event given that Nibiru has already been spotted by our scientists. According to Anu, Marduk will do everything he can to keep individuals weakened by fear and guilt.

Joysiah explained that some thought they were going through DNA Recoding because they were having unusual physical experiences. However, he emphasized that no one could go through this particular version of DNA Recoding without requesting it, whether formally or informally. He asked me to read the formal request Laramus had provided several months before to the group for those who felt they were ready to recode. Joysiah explained that most who thought they were experiencing DNA Recoding were going through the preparation needed to rid the body of all previous toxins. He said one would not be approved for DNA Recoding if they had not released the majority of the negativity residing in their body since they would endure too much discomfort when recoding. He said it was important to release as many *emotional* blocks as possible since releasing negativity *physically* was not a permanent situation. When emotional blocks were present, the physical body could rid itself of anger one day through a physical reaction to a situation but receive it back the next since the person still resonated with anger and kept attracting it.

Joysiah provided the following list as methods of preparing for DNA Recoding by releasing toxic emotional patterns:

- Energy work like Reiki, attunement, or craniosacral therapy;
- Acupressure or acupuncture;
- Toning (sounds);
- Eye therapy since the eyes are the window to the soul;
- Color and light;
- Repatterning or clearing techniques;
- Massage;
- Baths with baking soda and sea salt, essential oils, or Bach flower essences;
- Liver and colon cleanses;
- Activating crystals in the crown chakra through a form of massage;
- Chiropractic therapy;
- Movement, e.g., yoga, energy exercises; and
- Breath work.

Although Joysiah did not mention diet, I was given the following dietary information by Laramus regarding meat, fowl, and fish. It is beneficial to eat as little of this type of protein in the diet as possible in support of cleansing the body for DNA Recoding. Protein in the form of animal products creates a heavy energy in our system when DNA Recoding is attempting to lighten the energy field. Obviously, this is counterproductive to the process. Plus, meat and fowl are filled with antibiotics and hormones and fish is filled with pollutants. These chemicals interfere with the cleansing of the body, creating a continual dosage of toxins to eliminate. When eating meat or fowl, it is best to eat the antibiotic/hormone free versions. Additionally, animals which are raised in captivity for slaughter contain negative energy based on their living situation. We ingest the negative energy from the animal that has resulted from penned breeding and raising methodologies, again creating an ongoing intake of negative emotions that must be cleared. When eating protein, whether during or after DNA Recoding, the food should always be blessed in order to raise the vibration of the slaughtered animal to a higher vibration prior to ingesting it.

In regard to Segments One through Five, Joysiah offered the following pieces of additional information:

- *Segment One, Releasing Anger* – Liver cleanses are great for moving quickly through Segment One since the majority of anger is stored in the liver. There are a variety of liver cleanses available in health food stores. Colon cleanses or colonics also help release toxins.
- *Segment Two, Managing Anger* – Stuffing any anger will cause discomfort when recoding since it recreates the toxin that have been eliminated. It is important not to stuff any emotions when facing conflicts.
- *Segment Three, Clairaudience* – When this channel begins to open, there may be discomfort in either your right or left ear or headaches in your brow chakra area. There may even be some drainage, but this means the channel is opening. It is useful to avoid heavy electrical environments because it causes static in the channel and will not enable your guides to speak with you. This will persist through Segment Four since this is when the clairvoyant channel is being opened. Watching TV and listening to the radio can interfere with your progress. When using cable or radio waves, be sure to eliminate the electromagnetic radiation (EMR). This can be done by purchasing one of the many items that are sold to neutralize these harmful rays, e.g., Clarus clocks, Q Links. Or, simply buy a roll of blue surveyors' tape since the color of the tape neutralizes EMR. You can keep the roll in a drawer in the center of your

house and carry a six inch strip with you in your wallet. Although certain types of music are healing, the appliances that play the music might be detrimental due to the electrical currents. When listening to music, move the electrical equipment away from direct contact with the heart chakra. It is best to spend time opening and developing personal channels by getting back to nature. Moving away from electricity enables the genetic engineers to make more progress. During Segments Three and Four, work is begun on re-coiling the DNA strands in your astral body. However, memory of this work cannot be retained because you would want to stay with your guides rather than undergo the more challenging transition from a two- to twelve-strand being.

- *Segment Four, Clairvoyance* – When the third eye opens and you begin seeing entities on the astral plane, there is a tendency to experience fear. However, fear will keep you from moving through this segment. Acknowledge that you exist in another dimensional frequency, and no one can harm you if you do not vibrate with fear. Also, the amount of light in your presence creates a force field around you that does not allow astral level entities to disturb you.

- *Segment Five, Integration* – There are some things that will not clear in Segments One through Four because the crystals housing our codes are spread throughout the physical body. It will be necessary during this time to go back and ensure that everything has been integrated. Also, it is often impossible to fully complete each segment on the astral body because it may cause too much discomfort. The genetic engineers need to wait to complete the task when the body is ready, which is different for everyone. This is a time when copies will be left for longer intervals since more time is needed to work on the astral body, sometimes up to two days. You must train your copy to be productive while you are "gone." Integration is exciting because you can begin to transfer to other dimensions, simultaneously experiencing the multiple lifetimes you are playing at the same time that you reside on Earth. During this time, bleed-through information may occur in the form of vivid dreams. Segment Five is also a time when you must prioritize the path that supports your soul contract. The genetic engineers must be assured that you are committed to your soul contract before enhancing your power. Some will choose not to complete this segment since they will not desire to take on a planetary contract and all its responsibilities.

Finally, Joysiah gave a small amount of information about Segment Six, Owning Your Power. This is when your guides are ninety-eight percent positive that you will not back off your soul contract so you are given greater power. During Segment Six, your thoughts quickly manifest what you desire. Joysiah warned us to keep clean, positive thoughts since they manifest very quickly and negative thoughts could slap us in the face.

During the question and answer session, Mark, the person for whom I had linked the previous week, asked Joysiah about the interrelationships I had seen during his reading. I was surprised when Joysiah deferred to me, saying that "Lahaina has more understanding of this process than I do, and you need to speak with her." It was the first time any of these entities had referred to me as Lahaina, which took me aback. Plus, I did not know what information I had, but I whispered to Mark that I would look at it when I had a chance. I realized we know very little about who we really are and what experiences we have had prior to this limited linear reality. However, I was still surprised that I knew more about something than Joysiah.

I queried Joysiah on the reason I had not seen dark forms or attached entities in Segment Four. He asked, "Have you not been seeing pictures in your mind that gave you information?" I laughed since lately my mind had been filled with visions. He said every person experiences each level differently, particularly for me since I am constructed differently. I knew this was true due to my experience with Segment Three, as the presence of electricity did not seem to hamper my telepathic development. However, just to be sure, I had quit watching TV and avoided heavy electrical areas for the two weeks I was in this segment.

I was excited by the receipt of this new information and decided to create an article for publication, intent on distributing the DNA Recoding information to others. I wondered how many of those who came to Anu and Joysiah's channeling session would return for another. I knew our lives would change from this moment with the dissemination of the information to twenty-five people. Among those present that evening, there were some who would break through the sound barrier, opening up DNA Recoding to all human beings living on Earth.

MANAGING THE TWELVE-STRAND DNA ENERGY

I sprang into Segment Five on Tuesday after dealing with a very difficult situation that actually led to my understanding of my soul contract in relationship to my marketing consulting business. I had been questioning my current livelihood since, although successful as a self-employed entrepreneur, I no longer had the level of pleasure I did when I started the business. When I left corporate life to begin my own company, I was thrilled by the prospect of controlling my destiny. I have spent sixty to eighty hours a week over the last four years building my business into what it currently is. However, it no longer fulfilled me as it did in the past.

In the meanwhile, I continued to do the marketing consulting, making it more pleasurable for me by setting the intention for enjoyable clients who make the projects easier. I also asked to have opportunities presented to assist others, including myself, in their spiritual growth. However, a new client called for a research project, and I came to realize very quickly that this client did not fit my ideal of only working with pleasurable people. Unfortunately, this client worked for a company that operated in a particularly toxic manner. He was attracted to the company because he had his own toxic emotions, fitting nicely into the corporate culture.

As the project progressed, my new client determined I was not being objective in my work, perhaps influencing the outcome of the study. I was offended by this input since, as a marketing strategist, I sought truth through the eyes of the customer and would not be in business if I projected my agenda over the results. I wondered why I had drawn this negative energy. I asked Nephras for some answers.

Nephras showed me how my DNA Recoding energy was a threat to those strongly influenced by discordant energy. In other words,

I bound into the room, bursting with love and light which conflicts strongly with the fear and anger that most folks hold. I could "see" the group of clients sitting in our meeting room, surrounded by dark forms who were accompanying them because they fed off the negative emotions. This was the "psychic seeing" Joysiah had referenced in Segment Four. Nephras said when my strong light energy was introduced among those holding discordant energy, the net result was that those holding the discordant energy experienced discomfort. My client experienced fear in response to my presence, regardless of what I said or did, and he did not trust me. In essence, the dark beings were rattled by my strong light presence and created the same sense of mistrust in my client.

I asked Nephras what I was supposed to learn by this information. She said the lesson dealt with my recognition of my emerging power and how others would react to it. Due to the level being emitted, she said I needed to tone down my presence by being less verbal about my opinions, offering input primarily when asked rather than playing the leadership role with which I was familiar. When I "took charge" and relied on my male energy, I became too threatening to others due to the higher recoder vibration. Ultimately, my leadership aura would intimidate rather than heal others by creating fear as opposed to receptivity. Additionally, it was time for people to seek answers from within rather than tap into someone else's power. I thought this was excellent advice, realizing I did not need to project much to overwhelm others these days, as I had so many powerful beings assisting me in addition to my own growing power. I marveled at how much I continued to learn, even when performing a job of which I had grown tired.

I was also informed part of my soul contract was to continue my marketing consulting business for an undefined period of time. It was intended for me to bring my light into the business arena. Apparently, I was to act as a catalyst to others by "showing" the presence of my emerging recoder energy. If I limited myself to being surrounded by lightworkers ready for DNA Recoding, I would not have the opportunity to interact with a broad cross section of people. I could see how the dark energies around these particular clients reacted in my presence, dampening their enthusiasm through their awareness that the light was growing through DNA Recoding. I asked Nephras if I could clear the dark energy from these humans to assist them in moving toward the light. She showed me a process for temporarily removing the entities, explaining that the lack of dark energy would enable the person to be receptive to my energy while working with them. However, she said that a soul had the ability to recall the dark through their own free will. Essentially, I could provide people a window of opportunity through which they could choose to travel toward the light or not.

I spent some time visualizing the removal of the entities. Since I had not yet been trained in entity removal, I simply "zapped" them with my light. I realized my current business would continue for a while since it was part of my soul contract. After all, I had requested smooth transitions. However, I was not interested in placing myself primarily in negative situations. Again, I was being tested. I could either listen to non-physical beings and allow them to direct my life's course, or I could interject my own requirements. Being committed to the process, I told Nephras I would continue conducting marketing consulting until I had no heart for it. However, I wanted my guides to assist me in creating a big financial win in order to alleviate money pressures.

I recognized I had succeeded in moving to Segment Five, stimulated by my conflict with negativity and my resulting awareness. I felt that Segment Five would be short term and asked how long it would take. I was told I would be in it for approximately two weeks. Good! I wanted to get to Segment Six where I could begin manifesting more easily!

MY ASSOCIATION WITH
THE HALLS OF AMENTI

I had recently read about the Halls of Amenti. It was the first time I had heard of it and was still unsure what it meant. According to my dictionary of mysticism, it was the "Egyptian underworld," which did not exactly expand my understanding. When I initially read about the Halls of Amenti, my interest was stimulated by the description of the composition. The Halls of Amenti were created by thirty-two beings, sixteen Sirians and sixteen Nibiruans. I felt shock surge through my body when I read this, based on my knowledge that I was half Sirian and half Nibiruan. I checked to see if my heritage had some connection with Amenti and was told that it did. I decided to see how much information I could gain through linking.

Nephras said that the Halls of Amenti was a consciousness point, and I would understand the meaning after I had moved to higher recoding levels. She said I had been the keystone in the Halls of Amenti, just like the central keystone is fundamental to the structural solidarity of an arch. Nephras said that someone needed to be able to join the Nibiruan and Sirian energies when the Halls of Amenti were formed. I was the thirty-third, the connector point for the thirty-two other participants. I had been created with this role in mind, to act as the integration point. She also said I still existed in the Halls of Amenti in crystalline form as did all of the participants, enacting an existence there in addition to Earth. I knew from earlier information that I also existed as Lahaina as a member of the Nibiruan Council. This is rather mind-boggling since we are tuned to a single existence. I was actually in three places at the same time! I was relieved to know I only had to maintain my calendar for my Earth life. The thought of coordinating three schedules was too overwhelming.

As I listened to the information about the Halls of Amenti, I realized there was a connection to my Sedona lifetime in the crystal city. I also realized this had something to do with the information I had for Mark, per Joysiah, about the interlocking energy that he would initiate on this planet. Nephras affirmed my thoughts, saying that access to the Halls of Amenti could be achieved through a portal located in Boynton Canyon in Sedona. At one time, the Halls of Amenti had existed 2,000 miles above the Earth. Currently, it was supposed to be in Egypt, but Nephras said there was access to Amenti via the doorway in Boynton Canyon. She said this was where I hid the codes or blueprints under which we operated in the crystal city. The reason for hiding it from the invaders was that it was the key to linking beings throughout the universe into an interrelated whole. It was part of the galaxy's evolution toward Divine Union, because until we can align in totality, we cannot return to the Divine source. This is a major, major project for which Earth is a key player.

The Halls of Amenti is located within the Earth because it will be used to evolve us to a higher level of consciousness. Right now, the third dimension is a drag on the entire universe's evolution to God consciousness due to its density. Evolution will surge forward in a tremendous leap once humans move to the next stage of consciousness. When I heard this information, I confirmed my suspicions about Anu's generosity in helping us recover our twelve-strand energy. He was stuck until we moved, too! Essentially, the Halls of Amenti is part of integrating consciousness across the entire universe. No wonder I hid the codes from danger. Had invaders taken this energy source for their own purposes, we would have been severely hampered in our integration project, allowing dark to reign by keeping each group of beings, each star system, and each planet separate. I was excited to call Mark and give him the news since he was clearly part of the project and would be using this energy to boost us to the next level.

Nephras warned me not to visit Sedona. I had been invited to visit Sedona with Julia and Bobbie in August. They wanted to make a side trip after the Holographic Repatterning conference that was being held in Phoenix. I had experienced a reluctance about going, feeling I was not supposed to be on this trip. Now, I knew the reason. Nephras said that, based on my returning power and the level at which I was currently amped due to DNA Recoding, I could unwittingly spring open the portal to the Halls of Amenti based on my physical presence in Sedona. I was not to return to Sedona until I had achieved full DNA Recoding, after which time I could return to complete what had been started during the Sedona project. In fact, one year after completing DNA Recoding, my future husband, David, and I visited Sedona and performed a very powerful ritual in Boynton Canyon which opened the portalway to the information.

Before finishing my session with Nephras, I asked her to share my future mate's soul name with me. I knew my name was Lahaina, but I did not know his. I thought it would be easier to focus on my new partner if I knew his name. Nephras checked to ensure that his energy had sufficiently entered the Earth frequency prior to giving me the name. Otherwise, I might have interfered with the transference of energy that was occurring. She determined enough of his energy was presently in Kansas City and shared his name with me. It was Asalaine! Asalaine and Lahaina had a ring to it. When saying the names, I clearly felt the resonating tones. I knew from our names that we belonged together.

SOUL ORIGINATION AND HOW IT IMPACTS DNA RECODING

I visited N in order to speak with Anu about my DNA Recoding progress. Anu said he wished to give me more information on my lineage which always interested me since I was baffled by how a soul was conceived. He said there were two groups of beings from Sirius, Sirius A consisting of the Creator Lords who were feline in appearance, and Sirius B who were the galactic humans. The Creator Lords from Sirius A worked in conjunction with the Spiritual Hierarchies of various planets by genetically seeding these planets. They had left their mark on Earth in the winged lions and Sphinxes that proliferated in Egyptian art and architecture.

These feline creatures worked with a bird-like being called a Carian, which was symbolized on Earth by the Phoenix. The Carians were a protector race, acting as guardians to the beings seeded on planets by the Sirians. Prior to my soul's emergence into physical form, the Carians had evolved to etheric beings and were no longer mating. However, I received my Carian heritage, as well as my Sirius A lineage, from my mother, who was a cross between the Carians, Pleiadians, and Felines from Sirius A. Naturally, by now I was really confused, but I was impressed with the level of detail being delineated. Anu also mentioned that Joysiah, our master geneticist, originated from Sirius B. My father was from Sirius B, the galactic human civilization, but apparently a civilization with different appendages! Anu said I came from a great lineage which had gifted me with special abilities that would emerge as I continued my DNA Recoding.

I asked why I would spend only two weeks in Segment Five, the decision point when Joysiah and company determined if someone was ninety-eight percent aligned with their soul contract before returning their real power to them. I perceived the remaining segments to immediately augment my power and, although I truly manifested at an increased rate after Segment Nine, the power grew stronger and stronger over the ensuing years. Anu replied that I was already on my soul path by bringing the twelve-strand energy to Earth and recording it to share with others, so I did not need to remain in Segment Five for very long. Anu assured me I would continue my marketing consulting business in the short term to earn the money necessary to pay Jerry for complete ownership of the house. He confirmed that my future business would be more metaphysically-oriented and my manifestation of that business would occur easily.

I was excited by the prospect of helping others acquire greater awareness. In fact, I had already developed a new logo and company name for this venture. The new company was called InterLink and the logo consisted of a beautiful blue pyramid topped by a sphere. The pyramid and sphere were connected by a sunburst. I asked Anu why I could not support myself through a big financial win rather than the marketing consulting. He said I could win the money, but I was currently lacking the faith to accomplish this. He told me to work on my faith and the money would come. As I sat digesting this information, Anu said we had concluded our session. I said good-bye to this non-physical entity who had become a major part of my life.

ENTERING SEGMENT SIX

My son and I were in Pagosa Springs, Colorado spending our vacation with my family. My parents decided that we would go on a guided tour of the area as a means of becoming acquainted with the terrain. I was unexcited by the tour, vastly preferring to strike out and explore on my own with hiking maps. However, the other members of my family felt it was important to gather information from a guide and asked me to join them. I agreed, knowing they were tolerating my insistence on visiting Mesa Verde later in the week as it was known to attract huge crowds of tourists in the summer and was not an easy trip to make. In fact, my only reason for being interested in Pagosa Springs was its proximity to Mesa Verde, a sacred Native American power place of the past.

The guided tour turned out to be more than expected, a gentle reminder that enlightenment does not always result from planning or from sacred rituals. What do the Taoists say? Chop wood, carry water, revealing that it is often the mundane which moves us toward enlightenment. The morning portion of the tour consisted of visiting beautiful natural settings and chatting with our guide. In the afternoon, we drove approximately fifteen miles along a dirt road to a site called Silver Falls. By the time we had arrived, the sky was dark and threatening, and it looked like it would start pouring any minute. However, we piled out of the van and proceeded to climb the mountain to the falls.

As we hiked, it began to rain and the ground became very slippery. It was already difficult climbing due to the thin air at 7,000 feet above sea level. The lightning and thunder was dramatic, and the combined thin air, bad weather, and slippery ground convinced many in the tour group to return to the van. However, I proceeded, slipping and sliding on the rocks surrounding the waterfall as I pulled myself to the top under a sky of crackling bolts of lightning. I felt no fear! Usually, the mere thought of getting wet would have been enough for me to return to the van. I felt hesitant but enthusiastic, motivated to continue to the top.

I finally reached the summit and sat with our guide under a rock, letting the spray and sound from the waterfall wash over me. As I sat there, I could feel energy coursing through me. My fingers and fingertips were vibrating with energy, pulsing at a rate I had never experienced. I knew I had moved from Segment Five to Six and checked to confirm my intuition. Indeed, I was in Segment Six, the segment that focused on manifestation! I had gone on a guided tour, one I thought would pale in comparison to the sacred site I would visit at Mesa Verde, only to end up at a very sacred site in the middle of Pagosa Springs. I reminded myself that enlightenment can occur anywhere, even when playing the role of a tourist!

THE CONFLICT OF WARRIOR ENERGY WITH DNA RECODING

While I was on vacation, I heard from the editor of the metaphysical magazine that was publishing my articles. She had received the tape from our first channeling session and had listened to it, and she had left a voice mail message at my office to inquire about her own desire for DNA Recoding and how to proceed. I was excited when I retrieved her message since her personal interest would support the dissemination of the information. I told my office assistant to return her call and give her the telephone number where I was staying. The editor had gone through a difficult week as she and her husband, the owner of the publication, had determined there were pieces of their business that needed to be terminated. They were moving into a new phase of their lives, and it was a stressful time since the phase was undefined. Upon receiving my contact number, she called me in Pagosa Springs to ask if I could shed some insight on her upcoming transition.

I started linking for her to give her information about her soul contract in preparation for her reading of the formal request. Apparently, there were negative energies involved in a portion of her business, and her guides had initiated a house cleaning prior to her and her husband's undergoing the DNA Recoding process. She and her husband were to honor their soul contract by informing others of DNA Recoding through their publishing connections. Their passion for the subject was indicative of their soul contract and their commitment to be a part of it. Apparently, they were also incarnate members of the Nibiruan Council, just like N and I.

The editor asked how she and her husband had attracted negative energy when they were lightworkers who had come to Earth to accomplish good. Nephras showed me how she and her husband had partnered for eons to fight negative energies, coming up against the formidable Marduk on Nibiru when he turned a reign of light into that of darkness by dominating others through fear. Apparently, this couple had made a soul contract to battle the negative forces as a team. I saw them bringing negative forces upon themselves for the purpose of exposing them through conflict in lifetime after lifetime. However, their guides were telling me it was time for them to nullify their warrior contract and become peacemakers since it would interfere with their DNA Recoding contract. We are moving astrologically from the Age of Pisces which signifies reason to the Age of Aquarius which signifies love. The vibration of warrior energy and love is simply not a good match.

The editor was relieved to hear this information because she was ready to experience something different, particularly since her husband had elected to battle the IRS as one of the negative forces in this lifetime. I asked her to repeat the formal DNA Recoding request as I read it to her over the telephone. However, after she read the request, nothing happened. This was unusual for me because I always check to assure that someone will receive approval prior to having them read the request. Yet it was not being accepted. Then I heard Nephras say that my new friend needed to formally request removal of her other soul contract from her soul records prior to her new one being approved.

We were told that past attempts to bring higher consciousness to Earth had been unsuccessful due to the battle between light and dark. This time, we were to proceed as lightworkers without concerning ourselves about the status of the dark forces. They were free to do what they needed to do, and we were to do our thing. We were to pay no attention to them, which would ensure that there would be no resistance. This would ensure our success among those who opted for the light, leaving the others to take whichever path they chose. I finally understood why my guides were intent on moving us quickly toward Segment Nine so that a higher level of consciousness would exist on Earth prior to Marduk's return but, at the same time, were doing nothing to stop Marduk from returning.

I gave the editor the additional words the guides gave me to nullify her warrior contract and saw her request for DNA Recoding finally receive approval. She asked when her husband could undergo the same process, and I told her to fill him in on our conversation, work with him to remove his prior soul contract, and have him call me the next evening to read the request. I also told her to be specific when removing their former contract, specifying that she and her husband wished to remain together as a team but in the new rather than the old contract. She told me she would begin supporting DNA Recoding by publishing my article on the *How To's of DNA Recoding*.

ACCEPTANCE VERSUS FORGIVENESS

As expected, the owner of the alternative publication called me during my vacation in regard to his own DNA Recoding. Prior to his reading his request, I recommended we look at the barriers their publication had recently experienced since the latest issue had been in limbo for so long, experiencing one problem after the other, which delayed its publication date. They were also having trouble with the IRS. He said he had experienced great difficulty with an article regarding the subject of forgiveness that he had written for the delayed edition. I linked telepathically with Nephras to gain insight for him, and we were told that they would provide as much information as they could at this time but our current value system would make it difficult for us to understand the issues. We would have better clarity regarding the inappropriateness of forgiveness as we grew in awareness and, in fact, the article would ultimately have contradicted the essence of DNA Recoding.

Nephras explained that forgiveness was not part of Creator Truth because it was a value that assumed someone had done something wrong. The Divine Creator holds no judgment so there can be no right or wrong. Right and wrong is an outcome of the polarity of this planet, and it breeds judgment which separates beings. Separation keeps love from growing, thereby weakening our state. Nephras said a more appropriate value than forgiveness is acceptance because it allows everyone to exist and learn at their own rate. Acceptance is a value we must embody to successfully recode since past efforts at this endeavor have been thwarted by negative energy. Once we enter into judgment rather than acceptance of those that block us, just as Jeanne did when she redirected the laser that killed her Christ being and decimated the sending party's planet, we can no longer hold the love vibration. This also ensured that fear would not be present since this was a negative frequency which would undermine a recoder's success. Hopefully, as the light grew in strength, the beacon would be so strong that it would draw the dark toward the light through example rather than coercion.

I remarked about how this information about acceptance aligned with the information given to his wife the previous day regarding why they needed to disavow their warrior contracts. We finished the session by having him read his formal DNA Recoding request. The pieces were now in place to align us, and I awaited more information.

RECEIVING DNA WHEN IT IS LEAST EXPECTED

While we were vacationing in southwest Colorado, my mother suggested we visit Lion Canyon, which is a sacred Ute Indian pueblo near Mesa Verde. We had originally intended to visit Mesa Verde but were told that 700,000 tourists visit the site between June and August, and there is more irritation from crowds than peace from the sacred site. In fact, most of the sacred energy has apparently dissipated. We had heard of a tour company in Pagosa Springs that was authorized to bring visitors to Lion Canyon. Only 5,000 visitors were allowed to enter yearly because the Indians wished to preserve the integrity of the site yet allow non-Native Americans to learn about the importance of their culture. We opted for Lion Canyon over Mesa Verde and joined with a tour of twenty other visitors.

On the way, our guide told us about the mountain lions that had roamed the canyon in the past, hence its name. Knowing that lions were closely aligned with the feline race from Sirius A, I asked Nephras about any possible personal connection to the canyon. It was really handy to have access to an angel who answered questions at a moment's notice! Prior to the indigenous Native Americans residing in Lion Canyon, Nephras said the entire four corners area was connected to the Sedona area where I had resided as a crystalline deity during the crystal city project.

I knew this was not my first attempt at helping a planet evolve to a new stage of consciousness. The previous attempt was thwarted by invaders who came to take the knowledge currently protected in the Halls of Amenti, the power booster we need for this venture to be successful when the entire planet shifts consciousness. My immediate assumption upon hearing that mountain lions had been present was that the Sirians were involved at some time. They had left the lions as guardians of their energy when they left the area. Now, hardly any mountain lions were left as civilization had enveloped the area.

As we neared Lion Canyon, I knew the day would bring unexpected experiences, remembering my previous ties to a Sirian heritage. What better space to work on me than in a location infused with energy from my lineage? My anticipation grew as we neared the canyon, for a golden eagle arose from the brush and flew in front of our van for several hundred yards. It was a beautiful sight to ride behind the magnificent creature which had a six-foot wing span. Our guide was delighted with the eagle's appearance since there were few eagles left in the area and it was not the season for them to appear.

Lion Canyon was, indeed, a unique experience. The Ute Indians believed everything should be left as it was found, feeling that every animate and inanimate object went through cycles, and that those cycles should not be disrupted. The ruins were entered via the same narrow paths that the cliff dwellers used, accessed by long ladders that were hot to the touch due to the midday sun. However, once we were in the canyon, it was cool and pleasant. The ruins had not been reconstructed, and fragments of bone, corn cobs, and pottery shards were available to touch as long as we replaced them. What a treat! Our Indian guide was the son of the Ute Reservation Manager. He was wonderful because he allowed us to experience the canyon without any restrictions other than respecting the environment.

We began a one mile hike to Eagle's Nest, the highest cliff dwelling in the canyon. As we proceeded along the path, everyone became comfortable with their own pace so we no longer traveled in a group. I had been hiking the mountains all week and had adapted to the higher altitude so I was not short of breath like some of the others. However, about half a mile into the hike, I experienced severe vertigo, broke out in a cold sweat, and momentarily blacked out. My mother, who was sixty-five and accompanying me, had not encountered any problems other than a little breathing difficulty so I knew this probably was the unexpected experience I had been awaiting. I asked Laramus what was happening, and he told me they had just fused my eighth strand of DNA. They chose to fuse it in the canyon where the energy was extremely favorable. Well, great, but I felt lousy! It took some convincing of my mother and the guide, who had caught up with us, that I was all right and could continue. I felt shaky but quickly revived and was able to enjoy the remainder of the tour.

DNA Recoding Beyond Kansas City

We went to Durango to do what tourists do when they visit the Southwest, spend money on Native American merchandise. We walked around Durango, browsing the shops and visiting the original hotels that have been renovated to replicas of the Old West. I did not find anything I cared to buy since most of it was jewelry and clothing, and I was more interested in spiritual relics. In the afternoon, we entered a small shop that contained the type of Native American crafts that I liked, beautiful animal sculptures, dream catchers and fetishes that looked individually crafted rather than mass produced. There was a dream catcher that immediately caught my eye, filled with crystals, animal skins and other natural elements. It was a very powerful piece.

I asked the woman in the shop the price of the dream catcher. It was more than I wanted to spend, but I told her I would be back if I wanted it. The dream catcher nagged me all afternoon. I knew it was something I had to purchase. I returned to the shop, and the owner laughed when she saw me. She said she had just finished telling another person who wanted the dream catcher that it was sold because she knew I would return for it. I was impressed that someone would turn down a definite sale for a prospective sale that had not yet occurred. I thanked her for her faith in my interest despite my previous lack of commitment. We chatted briefly as I purchased the dream catcher, and she took the shipping information and gave me her business card. Her name was Donna. When I left, she hugged me good bye and wished me enjoyment of my purchase, a gesture I found strange since I did not know her at all. I knew the minute she hugged me that her energy was Nibiruan because I could feel the connection. I left in a rush to meet my parents so we could return to Pagosa Springs.

My guides nagged me all the way back to our resort: call Donna, call Donna, call Donna. I could not get them out of my head! What was I going to tell her? Was I supposed to call a stranger and tell her she was Nibiruan? How would she react? This had never happened to me, and I did not know how I would handle it. But I knew I would call her because I could not stand the noise in my head. So much for wanting to be able to channel

... now I had more company than I desired at times! I called Donna when we returned, told her I had just been in her shop, and I felt very impulsed to call her based on direction from my spirit guides. I told her I probably would not be calling had she not connected with me over the purchase of the dream catcher.

I decided to plunge into my topic, and I asked Donna if she knew she was a very old soul who had lived in other dimensions before coming to Earth. She said she had guessed that she might be based on feeling different from others, but no one had ever confirmed this information for her. I told her my sources said she had lived on a planet named Nibiru, and I had been asked to share this information with her. I felt bizarre imparting this knowledge, but so far she had not hung up on me. I asked her if she knew about DNA Recoding and the need for twelve strands to move to the next stage of consciousness, and she said she had read some books about it. Thank goodness, our guides prepare us for what is coming! I told her about my involvement in DNA Recoding and promised to send her my write-up about the various segments. I would also send the tape from our first channeled session. I told her to call me if she was interested in the subject matter after she had reviewed it.

Donna did call several months later, and she said she was interested in staying in touch. I worked with her spiritually, conducting several telepathic sessions as well as a soul clearing on her following my workshop in Colorado where I learned how to do so. Through Donna, I also met, via telephone, a group of individuals who lived in Durango and were interested in soul clearings and DNA Recoding. I have worked with them, helping to establish a network of DNA Recoders in another part of the country. What an odd experience from the day I met Donna until later when I had worked with many of her friends! I never knew when I was going to encounter another soul who would gravitate positively toward the DNA Recoding information or what would clue me into their origins. However, I had learned that I needed to trust the situation and listen to my guides. They were not going to embarrass me, and they ensured that others were prepared to hear about the subject of DNA Recoding when I brought it up. Again, my issue with faith had arisen. I promised myself I would spend more time believing and less time analyzing.

USING CREATION ENERGY

N called to tell me she had entered Segment Seven, "Removing Illusions," and had some preliminary information about it. I eagerly asked her to share what she knew, and she described it very obliquely as follows: "One will feel the presence of a light at the end of a long dark tunnel which symbolizes one's mission, and one must traverse the tunnel to reach the light. One's personal power is the torch that lights the way toward one's mission. Every time an obstacle is hit, the torch should be shined on the obstacle, thereby exposing the illusion that has been created."

Later, I asked my guides to add more information on Segment Seven since the gateway had been opened by N. They told me that in Segment Six, one learned how to be a "maker," opening avenues to energy that would support our manifestations. Now, in Segment Seven, one has become a creator. Creators manifest any reality they choose since they realize they create their world by placing attention on what they want and removing attention from what they do not want. Whenever a perceived obstacle is hit, a creator shifts to a more beneficial reality by focusing on the goals or objectives he or she desires without creating resistance due to the presence of an obstacle. Unfortunately, one also acts as a creator when hitting a perceived obstacle and choosing to identify it as a problem. The more the obstacle is perceived to be a blockage, the greater the barrier it causes. As a creator, you can create any reality so it is important to remember to choose the path of positive rather than negative perception.

MAKERS VERSUS DOERS

I remained confused about Segment Seven, Removing Illusions, and how it differed from Segment Six, Owning Your Power. I finally asked Laramus for clarification. He said that first I needed to understand Segment Six. Laramus said Segment Six was tricky since we were no longer relying on our guides to generate manifestation energy for us. We were not pleading for outside assistance because we perceived that we could not fulfill our objectives by ourselves. We were finally going solo.

This was different for most of us who had been using creative visualization as a means to manifestation. We had been taught to state affirmations in present tense and ask our guides to use their energy to support our requests. However, after reaching Segment Six, my guides had gently (and sometimes not so gently) chided me about using my own energy instead of relying on theirs. For example, if I desired financial abundance, I was to experience the feeling of having the abundance by generating the emotions that were part of that situation. I needed to *feel* rich to be rich. If I wished to have my life mate Asalaine join me, I should view myself as a radio frequency that broadcasts and sends messages to my future partner, feeling my energy projecting in his direction. I should feel the intense attraction and heart connection. Also, I was to support that broadcast signal with the feelings I would have while with my life mate, experiencing the emotions of sharing time or making love with a significant other. The more intense the feelings I generated, the faster I would be able to create what I desired.

For those who have read *The Tales of Alvin Maker*, it reminded me of Alvin because now we are the *maker* rather than a *passive receiver* of what our guides do for us. I had been stating my affirmations, expecting my guides to intercede on my behalf rather than using my own energy. I was becoming what my guides had always been to me! I understood that I could always ask my guides to support my efforts as they could not intercede unless I requested. However, my guides now played the role of aide rather than maker or doer since that was my role. Once we understand that premise, we are ready for Segment Seven because we are no longer thrown by unsavory events. We understand we have the choice to include them in our experience or edit them for a more joyful experience. We are totally responsible for every experience we have.

I was excited to receive this information because I knew I was capable of manifesting but was unsure how to unleash the energy. I decided to experience my manifestations emotionally, which is essentially energetically, by focusing on manifesting my life partner.

SOUL GROUPS AND LINEAGE

I asked N to channel the male energy that was responsible for my soul inception. I wanted to talk to my Father! This session resulted in a wealth of information, including clarity regarding my lineage. Based on my being a mutable, which was a soul designed to communicate with all beings in the galaxy, I surmised that I had to have reptilian lineage since there were many references to the existence of reptilian races in channeled material. I did not relish the thought of ties to scaly creatures – in fact it made me shudder but I knew the reptiles represented a large galactic population. I assumed I would need some tie to the reptilian lineage if I was the communicator they described, a being able to talk to all races. I felt a little like an interplanetary United Nations.

My previous channeled sessions had only surfaced the Sirius A and B ancestry as well as the Nibiruan/Pleiadian ancestry. I figured Dad could provide the answers! N went into a trance, and a being named Natara emerged in order to answer my questions. Natara said he had originated from Sirius A, the feline people who called themselves the Elders or Creators because they were responsible for seeding other planets with new civilizations. They were involved in seeding other planets since they had already completed their work in their own universe. I asked Natara if he had any association with Lion Canyon, the location I had recently visited on the Ute Indian reservation, and he said that was an "energy point" for Sirius A. I always felt as if I was on an expensive long distance international call with these entities so I did not press for definition. I wanted to gain as much knowledge as possible while they were briefly present. Natara also confirmed they had worked on my energy while I was in the canyon because I was in an optimal setting for the Sirian vibration.

I asked Natara how he could be from Sirius A when I had been told that my originator was a galactic human from Sirius B? He said that I was fostered by my Sirius B father, named Gunnaia, but I was actually a fragment from Natara. That piece of information made me feel less than significant! He explained that the Divine Creator had desired to experience more aspects of life so it released fragments of itself to seek other types of dimensions.

Those fragments then fragmented themselves to increase their repertoire of dimensional experiences. I asked how many fragments existed, and Natara said they were too numerous to count. I also asked how the fragments returned to the Divine Creator. Natara said the fragmented souls returned through the individual Divine plans that were created for each of them.

Natara said he had been able to mate as a more evolved being with a less evolved female to produce my soul because he worked through energy patterns that denoted a common denominator of creation for all civilizations. Once my soul was created via the two fragments, it was fostered by my Sirius B father Gunnaia. Obviously, by now I was confused, and Natara acknowledged my confusion by saying that it was a complex process and beyond my current understanding. I asked how the reptilian piece of my heritage had been created, and he said that my physical vehicle had been seeded with their DNA. Natara said the ancestry of souls becomes even more complex because, for example, my son Drew's soul originated from Natara, too. However, Natara did not work with a female energy to create Drew. Drew originated entirely from Natara, hence his extremely strong male energy. I asked Natara if love was an aspect of these soul "matings" or were they more aligned with test tube pregnancies. He assured me love was always an important element, since without love, the new soul's frequency would not be complete.

Natara said Asalaine, who would come to Earth to be my life partner, was part of my soul group. I asked him to define soul group, and he said it was a group of beings who resonated at the same frequency and made a commitment to walk the same evolutionary path. Soul groupings could be large, like the Nibiruan civilization, or they could be smaller subgroups existing within subgroups of the larger soul group. Natara said all of my soul group was not on Earth at this time, but we would eventually be brought together since we were all working on the same plan. I asked him, what plan? He told me I would remember eventually, but they had purposely blocked my memory so I could uncover my path within the context of normal human development. He said it was sufficient for me to know they were supporting me in my soul contract and would allow me to remember when they were assured I would not allow my ego to get overly inflated from the information. I assured him that would never happen since I felt a very deep need to exercise the responsible use of power.

I asked Natara if completion of my contract would "promote" me to a higher consciousness than Earth since I had originally come from a higher consciousness. I was unsure what else to call it, but Natara understood the concept of promotion. He said I would move well beyond my current consciousness when I left Earth, but the level depended on my ability to serve. Now, this was tricky because I was still unsure exactly what I was supposed to be serving. Natara must have heard my thoughts because he said I honored him through my work since I was a fragment of him, and they did not choose the members of their mission lightly. He said that it was joyful to speak with me, and that now Anu desired to speak with me. Anu returned and said I would be awed if I realized the amount of support around me at this time. He said if I could "see," I would realize how much assistance I was receiving for this mission. Anu said good-bye, and N returned.

ANOTHER WALK-IN!

My roommate Julia recently discovered she was a walk-in, a shocking experience for her since we determined it had happened within the past year. It is quite nerve-wracking to discover that the person you thought you were is not the person you are at all. This happened to me when I discovered I was a walk-in, although I think it was less traumatic since it had occurred when I was a young child. I started thinking about the character traits I had prior to walking in and the ones that surfaced afterwards. There were clear differences that emerged once I thought about it, despite my youth at the time. Yet, since we carry the memories of the original soul who resided in the body, it is difficult to separate who we are from the original soul. It is the ultimate identity crisis!

Here is what happened with Julia. I had been taking a correspondence course on soul clearing and de-possession from a new teacher, Venessa. In fact, I was scheduled to attend an apprenticeship weekend in early August which I anticipated with excitement. I had been listening to Venessa's audio tapes and reading the materials that accompanied her soul clearing course. I was at the point where my homework required reading the soul or Akashic records for five people and sending the information to Venessa for review.

I asked Julia if I could read her soul records for practice. To read the soul records, one must first determine that the correct soul information is being tapped. Therefore, one of the first questions is whether this person is mono-souled and has a single soul existing in their body for this lifetime. Since Julia had already had a soul reading where her Akashic records were accessed in the past, she expected me to receive a "yes" to this question. However, I did not receive a "yes." We were perplexed. I decided to break the question apart and restate my query to try to clarify the information. I received a "yes" to the mono-soul portion which meant that Julia was not experiencing an entity possession or the residence of multiple souls in her system. However, I received a "no" to the portion of the question asking if a single soul resided in her body for this lifetime. Immediately, I realized Julia was a walk-in, asked for confirmation, and received it.

I told Julia what I discovered. She stared at me in complete surprise, then violently protested the information. I quickly received additional information that she had walked-in within the past year and asked her if anything unusual had happened last August or September. Suddenly, she recalled a road trip she had made to MacPherson, Kansas during which time she kept fearfully repeating to herself as she drove that "I'm going to die." When she arrived in MacPherson, she blacked out for thirty minutes in the parking lot where she exited her car. She was meeting her friends at a restaurant, and they saw her pass out and furiously tried to revive her. This is typical of a certain genre of walk-ins who make the swap during one propitious moment. I call it a flash cut because it is instantaneous and often accompanied by lack of consciousness, whether from fainting or from anesthesia due to surgery. It is important to understand that walk-ins are not possessions when a demonic energy overcomes a positive being. A walk-in is a soul exchange, and each soul has a previous contract with the other. Yes, I confirmed, the episode in the MacPherson parking lot coincided with the walk-in event.

Julia was distressed, trying to understand what part of her was Julia and what part was someone else. I decided to link for her to try to provide some insight. We discovered that Julia was born in a soul grouping of four, much like quadruplets. One soul was her husband she was currently divorcing, one was the original Julia, one was the current walk-in, and one was the man she would meet who would become her life mate. The original Julia had a contract to bring her to the point of emergence, surviving an emotionally abusive childhood and a difficult marriage, but not breaking ties with family or husband. The walk-in was to enter Julia's physical body without remembering who she was and bring Julia to freedom. Again, this is typical of walk-ins who must clear the negative programs and achieve the soul contract of the original soul as well as their own soul contract. Most walk-ins are highly evolved souls since this requires doing double duty during a single incarnation. I was not surprised that Julia was receiving this information on July 22, the very day she had filed for divorce, since that act completed her contract with her husband and fulfilled the walk-in's contract.

I asked for the walk-in's name and was told it was Pelauria. We proceeded to complete the Akashic record reading to determine if Pelauria's archangel realms and soul training were different from Julia's. Not surprisingly, they were entirely different. Pelauria carried a different soul imprint with different experiences than Julia. Pelauria would need to get to know herself.

HOW POLARITY CAN AFFECT US

Again, I attempted to proceed on my soul clearing homework assignment, this time asking my son, Drew, to work with me. I did not know what to expect after my session with Julia, but I decided it was important to practice. Again, I experienced a glitch since Drew held a compassionate connection with a negative person from a previous lifetime. This meant that he had a past life association with a murderer or slanderer or abusive parent who had remained in a negative mindset and, upon dying, entered the negative astral planes surrounding Earth, or hell as we call it. The negative person becomes a non-physical negative entity, but it continues to hound people from its past lifetime, now in non-physical form. Despite the fact that Drew was a lightworker, he would recognize this unsavory entity due to past associations. It might have been an abusive parent whom he attempted to love or even a partner in crime in that lifetime. The compassionate nature of the connection had the capacity to draw Drew into darkness, for example, substance abuse, stealing, and it needed to be removed.

Now that I have conducted numerous soul clearings, I have a greater scope of understanding regarding the number of dark alliances and connections we carry in our soul imprint. As fragments of the Divine Creator, we left the Source to increase our experiences while simultaneously expanding the repertoire of the Creator. This meant we lived both positive and negative existences in order to experience each side of polarity. By wearing both the white and the black hat, we are able to find a place of balance because we have lived the extremes. However, in the process of experiencing darkness, we sometimes create bonds that are never broken. These follow us into subsequent lifetimes and sometimes create problems we cannot resolve on a conscious level. Had Drew continued to live with a link to the negative entity from the past, it might have negatively impacted his current life through unconscious suggestions that eventually surfaced into conscious choices. I proceeded with the request to clear his past life association, happy to release him from a dark presence, but not realizing the implications this type of work had for me.

EXPERIENCING A PSYCHIC ATTACK

Clearing my son Drew from the compassionate connection he held with a negative entity led me to some of my own life lessons. The night after I cleared him, I dreamed about being pursued by some vicious looking creatures that had huge snapping claws like a lobster, legs like a scorpion, and the body of a snake. They were evil, mean and relentless. In my dream, I was fighting and kicking them away from me with all of my strength, feeling their weight to be about the size of a small dog as my foot contacted their bodies. All of a sudden, I awakened, realizing that this dream felt very real and these horrible creatures were seemingly trying to enter me through my feet.

My heart was beating furiously as I tried to run a large amount of white light through my body, but I encountered two problems. First of all, I was too depleted of energy to resist the invasion due to the negative energy that had already entered me. Second of all, my arms and legs felt paralyzed and my head felt crushed by a tremendous pressure that did not allow me to send commands from my brain to my body. Apparently, part of my astral body was still away, being altered by the nightly work conducted by my genetic engineer, Laramus. I had partially returned to protect myself, but Laramus did not have time to return *all* of me. So, I was a mixture of me and my copy who resided in my body while I was gone each evening.

I immediately called to the Divine Creator and the archangels to help me. I asked them to assist me in pushing the negative beings out of my body. I felt these gruesome entities being removed, and enough of my own energy returned to enable me to participate in the extraction. I still felt horrible, but I was also angry. How could my guides leave me unprotected? I trusted them! Obviously, my copy did not have the same level of power I did to fight invasive energy. I told my guides they could not work on my astral body if they did not adequately protect me. They apologized for the event, but somehow I felt there was a lesson in it for me in regard to holding my power. There was also a lesson for them. They realized they needed to train copies to prevent any invasive energy that might attempt to enter a recoder when they were exposed and vulnerable during sleep.

The next morning, I called Bobbie for advice. She said she did not know I was "traveling through the universe" doing soul clearings. She said I should know better than to tackle negative entities without protecting myself while sleeping, since it is a vulnerable time period. I had not known this but vowed to never expose myself again. She told me to ask my healing guides to assist me by running light energy through my body continuously for several days as she saw traces of the negative energy still inside me. I immediately solicited help from my guides, and I felt my feet tingle all day as the energy they sent coursed through me. My head ached, but it was slowly improving.

Protecting ourselves energetically is an important lesson for those recoding. First of all, we attract negative energy that is looking for an interesting playing field. Battling empowered beings is fun! Secondly, we must accept our power. I have always been squeamish about the dark side and felt it was not my job to get involved with it. However, if I am to own my power entirely, I must overcome any fears I have, whether physical or energetic.

I asked my protector guides how to ensure I did not encounter any other negative energies while sleeping. They explained how to create a positive force field of love and light around my body prior to falling asleep by envisioning six layers of white light outside my aura. Six represents love and harmony in numerology so the high vibration of the white light combined with the numerological meaning of six would create a strong positive energy. I was grateful to receive a method for protecting my vulnerability, although I did not envision sleep would come easily for a while. I had felt jumpy all day, and my scalp kept tingling as if invisible energies were brushing against it. I kept remembering the vicious appearance of the scorpions and the thud of my feet against their bodies, shuddering at their frightening demeanor.

EXPOSING ILLUSION

I entered Segment Seven, Removing Illusions, arriving immediately after making the mental decision that the scorpion creatures could not harm me. Remember, Segment Seven is about creating our own reality by exposing illusions, and the scorpions were my first seemingly real brush with a negative energy. Although it felt very real, it had to be an illusion since we are fragments of a Source of pure, positive perfection. Darkness is created in order to provide contrast to that perfection. I could either pay attention to the darkness and remain in its grasp through my fear, or I could ignore it and allow it to dissipate.

Prior to letting go of my fear, I had a very difficult time falling asleep after my run-in with these creatures. I was in a hotel in Charlotte, North Carolina after a day of marketing consulting with an East Coast client. As bedtime came and went, I realized how afraid I was to fall asleep, despite the fact that I had been taught how to protect myself with the six layers of white light. I toyed with the idea of calling Bobbie for emotional support, but it was past midnight, and I did not wish to awaken her. I decided to be brave and try to reconcile my fear. I reminded myself I really was not alone since my guides were always there to assist me. I asked for them to remain with me during the night and protect me.

Then, it occurred to me that I needed to get over it. If I were to recover my power, I could not be whimpering in my bed, afraid to shut my eyes due to some non-physical creature that visited me from a negative astral plane. All energy has a pattern, and that pattern can be manipulated according to how we manifest our own energy. I could not allow a dark force to cower me by thinking it was more powerful than I was. I had to believe in my ability to be safe through my own sense of self-empowerment. I decided to visualize my six layers of white light and fall asleep, confident that the scorpions or other such entities could not reach me if I chose not to allow them near me. Besides, Tammuz was clamoring for me to fall asleep so they could complete their work that had been abruptly abbreviated from the previous night. Although I was unsure how soundly I slept, I placed protection around me and willed myself to sleep for a short four hours.

When I awoke, my entire body was vibrating. My feet were buzzing, and I was experiencing spasms throughout my body. At first, I was frustrated, asking my guides why they had not done a better job of correcting the previous night's work and putting me back together. I heard them tell me they had made repairs, and I realized I was vibrating because my energy was getting lighter. I had reached Segment Seven. I had embraced my power in regard to the scorpion illusion of danger and fear and had squelched it. I congratulated myself.

I lay in bed, feeling the round of spasms that accompanied my new vibration. I asked my guides how long the spasms would last, and they said "forever." They explained the spasms were a result of lightening my energy, and they could not be controlled. I was disappointed because the spasms were very annoying. Then, I realized they were continuing to teach me the creator aspect of

Segment Seven. Nothing is forever if we do not choose for it to be that way. I told them I refused to accept eternity as an answer, and they better return to the drawing board to rework the solution since I expected them to find one. They laughed at me, delighted I was recognizing and appreciating my new self-empowered role.

INFORMATION ON SEGMENT EIGHT

N came over to check the taping equipment for our second public channeling. She had just entered Segment Eight which was called "Releasing Fear," and I asked her to share what she knew thus far. N said Segment Eight was the time when most of the work was conducted on how our brain processes information. By Segment Eight, most of our DNA strands are re-coiled and activated in our energy or astral body. At this point, I had eight re-coiled, and I was in Segment Seven. By reprogramming the way our brain communicates information, the DNA is able to absorb the additional information from twelve levels of consciousness. The entire firings or synapses of energy sequences operate differently once this work is completed.

N said life had become incredibly easy for her. She was finding opportunities at every turn, both business and personal. Whereas Segment Six was a time to take back power and begin feeling the importance of our role as a maker, Segment Eight provided us with the ability to manifest quickly. This is when we reap the rewards of learning how to harness our own energy rather than being on automatic pilot while our guides assist us. When we recognize the potential of our own will, we can move mountains.

MY RECALCITRANT CARETAKER

I was extremely enthusiastic about DNA Recoding because I felt I was on a mission to unearth a process that would assist me in finding my true potential and power. I spent a portion of each day focused on what I was experiencing and recording it. However, others did not necessarily gravitate to DNA Recoding with the same level of enthusiasm. Oh, in some cases, there were people who embraced it with a passion equal to my own, grabbing any opportunity to learn more about it. But others were casually interested in it since they did not see it as a key life event. Still others attempted to proceed through the segments but wavered in determination whenever they met a challenge.

Although I was fully committed to the process and continued to take people through their soul contracts and the approval, I also empathized with those who found the path difficult. There were days when I wanted to return to a less tumultuous life, one filled with fewer major events. And there were times when I felt crazy since I spent more time having conversations with beings who were not physically present than I did with those in my everyday life. Then I remembered the mundane existence facing me if I did not recode: one filled with fear, anger and routines rather than joy, love and flexibility. Fortunately, those who followed in my DNA Recoding footsteps did not experience the same level of chaos that I did. Partially, this was due to my being one of the first to experience the process, and there were many glitches to resolve. Also, I had asked for a robust menu of experiences in order to be able to gain insight into any and all difficulties others would face so I could better assist them.

I had been moving through Segment Seven, Removing Illusions, and it was, thus far, the most difficult level. Segment Seven is the one where we must use our growing power to light the way through the illusion of obstacles. Obviously, my fight with the dark energies who "slimed" me was part of that course. However, there had been other setbacks with which I had less success. For example, the editor I had assisted in DNA Recoding called to inform me that she and her husband had decided to sell their publication. Unfortunately, all of the articles I had expected to see in the upcoming issue were postponed until a buyer appeared. I was extremely deflated by this news since I had worked hard to meet short deadlines in order to be well represented in the publication. I had not quite accomplished the knack of living without resistance, shifting attention from what I did not want to what I desired when a block occurred, because I brooded over the loss of exposure. Instead of focusing on new and better opportunities which indeed occurred, I focused on what I had lost.

Segment Seven is also a time when the genetic engineers work on our astral bodies for longer time periods. It was necessary for them to have access to our astral body for two or three days at a time, because they could not accomplish everything during the evening hours when we are asleep. They were replacing my astral body with a copy, or "caretaker" as they preferred to be called. These caretakers certainly had a host of shortcomings, as I eventually discovered, although they never harmed me or anyone else, and they never undermined me in important items. First of all, they needed to be trained, or they would change my agenda to whatever they pleased. This could mean they would do nothing when I was faced with an important work deadline, or it could mean they would binge on sweets after I had spent the last two years weaning myself from sugar.

Apparently, caretakers are young souls who have never experienced physical form. They are volunteering for this assignment as part of their own soul growth. Therefore, they are very interested in experiencing the easy and enjoyable side of life and feel little need to exercise any discipline. Just imagine what it would be like to eat ice cream or soak in a hot bath for the first time. Additionally, caretakers have no emotions since they are not vested in anything in our lives. They act emotionally detached since they have not participated in any of the events that make us who we are. My detachment from my life and particular outcomes was immediately noticeable by those who knew me well since I have a very focused, driving personality.

During our second public channeling session, Joysiah spoke at length about the frustration we felt with our caretakers, telling us we needed to train them or they would act more like a "house sitter" than a "housekeeper." He said the first thing we should do is send our caretaker a mental message of our intentions during its tour of duty as our astral body replacement. For example, we expect our caretaker to be responsible rather than frivolous. We expect our caretaker to care for our children as if they are their own. We expect our caretaker to assume our emotional, mental, spiritual, and physical blueprint and react to situations just like we do. Joysiah said we could even write a list if it made us feel reassured. It was also important to grant permission to caretakers to read our soul records since no one was permitted into our records unless we allowed it. By allowing access to our soul records, we had greater likelihood of the caretaker's reacting similarly to ourselves in all situations.

Kryona was my caretaker, and I was trying to train her. After experiencing a weekend lacking in emotion and filled with lethargy due to her presence, I decided to have a mental talk with her. Besides, all of my friends were asking me what was wrong with me since I was very listless. They knew I was not acting like "myself." I realized Kryona was doing the best she could, but I wanted to experience the elation that was becoming part of my everyday experience with DNA Recoding. I did not want to feel like a robot. I told her she needed to attempt to experience joy on a daily basis while here, and she needed to be productive. I also told her I had worked too hard to reduce the amount of sugar in my diet, and she needed to curb her sweet tooth. She agreed to cooperate. In fact, she said I could trust her to occupy me full-time, even while I was doing my marketing strategy work. She felt that she could free me up for more astral body work in order to expedite DNA Recoding. At this point, I did not entirely trust her with my client base!

I struck the following agreement. I figured that since we live in an energy state, we can distribute energy any way we want. I said I would allow her to occupy seventy-five percent of me to work with my clients and write a report. If the report was good, I would allow her to maintain her seventy-five percent during work days over the next few weeks to expedite my astral body work. However, I wanted to be fully present during weekends. Since DNA Recoding, I had discovered a greater joy of life, and I especially did not wish to relinquish that feeling during my free time.

I also asked Kryona to feel free to do anything better than I did it if she felt more capable. I gave her permission to eliminate any of my bad habits. I figured I might as well maximize someone else's talents instead of trying to exercise complete control. Unfortunately, I could not ask her to be more energetic. The caretakers seem to have low energy levels, perhaps because they are unfamiliar with the density of this planet. I was taking naps during the work day, something unheard of in my typically high energy lifestyle. This is a major complaint from other recoders who are not accustomed to feeling tired during the day. They noticed the lethargy and lower energy levels when their caretakers were present. Unfortunately, we must accept the low energy level until the caretakers have time to acclimate to the density of energy on our planet. Fortunately, the use of caretakers is brief, and they acclimate rather quickly to our lifestyle and energy.

Kryona wrote an adequate report for me, although there were a few details missing. All things considered, I felt she was a sufficient replacement. I left town with seventy-five percent of her and twenty-five percent of me in my body, deciding I would like to be partially present to ensure I did not lose any clients. I was starting to feel like Sibyl because I was carrying on multiple conversations inside my brain, some with my guides, some with my genetic engineer, and now some with Kryona. I was glad there was no one intimate in my life because I could not handle one more point of contact. I was also thankful my son was at camp for three weeks since it was hard to convince those who knew me that everything was fine. I checked to determine how long I would need to endure my multiple personality and was told the work would be completed in six days. This was not an extensive time commitment when considering the positive outcome from DNA Recoding.

SUMMARY

JULY DNA RECODING LESSONS

- All beings in our solar system are tied, in some way, to each other. Our evolutionary return to the Divine Creator energy of pure, positive perfection is hampered until everyone in the solar system sufficiently raises their vibrations. For this reason, advanced civilizations like the Sirians and Pleiadians are very interested in assisting us in increasing our consciousness since they are tied to our progress.
- DNA Recoding is a key part of reducing the effect Marduk will have on this planet when he returns on Nibiru's next passing by Earth. This event is to occur in

our lifetime, as scientists have supposedly already spotted the returning planet. Raising our vibration via DNA Recoding will circumvent Marduk's attempt to reinforce fear as a primary motivator, thereby increasing our success at moving into an enlightened period.

- Fear can undo what DNA Recoding has done during our progression through the segments. It is very important to remember that fear is an illusion that has been established on Earth to limit us from realizing our true potential.

- Recoders will need to rid themselves of the majority of their toxic energy, mostly in the form of anger or fear from this life as well as past lives. In fact, there may be physical discomfort during some of the work, depending on how much negativity has been cleared prior to beginning DNA Recoding. It is recommended that we utilize liver cleanses for removing anger from the body since the majority of anger is stored in the liver.

- During DNA Recoding, it is beneficial to eat as little meat, fowl, and fish protein as possible in support of cleansing our body for DNA Recoding since meat and fowl are filled with antibiotics and hormones and fish is filled with ocean pollutants. These chemicals interfere with the cleansing of the body, creating a continual dosage of toxins to eliminate. When eating protein, we can raise the vibration of the energy by blessing the food prior to ingesting it, thereby circumventing some of the negativity associated with the way animals are raised in captivity and slaughtered.

- It is important to *release* those whom you feel anger toward rather than *forgiving* them. Forgiveness is not part of Divine Truth because it sits in judgment, assuming someone has done something wrong while the other has done something right.

- Segment Three, Clairaudience, is when the clairaudient channel begins to open. If we resist what we begin to hear, there may be pain in either the right or left ear or in the brow chakra. It is useful to avoid heavy electrical environments where the electrical current flows in a random state because it causes static in the telepathic channel and may result in nausea or achiness.

- Not everyone will see non-physical entities from different astral planes with the naked eye after clearing and completing Segment Four, Clairvoyance. For some, these entities will be seen psychically through the third eye or telepathic vision.

- During Segments Five through Seven, caretakers will be present for greater intervals since the genetic engineers will need your astral body for longer time periods. It is important to make a "to do" list for a caretaker in order for them to be productive during a recoder's absence. Caretakers are young souls who wish to experience life on Earth. Caretakers have no heart connection to your life since they are copies, and they will be more neutral and passive in their responses to your friends and loved ones. It is helpful to give them permission to review your soul records so they have a frame of reference for how you want them to react to your life experiences.

- Segment Five, Integration, is exciting because you can begin to transfer to other dimensions, simultaneously experiencing multiple lifetimes. During this time, bleed-through might occur which may come in the form of a dream or flashes of deja vu.

- By Segment Six, Owning Your Power, your guides are ninety-eight percent positive that you are firmly committed to your soul contract and life path. You begin to receive greater levels of power. It is the segment that enables the mind to manifest what it desires very quickly. This is a time to maintain positive thoughts since negative thoughts can also manifest. Your guides now play the role of "aide" rather than "doer" since that is now your role. However, at this point, fewer than half of the twelve strands of DNA are connected, which limits your manifestation ability.

- Segment Seven is called "Removing Illusions" and is a release of multiple layers of density, peeling each layer back just as layers can be peeled from an onion. This is when your density begins to truly lighten. In Segment Six, you learned how to be a *maker*. Now, in Segment Seven, you have become a *creator*. Segment Seven is difficult because you move from the realization of yourself as the power source in Segment Six to running the gauntlet of illusion to test that power.

- By Segment Seven, you will probably begin to attract attention from negative energy that would like to keep you bound by fear and guilt. They are mesmerized by your light since it is ultra-powerful and would be a tremendous boost to their own energy. If you are not already performing a daily energy clearing routine, now is the time to start.

- Segment Eight is called "Releasing Fear," and it is the time when most of the work is conducted on the way the brain processes vis-à-vis the incremental DNA strands. By Segment Eight, most of your DNA strands are fused and activated in the energy body. The firings or synapses of energy sequences throughout your brain will now operate differently. By reprogramming the brain, the DNA is able to support the additional incoming information from twelve levels of consciousness.

CHAPTER FIVE

AUGUST • 1996

FEELING BAD BEFORE FEELING GOOD

Segment Seven was the most difficult segment I encountered; difficult because I did not know if it was me or my caretaker reacting to situations. Sometimes, I could not differentiate between my responses and Kryona's, so I was unsure if I was solely responsible for my actions or if another soul was involved. I had felt dull and listless since Kryona began caretaking my body, a reaction to my caretaker's lack of emotion for a life she has not lived. I was present, yet not present.

I had set the condition for Kryona to leave for the weekend so I could enjoy myself. I missed the positive feeling that I naturally brought to myself when I was whole, a feeling that Kryona had difficulty creating since she was too far removed from my emotional responses toward my life experiences. However, I discovered upon returning from a lengthy business trip at the end of the week that I had to fall asleep for my caretaker to exit, and Kryona had decided she wanted to stay a little longer. She said she liked Earth and wanted a few more experiences! I had been invited to a gallery exhibition, and I just had time to shower and change between the arrival of my flight and meeting my friends. There was no time to fall asleep to swap out Kryona. I went to the exhibit in our seventy-five/twenty-five percent configuration but, typical of Kryona's energy, I felt disoriented and had difficulty connecting with my friends.

On my way home, I rented a video because I knew I could not sleep, partially because Kryona wanted more time, and partially because I had developed a pounding headache based on my lack of sleep that made it difficult to relax. When I returned home, I took a hot bath, hoping it would relax me enough to fall asleep, but I emerged equally agitated. I decided to watch a video which ended at 1:20 AM I was still wide awake and by now my headache had traveled down the side of my neck. I do not like to take medication, but I knew Kryona would not leave until I slept so I took two extra strength aspirin, hoping when I awoke in the morning I would feel like myself again. I finally fell asleep around 2:00 AM.

When I awoke, I felt very depressed and had no energy. I thought perhaps Kryona was still present, but I checked and determined she was not. How could I be back and feel so low? Then, I realized that a major percentage of me had been with my "real" family for almost a week. Despite the fact that my memory was blocked, I was experiencing profound homesickness. I could not pull myself out of it. I spent the day floating in the pool, trying to orient myself. I was also feeling depressed about the DNA Recoding process because I knew I had ten strands of my DNA re-coiled and wondered when I would start feeling dramatically different. My friends did not relate to this attitude because they knew how psychic I had become over the last few months and how quickly I was manifesting positive experiences. I still felt less evolved than I expected I would be at this point in my DNA Recoding. How could the next level of consciousness feel so bad?

On Sunday morning, I spoke to N because the depression had not cleared and I was growing increasingly concerned. She empathized with me, reflecting how difficult Segment Seven had been for her as well. Segment Seven exposes all of our remaining fears, forcing us to address and remove them. When we come to Earth, we have programs that are placed in our body to assist us in learning the lessons we have come to experience. Otherwise, we would simply duplicate the pure, positive experiences of the Divine energy of our origination. We plan our dysfunctional behavior, then attempt to rise above it. Some of those blueprints actually enhance the level of certain fears to supplement our learning experience. I guess we graduate magna cum laude if we overcome the fears that have been intentionally magnified. This seems unfair to me from my perspective, but I guess when we are in spirit form, we enthusiastically seek challenges in order to ensure our soul grows.

During Segment Seven, we are forced to face the deepest fears we came here to conquer. Then they can be removed. My remaining fear was a fear of being controlled by others through mental or physical possession. Well, they had certainly tested me on that one with that nasty scorpion energy. I was also being tested via my caretaker who did not want to leave. N advised me to "let go" of everything in order to bring Segment Seven to closure. I did not know what "letting go" meant in this context so I was unsure how to proceed. In the meantime, I repatterned any negative energy frequencies as they arose, staying as clear as possible during this time frame. I hoped I would grasp the meaning of "letting go" soon since I disliked living in a negative state.

VISITING THE HALLS OF AMENTI

Jeanne and Mark, the couple I had assisted in requesting DNA Recoding, came over to help me learn more about the Halls of Amenti. I had two reasons for asking their help. First, Jeanne used a process called "flowing" where she is able to take people on guided visits of other dimensions. I had asked her if she would be willing to take me to the Halls of Amenti to determine how I was involved. Secondly, Mark had been involved in the web, or grid energy, that was established as part of the Halls of Amenti which will be used as a booster to move us to expanded consciousness. This was the reason he had entered his lifetime in "group think" regardless of the unpleasantness of the situation. He needed to understand how to coordinate energy to develop an interrelated platform for moving our individual energies from one stage of consciousness to the next. I had already shared with them the information I had received about the Halls of Amenti regarding Mark's involvement and my own. They were as interested as I was in exploring this sacred realm.

When they arrived, Jeanne asked if I had permission to visit the Halls of Amenti energetically, knowing that I was not currently allowed in Sedona due to the codes I carried in my body which could open the portal to the Halls in the future. I told her I had already verified we were able to visit, learning that traveling astrally would not interfere with the energy there. Jeanne prepared us for flowing, having the three of us lie down and hold hands with Mark in the middle. She verbally moved us into a meditative state, proceeding to take us to the entry of the crystal city, the one I had told her I frequently saw hovering over the current site of Sedona.

Jeanne described the route we were taking into the crystal city as the three of us explored our own visualizations. Per Jeanne's description, we proceeded over a bridge that spanned a beautiful crystal waterway that meandered throughout the city, filled with tropical fish and careening waterfalls. We saw how the tropical fish of today contained the same crystal coloring of that spectacular city. We also saw how the water derived energy from the crystal nodes that protruded from the main temple, and how people used the water for drinking and bathing as a source of good health and spiritual nourishment.

Jeanne verbally helped us proceed through the temple to the area that would take us to the Halls of Amenti. We saw a pyramid topped by a floating sphere to the left of the temple, with access through a walkway. I gasped when Jeanne began describing the pyramid and sphere. I could visualize what she was describing, and it was my new InterLink company logo. I was stunned to see the past lifetime meaning those shapes had to me. I knew the shape of a sphere and a pyramid held sacred meaning in terms of the science of geometry, and I had selected the logo based on the sacred geometrical principles they represented. However, I did not know the InterLink logo actually marked the entry to the Halls of Amenti.

We entered the pyramid and descended a stairway behind the podium that led to the portal of the Halls. At that point, we diverged. Jeanne said, "We are moving down a long, narrow hallway and we are entering the appropriate door which is the second door on the right." I interrupted her to say, "I will proceed down the hallway as well, but I will enter the room that is straight ahead." Mark said he needed to enter a room he saw on the left. My room was filled with white light. As I moved into the light, it transitioned me into the actual Halls of Amenti.

Initially, we were perplexed by our different locations since we had been traveling together until the divergence. Later, we realized we each had played different roles in the crystal city which is why we went to our respective positions. Jeanne had been the keeper of the codes that were inscribed on the crystal tablets. Mark was a crystalline deity in the Halls of Amenti. I was the keystone within the Halls. Jeanne said they would follow me to my destination. I entered an oval room that was encircled by thirty-two crystalline deities, Mark being one of them. Each one wore the Egyptian headdress I had seen on busts of Nefertiti or Tutankhamen. There was a frieze of different scenes around the top of the room that integrated the energy of the various deities. I sat in the middle and began communicating with all of them. Jeanne asked for those of the thirty-two we knew as Earth incarnates to please step forward. Mark was one of them and there were four others whom we could not seem to recognize. Mark was told that it was his job to identify those of the thirty-two beings who were incarnate and bring them to awareness of their dual existence, one part on Earth and the other part in the Halls of Amenti.

Jeanne brought us out of the Halls of Amenti and out of our trance. The experience was awesome, more so because the three of us were connected by our work in the crystal city yet unaware when we initially met. In fact, Jeanne and Mark had met the prior year at a singles party at Unity Church. The sequence of activities that had brought us together in incarnate form was astounding. Additionally, I had never traveled someplace astrally with others who could see the same scenes. It was very powerful to experience the richness of my own visuals as someone else simultaneously described it.

THE NUANCES OF SEGMENTS SEVEN, EIGHT AND NINE

I took a long walk in the woods to communicate with my guides away from the interference of electrical energy. I told my guides that my motto for Segment Seven was "seven sucks." Yet, despite my difficulties, I had ten strands of DNA aligned and fused in my astral body. I wondered why the presence of so many strands did not ease my progress through Segment Seven. I was still fuzzy about the differences between the manifestation aspects of those two segments and the purpose for the stress imposed by the negative experiences that arose in Segment Seven.

Based on the input I received from my guides, I determined that Segment Six was a time to incorporate our newly acquired powers. It was a transition from the "help poor little me" requests of our spirit guides, to the recognition that we own our own power and need to begin flexing our manifestation muscles. However, at this point, the unconnected strands of DNA limit our ability to move to complete manifestation. Segment Seven required us to test our new skills based on receiving additional DNA strands. We were thrown obstacle after obstacle which were associated with any past fears lingering in our consciousness. We had the choice of accepting or rejecting the obstacle based on the fact that any obstacle lying in our path was an illusion. If we had learned our lesson well in Segment Six, we would understand that we manifest our own destiny and can create any illusion we choose. Segment Seven is tough because we move from the realization of ourselves as the power source to a running of the gauntlet. It is as if everything we believed in Segment Six is being put to the test. Yet, for me, Segment Seven was completed when I threw up my hands and said, "Enough of this, I don't choose to live this way." It was the "letting go" that N had recommended.

Finally, we enter Segment Eight which clears the illusions from Segment Seven and allows us to completely manifest as long as we use our *own* power to create the manifestation and not the power of our guides. By the end of Segment Eight, our blueprint that holds fear is reprogrammed because our fear implants are removed. These implants were placed in our bodies prior to incarnating on Earth in order to allow us to maximize a soul experience that uses fear as a prevalent emotion and motivator. With the advent of Segment Eight, we have ten re-coiled strands of DNA to assist us in addition to our recognition that we are the ultimate commanders of our path. We recognize that the elimination of fear defuses our magnetism to violence, and that we create safety by our own ability to manifest clean emotions like love. We are closer to Spirit than we have ever been while living on Earth in physical form.

I had assumed the additional strands of DNA would have provided me with more abilities by this time. Anu had predicted that people would assume they could walk on water like Christ by the time they had cleared the nine segments. He had explained that all of us will be able to move mountains by the time we finish DNA Recoding. However, we must learn how to harness our energy to enable us to do that. Naturally, living life without fear was just about as empowered as one could get on this planet, but I guess I expected more. I had become highly psychic and was rarely in a situation where I could not obtain an answer to a life event. I was also able to manifest quickly and easily. But something was missing. It seemed I had been given a pair of wings with no flying lessons.

I felt that I needed to choose an area of interest and funnel all of my newly enhanced energy into it. I wished to conquer the field of manifestation, bringing to others the skills that I was obtaining in that area. I wished to use soul clearing techniques and repatterning of negative frequencies to remove the blocks others experienced that prevented them from moving into their manifestation power. So many people on this planet do not believe they can have whatever they want. I wished to be able to teach others how to quickly and easily manifest so they could bring joyful experiences to their lives. I understood that graduation from the nine segments was only the beginning. I felt myself slip into Segment Eight as I viewed that obstacle and decided to have fun with it rather than feel defeated.

MORE ABOUT MANAGING CARETAKERS

As much as I appreciated Kryona assisting me while my astral body was away for extended time periods, I was relieved to no longer need my caretaker as the remaining work on DNA Recoding could be done during my sleeping hours. However, my friends and associates who were undergoing DNA Recoding were having a particularly difficult time adjusting to caretakers. Julia, my roommate, was particularly unhappy since she felt flat and emotionally removed from her life, a telltale sign that a caretaker was in charge. She was enjoying her separation from her husband and had begun to date. But her caretaker had thrown a wet blanket over her enjoyment because she was not emotionally vested in Julia's life. My friend, Pat, had named her caretaker Rachel, and was trying to get along with her. However, she also found her emotionally vapid and particularly uninterested in working which was putting Pat behind schedule. Both women were experiencing binges with junk food, a habit they had relinquished long ago in exchange for a healthier lifestyle. However, both also confirmed they planned to endure their caretakers since the objective of twelve aligned and connected DNA strands was worth this interim aggravation. Per Joysiah, I advised Julia and Pat to allow their caretakers to read their soul records because our body-sitters were not allowed to assess our personal records without permission.

I informed Julia and Pat that I initially resented giving up a part of myself by allowing another soul to manage my astral body functioning. Both Pat and Julia agreed that having a caretaker was uncomfortable, and they, too, would be glad when it was no longer necessary. Similar to my experience, people noticed that Pat and Julia seemed distant and remote. I empathized and told them the caretaker's occupancy time frame was, thankfully, brief. I came to understand that my caretaker was doing me a favor by allowing me to "disappear" for several days at a time because she enabled me to regain my DNA. In exchange, I attempted to enhance my caretaker's Earth adventure by attempting to have a variety of different experiences during her presence. I explained to my friends how I had decided to be one-fourth present during Kryona's occupancy and, therefore, be able to act as a partially present tour guide. I also had given Kryona permission to override me on anything she could do better, as long as it was in my highest good.

EXPERIENCING TWELVE STRANDS

I had transitioned into a state of continuous joy and elation which was a distinct departure from the oppression felt during Segment Seven. It occurred to me that all of my twelve strands must be re-coiled based on the positive feelings I was experiencing. I had recently entered Segment Nine, although the genetic engineers were still working on elements of how the circuitry in my brain would work in tandem with my new strands. I felt great pride at completing DNA Recoding, since I was under the false impression I was done with the process (having yet to uncover the remaining four phases of the process). Later, I would discover the additional steps to take before truly experiencing the power of DNA Recoding.

Segment Nine is called "Freedom from Guilt." This was when all of the twelve strands of DNA are re-coiled and implants that stimulate feelings of guilt are removed from our system. Just like fear, guilt is programmed into our system in order for us to deviate from the pure, positive perfection of our Source. This way, we have the ability to experience creator energy differently from the Creator. Naturally, I felt pure pleasure when my guilt implants were removed in addition to the fear implants that had been deleted during Segment Eight.

This was the first time in my life I remember making decisions that were not motivated by feelings of fear and guilt. Although I still resided in the Earth's density, my energy had significantly lightened because I was vibrating at a much faster rate. I felt like an orchestrater of experiences as I was able to move energy quickly and easily compared to the past, and I was experiencing more of what I wanted. Strangers seemed to pay more attention to me since I projected an outer glow from my increased vibration. I was enjoying every minute of Segment Nine compared to the difficulties that had arisen during the earlier segments. Making decisions and dealing with life problems was becoming increasingly easy. Even when life did not proceed smoothly, I retained a greater sense of appreciation that everything was as it should be.

I had gone through DNA Recoding rather quickly, given the newness of the process. It appeared that I would complete the nine segments in five months, slightly over half the projected time period of nine months that my guides had initially given me. However, Joysiah told me that everyone might not proceed as quickly. For one thing, I was extremely motivated by my soul contract to bring the twelve-strand energy to Earth, and I proceeded through DNA Recoding with little fear. Secondly, Joysiah had enabled me to move quickly since this was a learning experience for him and his team, and they wanted me to complete the process for the education of the genetic engineers. Thirdly, I was privy to repatterning techniques which cleared me quickly from negative frequencies that were hampering my DNA Recoding process. If I had addressed my blockages from an emotional perspective, it would have taken longer to clear them through introspection and change.

As Joysiah had predicted, some people experienced longer time frames than mine. However, ironically, I found that many of my clients moved through DNA Recoding faster than I did. By the time they discovered DNA Recoding, they had been practicing many of the clearing modalities I had encountered such as energy repatterning, past life regression, and soul clearing. There were also more and more practitioners of DNA activations that moved people rapidly through the nine segments. Sometimes, someone would call me to discuss DNA Recoding, and we would determine they had already completed the first nine segments and simply needed to plug the energy into their endocrine system, a stage I discovered was necessary several months after supposedly completing my own DNA Recoding. I had one client who was so thoroughly prepared to experience the additional DNA energy that he completed the entire process in seven days! Obviously, he had conducted a great deal of pre-work to enable this to happen.

Joysiah had asked me to check with him prior to using repatterning techniques on new recoders to ensure I did not expedite the process beyond the capabilities of the genetic engineers. He said I needed to honor the readiness and commitment levels of others, as well as the necessity to sometimes move slowly to remove blockages which could cause discomfort. A slower rate would allow those with larger issues to proceed through the segments more smoothly. Initially, Anu and Joysiah were overjoyed to see me proceed so quickly in order to bring the full DNA energy to the planet. However, based on the stress it had caused me at times, they desired a more enjoyable experience for future recoders.

TWELVE LEVELS OF CONSCIOUSNESS

I flew to Colorado to train with my new teacher, Venessa, on her soul clearing techniques. The work was fascinating and provided additional insight into my DNA Recoding experience as well as confirmation of certain aspects. Knowing that my soul destiny contract involved teaching DNA Recoding, I wondered why I was so interested in learning soul clearing. Venessa provided an answer on the first day of class. She said that older souls who had lived elsewhere before journeying to Earth for additional soul growth could not return to their original realm or proceed to new experiences if they carried negative energy from prior lives. They were not allowed to leave the Earth realm because it would be like breaking quarantine, essentially intro ducing a negative energy that would harm others who might live in a clean environment. Soul clearing was the ultimate detox, clearing negative energy and blockages created by trauma retained in our soul memory in one session.

Based on the soul clearing Venessa had done for me several years earlier, I knew it was easy to be carrying blocks and barriers without knowing it. For example, I had been the recipient of monitoring implants placed during a series of ET abductions I had endured as a child. I needed to remove these implants since they maintained a link to an intrusive society which might misuse them at a later date. However, I had no knowledge of them until they were uncovered during my soul clearing. My life had changed dramatically after that, as the implants had been placed in my third eye and blocked my ability to meditate or receive psychic transmissions. Right after my soul clearing, I began my automatic writing. Based on my practice sessions on recoders, I was aware that, like me, some of them had prior negative influ ences that required clearing, whether it be a conflicting soul contract or a curse or a compassionate connection with a dark being like my son had experienced.

In the evenings after our training sessions, Venessa channeled an entity named Maria for our education and enjoyment. Maria was a lively entity with a German accent and a wonderful sense of humor. We looked forward each day to hearing from Maria. On the first evening, Maria said she wanted to share information on Goddess energy, and she asked if anyone had questions. She requested that each of us state our name prior to asking our initial question so she could associate our energy with our request.

Of course, I had many, many questions these days! However, I politely sat there as the others introduced themselves by first name and asked their questions. When a lull occurred in the barrage of questions, I took the opportunity to introduce myself to Maria as Anne. Maria immediately responded that she did not recognize that name with my energy. I was perplexed and unsure what to do. Then, it occurred to me to introduce myself as Lahaina. Maria said, "Ah yes, Lahaina," in immediate recognition as if we had known each other for thousands of years. This was wonderful confirmation for me since I had never told Venessa my soul name. I really was Lahaina! I proceeded to ask Maria about my twelve strands of DNA, looking for further confirmation regarding my progress. Maria said, "Yes, you have twelve strands," in a tone that implied, "Don't you know this, you sweet moron? Don't you have anything interesting to ask me?"

I asked Maria why I did not *feel* extremely different with twelve rather than two strands. I said I was unsure what to tell others to expect as a result of DNA Recoding. Of course, I also did not realize at the time that I had not completed the process. Maria explained that two strands of DNA gave a human being access to two levels of awareness and information, whereas twelve strands provided access to ten additional levels of awareness. Essentially, our superconscious could visit a larger database of information, plus hold the capacity to *understand* the incoming information. Later, Venessa and I discussed how the twelve strands became integrated into the physical vehicle. We saw this as a process that occurred over time since a quick integration would probably scorch our circuitry. In fact, Venessa surmised that those who seeded the twelve strands energetically through the DNA Recoding process might never be able to carry twelve physical strands during their current lifetime. She proposed that our purpose was simply to ground the energy on the planet to allow future generations of individuals with twelve physical strands to exist.

However, Venessa and I also felt a further integration of the twelve DNA strands would occur for those who energetically carried twelve strands. For example, as the Earth's electromagnetic field continued to lighten in our transition to a new consciousness, a soul living in a two-strand physical body would begin to access more and more capabilities from the twelve strands that existed in their energy field. The lightening of the energy allowed a better transmission between the physical and energetic fields. Later, I would discover that we could actually plug into the twelve-strand energy through our endocrine system, which further enhanced my usage of the energy.

Based on this refined understanding of DNA Recoding and with the help of my genetic engineers, Laramus and Joysiah, I rewrote the information package that I was distributing to those interested in the process. I felt it was important for recorders to understand that they may not immediately turn water into wine or walk on water after they finished the nine segments. However, the twelve-strand energy held the potential we needed for our soul evolution. The following information was included:

"When a third dimensional being regains twelve strands of DNA, those twelve strands are attained energetically through the astral body since the third dimensional body is currently too dense to accept the higher vibration created by more strands. This is the first step to experiencing an expanded level of consciousness. The next phase consists of plugging the twelve energetic strands into your endocrine system. Eventually, the twelve strands will be integrated into the physical body as the energy field lightens on Earth. Bear in mind, those who have energetically attained their DNA and have children will be able to seed a soul with a higher vibration that is capable of housing twelve coiled strands in his or her physical body. In the meantime, your life experience is improved through the gaining of access to twelve levels of awareness and information versus the current two levels. In addition to having access to greater awareness, all fear and guilt implants are removed as a part of the DNA Recoding process, again a significant improvement. DNA Recoding is not to be confused with ascension which allows a soul to consciously move back and forth between dimensional experiences. However, DNA Recoding ultimately guarantees that you will ascend since only fully activated beings can properly activate their energy for the event."

ELIMINATING MY RESISTANCE TO ARCHANGEL KAMIEL

There are seven archangel realms which are actively involved in bringing teachings of love, light, and truth to the Earth realm. These seven archangels align with our seven primary chakras. If we live with our seven primary chakras aligned and balanced, we experience love, light, and truth every day. As an older soul, I had come to Earth with a specialty in a particular archangel realm, my specialty for assisting and being of service. My primary archangel realm was Gabriel which is the realm of teaching and communication. During our training, Venessa taught us how to evaluate our receptivity to all of the seven archangel realms since we should enlist the support of every realm, even if it is not our primary one. Essentially, we determined what percentage we were "open" to each particular realm. As I learned, this is an exercise that must be completed prior to plugging the astral body DNA strands into our endocrine system, and it is shared in a later segment of the book. Most of my percentages were high. Understandably, I was open one hundred percent to the Gabriel realm. However, I was only fifty-three percent open in the Kamiel realm, which is the realm of power.

During our lunch break, I took a long walk in the mountains outside Venessa's home. It was wonderful because I was completely alone and could hear my guides very easily due to the lack of interference from electrical power. As I walked, I asked my guides why I had been halfway shut to the power realm when it was so important for me to feel empowered in order to accomplish a significant task like DNA Recoding. They told me I had shut myself off from my own power because I did not trust it. When I had been given a great deal of responsibility and believed in my own power in the crystal city of Sedona, I had been forced to make decisions that hurt my society. I was afraid to take my power back because it would mean I would have to, once again, be responsible for difficult decisions. This was why N initially spearheaded DNA Recoding. My guides had been concerned that I would reject the information if it had come to me first based on my rejection of my power. I cried as I realized how I had not allowed myself to flourish because I had thought the outcome might not be positive. My guides kept asking me if I wanted my full-fledged power back, but I resisted. What if I had to make decisions that hurt others again? What if I just wasn't up to it?

Then I realized that if I did not accept my power, I would never successfully complete my work during this lifetime. I wept as I pushed my hesitation aside and agreed to fully accept my power and the responsibility that followed. However, this time I would not be alone. I would draw on the strength of my guides and the Divine Creator to ensure I walked the straightest path to my objective, making decisions that would heal rather than harm others. However, if harm occurred, I would know everyone experienced exactly what they needed to experience, based on the principle of Divine Order. I felt a tremendous burden lift from my shoulders, replaced by a feeling of calmness. I knew I had cleared a major obstacle by releasing a block to my power that I had held for the hundreds of lifetimes subsequent to that fateful experience at the Halls of Amenti in the crystal city.

WHERE IS MY FUTURE MATE?

It was time for our nightly channeling session with Maria. This time, when questions were asked, I focused on the whereabouts of Asalaine, my future life partner. I asked Maria when I would meet Asalaine since it was late July, and I had been told I would meet him by the end of the summer. Maria informed me that I had to "clear that other man" from my energy field before Asalaine would appear. I was surprised because I had done a great deal of clearing to energetically release who I assumed was Jerry. I thought I had cleared most of it. Maria said I had cleared my *own* issues, but *Jerry* had placed a "wedge" under the door leading to Asalaine. Although Jerry and I were finished on a conscious level, Jerry had not done any clearing work on a subconscious level, and he still had my energy and his intertwined. Thinking of all the energetic cleansing I had done, I wondered how those experiencing death or divorce ever released themselves from each other without conducting some clearing work. There must be a tremendous number of ties that remain linked for years despite the dissolution of the relationship. Eventually, I designed a ritual to break these ties which my divorced clients deeply appreciated.

I asked Maria what I should do to dissolve Jerry's tie since our relationship was finished for this lifetime. She said I needed to use love to release it. She told me to envision a door with a wedge under it, the wedge symbolizing the energetic block that Jerry had created. In typical male fashion, Jerry's attitude was "If I can not have her, nobody can" despite the fact he was already involved in another relationship. Maria instructed me to connect with the Divine Creator and bring white light into my third eye, place my hand on my third eye while formulating the intent of dissolving the tie, and move my hand to my heart chakra once I stated the intention. Then, I was to transfer the heart energy that held my intention in pure love onto the wedge under the door and dissolve it.

Instinctively, I moved my hand out from my heart to pluck the wedge from underneath the door, but Maria stopped me. This, in itself, was impressive since Venessa channeled with her eyes closed! Maria said, "You cannot use force to remove the wedge. Force creates resistance which defeats your objective. It must be dissolved with pure love." I relaxed my hand and continued to send pure love to the wedge. I saw it blast apart. When I opened my eyes, I asked Maria when I would encounter Asalaine. She said, "Today, tomorrow, whenever you wish!"

Later that day, I took my lunch time walk in the mountains and asked my guides where I should go to meet Asalaine. They told me to "go to a park where people walk dogs." I laughed, saying "I have a cat. I don't have a dog." Their response was "Go anyway!" I was traveling almost every day through the end of August. I light-heartedly resolved to explore dog walking after Labor Day.

MORE COMMUNICATION PROBLEMS

Venessa channeled Maria for us one last time on the morning we were planning to leave. Since I had all the information I needed about Asalaine and my twelve strands of DNA, I decided to ask about my role in the Halls of Amenti. Although I was capable of receiving my own information, I liked to receive confirmation from others, especially those who had not been privy to the information I had been receiving over the last few months. I was not about to miss an opportunity to ask questions. Venessa was not well-acquainted with what I was doing with DNA Recoding although she knew I was involved in the process, and Maria was a new entity she had recently begun channeling. With the understanding I would be receiving a fresh and unbiased perspective, I asked Maria my role in the Halls of Amenti.

Maria said she had to obtain permission to open the doors to the Halls of Amenti to view my role. I waited patiently as she checked, then she returned and said she could open them for just a few minutes. She instructed me to ask my questions quickly as time would be limited. She confirmed that I was, indeed, present in the Halls at the same time I lived as Anne on this planet. She also confirmed I acted as the keystone in the Halls for this project. Here is what she shared:

"I have to translate through a different energy field to make contact. You are both here and in the Halls of Amenti at the same time. This is why you have an energy translation error for your body. Your clothes have never fit quite right, but they will within the next few months. You need to bring the two places forward through the work you do with the body, not for this place to become that place or for that place to become this place, but to combine the coded information for both places to bring two parts of the code together. It is not a soul contract for spiritual work. It is a soul contract for physical work. The female body issue you work with is the translation error for the information coming through. Make your clothes fit, and this will resolve itself. You are the keystone of this particular project. But it is a part of many great projects for Earth. It is a specific teaching you have in a different energy interpretation. It is a teaching you have brought to other worlds. It is similar to your work in the crystal city of Sedona, but it is more. It is your training for many, many, many interpretations and many worlds so you can bring a certain teaching to a different world with the same need. You have to follow your soul plan, because I have difficulty reading this because of the challenge of the type of language plan you wish to bring here to interpret. It is the challenge of the system of the planet not wishing to expand. But of course it will expand. The challenge is because of the lack of current expansiveness on the planet so you cannot keep the door open for great periods to bring the expansiveness in. It is time to try to ask it to open, even for a little bit, because it brings expansiveness for all. Ask, how can you open the door more, even for a little bit? Even if you open it a little, it allows the energy in. You have to set the energy vortex to allow the door to open because it is bringing information with a vibrational energy that is not accepted well by planetary Earth. So, it is a challenge. But you have done this in other systems. You are practiced."

I was mystified by this information, hoping it would become clearer after I worked with opening the doors to the Halls of Amenti. After the channeling, another woman from the seminar, Kay, came over to me and said, "Do you understand what Maria meant by the translation error?" I said I did not and would she please explain it. Kay said her interpretation was that the translation error was due to the lack of heart energy in the Halls of Amenti. The energy was blocked from Earth because this planet's frequency is based on heart energy, a foreign element in other dimensional experiences. In fact, my greatest struggle to adapt to this planet has centered around opening my heart energy. I had spent the last ten years painfully peeling back layer after layer to get to the essence of why I came here to experience this planet. My heart is finally open, which is why I knew they would send me Asalaine, a male energy who also hosted an open heart and can support me in this venture. Kay said if I wanted to access the Halls of Amenti, I needed to conduct a transference of energy, taking in the energy from the Hall and projecting my heart energy. Because I resided in the Halls, I would be capable of making the transference. However, the doors would only open briefly so I had to act quickly. Over time, the doors would remain open for longer periods of time as the energy from the two locations merged.

I worked with the energy of the Halls for a long time. It was frustrating because I always felt pressed for time. It was like stepping on a pad that opened automatic doors and needing to complete all of the work during the interval between when the doors slide open and closed. Ultimately, my future mate, Asalaine, and I would travel to Boynton Canyon in Sedona at the end of 1997 and perform an energy ritual that opened the doors. When we did, we felt the sadness and oppression associated with the area immediately lift from the hulking shoulders of the mountains. I felt my immediate work with the Halls of Amenti was complete.

WHERE, OH WHERE, IS MY PERFECT MATE?

My friend Wendy visited in order for me to practice my newly learned repatterning and soul clearing techniques. After our session, we sat on the sofa and chatted about the recent events in our life. Wendy lived in an older section of Kansas City, and the historic homes in the area surrounded a beautiful park. She had recently purchased a dog. She told me the dog was leading her to meet a number of her neighbors since the residents of the area who owned dogs had initiated a daily habit of meeting in the park to chat while their dogs played. Wendy said she had met an interesting man during her daily visits to the park. They were getting to know each other since they briefly met every day during the 6:00 AM and 7:00 PM neighborhood dog walking event.

She spoke about this man's intensity, his well-developed feminine side which made him a non-competitive and agreeable confidante, and his familiarity with metaphysics. In fact, he was a teacher of Polynesian or Huna spirituality. He was also a chiropractor who had expanded his practice into alternative healing by becoming a clinical nutritionist. He had recently been divorced, and he had already asked Wendy if she was interested in dating. Wendy has always known exactly what she wants, and in this case she flatly responded "No." She told her new friend she enjoyed their conversations but was not interested in dating since his intensity fatigued her after a period of time. In fact, she had been thinking of asking him if he wanted to go out with her friend, Sharon.

As I listened, alarms were going off in my head. I thought over and over again, "This sounds like Asalaine!" I asked what type of dog he had, thinking it might be a Scotch Terrier, but Wendy said it was a large dog and she did not know the breed. Half expecting the answer to be "no," I asked my guides if the man in the park was Asalaine, and the answer was "yes!" I sat there stunned, partially in disbelief and partially full of faith that everything was proceeding as had been promised. I said to Wendy, "You can't fix this guy up with Sharon. This is my guy. This is Asalaine!" Wendy gave me a blank stare and asked, "Who is Asalaine? This man's name is David."

I gave Wendy the background on Asalaine since I had never shared my search of my perfect partner with her. When I finished the story, she expressed her excitement at being the link that would bring two perfectly suited life mates together. We debated what to do since David was interested in Wendy and was unaware of me. I knew I couldn't just call him and say, "Hey David, our guides have informed me that we are perfect life mates and meant to spend the rest of our lives together!" Wendy knew David was away for the day since she was aware of his presence via their daily dog walking, so we decided she should leave him a vague message on his answering machine. She called and told him she had a friend whom he should call due to this friend's interest in the channeled Abraham material, information for which David displayed a particular fondness. She left him my name and telephone number. I laughed because I had no familiarity with the Abraham material at the time and was unsure how I would back out of the white lie when David called.

I had hoped to hear from David during the weekend because I was free to meet him on Sunday afternoon. I was intensely curious to encounter this man who was, according to my telepathic information, my future life mate who offered the ultimate in synergy by carrying the same grid structure. I was also incredibly nervous, wondering if he would like me or I if would like him based on our similar energetic patterns. What if my guides were wrong? After all, they were not living in physical form. Maybe their taste in men and mine did not correspond. In an effort not to discreate what I had just created, I made a massive effort to assume if he was really Asalaine, we would have an intense mutual attraction.

I left the house early Sunday morning and missed David's call. He called at 11:05, and I had left at 11:00. His message said he was responding to a message left by his friend, Wendy, and he would be happy to talk to me on Monday when he returned from a conference he was attending over the weekend. In an effort to prepare him for our conversation, I called and left him my own message. I thought it would help if he heard my voice. In an effort at honesty, I told him I was unfamiliar with the Abraham tapes per Wendy's initial message, but I had received information from my guides that we should meet because we shared common business interests. It was awkward knowing more than the other party. I was entering the situation with a certain set of expectations. I did not wish to create the same set of expectations for David, perhaps making him nervous or causing pressure. I figured the pretext of working together would suffice for meeting, and we would know in the first fifteen minutes if it was more than that. I awaited his next call.

Asalaine and Lahaina

David called my office early Monday morning. My assistant answered the phone, then called to me, "Dr. David is on line one." My heart leaped into my throat, and I started sweating. I thought how silly it was to have such a school girl reaction, but I could not seem to control my nervousness. What was I going to say to a life mate I had never met? At least, I knew from Wendy that he was tall, physically fit, and nice looking. He was rather disadvantaged because he knew nothing about me.

I picked up the telephone and said, "Hello," and I repeated what I had left on his message recorder, that my guides said we might have a mutual business interest, and they recommended that we should meet. I explained how I had been told months prior that I would be meeting a chiropractor in his fifties who lived in Kansas City, was involved in healing, was well-acquainted with metaphysics, and, of course, had a dog. The soul name of this man was Asalaine. I asked if he had ever heard that name in relationship to him. He said no, and I could hear the lack of warmth and trust in his voice. I felt like I was using some cheap, metaphysical pick-up line in the genre of "What's your astrological sign?" His tone suggested that he felt the same way. I struggled with what to say next to break the ice and I heard my guides said, "Tell him your soul name. Say that you're Lahaina." I took another shot and asked him if he had ever heard the name "Lahaina." There was an immediate adjustment of the energy as I felt him connect. He said, "*Who are you?* I just got a hook-up. You know that rush you get when you gain immediate insight? That's how I feel."

David said he knew the name, Lahaina, and it meant something to him, something from the distant past. I asked if he was thinking of the town in Hawaii? He said "No," but that he taught Polynesian metaphysics, thinking that might be the connection. Later, we would determine that one of our happiest lifetimes together was when we lived as two Polynesians in the Hawaiian Islands. During that lifetime, I had used the name "Lahaina." I asked David if we could meet for an hour and explore if there was any credence to our "business" connection. He agreed, and we struggled to match calendars. I was leaving town for a week, and he was busy with his patients and his weekly radio show on alternative medicine. We settled on meeting at 3:00 PM the following Saturday after he finished his radio show. We planned to meet at a restaurant in a bar and night club section of Kansas City. He kept stressing he only had thirty minutes to an hour free due to his busy schedule. Clearly, he was hedging his bets, and I did not blame him. I was disappointed to wait another week, but knew either he or I had unfinished business to resolve or we would have connected sooner. I hung up the phone and prepared to wait.

SEVERING CONNECTIONS, AGAIN, WITH JERRY

I had to call Jerry due to some unresolved finances regarding the house. The call led to a series of emotional conversations throughout the day. I was disappointed in my heated response during the conversations since I thought I would feel more neutral. However, at the end of the day I reached a place of resolution and calmness that has remained with me ever since. Our intense conversations were emotionally difficult but also very cleansing. We both had felt we were meant to be together forever, that ours was a divine soul complement relationship that would transcend time. It had been difficult to resolve that soul mates were not necessarily supposed to remain together.

As my guides explained later, soul mates were often characterized by relationships full of passion because the two individuals had emotional issues to resolve from prior lifetimes. If the relationship was not passionate, most couples would not remain together through the clearing of their discordant energy. Jerry and I had been soul mates and had cleared our past. Now, we were free to find our life partner. Somehow, through the course of our conversations that particular day, we were able to put our lack of understanding to rest. We could honor the relationship we had together and know the love would not die at an eternal level, while also honoring the fact that we were not meant to be together any longer as life mates. There was no negative emotion left, only a feeling of peace. I knew by the end of the final emotionally intense conversation that I had completely let go of him and vice versa. I also knew that this was why I could not meet Asalaine the previous weekend. Sometimes we need to clear and come to peace with certain aspects before we can move forward, especially when we are so emotionally bound.

Later in the day, Wendy called to tell me of her conversation with David in the park that morning. Apparently, he had not entirely bought my "business" excuse for getting together. I guess when an unknown female calls and claims her guides suggest a meeting, that carries a hint of a come-on. Later, David would tell me that some women had tried this tactic in the past without success since they knew about his interest in metaphysics which is why his suspicion was raised.

According to Wendy's most recent meeting with David that morning in the park, he was more interested in asking Wendy about my personal rather than professional habits. Wendy told David that he "owed her" for getting us together because I was the "sexiest" friend she had. I was dismayed by this promise because I did not feel I fulfilled her description. I hoped I lived up to her portrayal in his eyes when we finally met since I had always been unsure of my feminine energy, an aspect of myself that David would help me fully uncover in the future.

Wendy also said David shared an experience that had occurred over the weekend with his recent ex-wife. Apparently, she was also at the conference he was attending. When he saw her, which was prior to receiving my message, he looked at her and felt totally disconnected from her energy. He felt released by the emotional ties of the relationship. As he was driving home from the conference, he felt a lifting of the heaviness he had carried for months. He felt liberated and began singing due to his incredible feeling of joy and freedom. He told Wendy he knew at that moment he was ready for someone else, the ultimate partner he had never had. When he returned home from the conference, the message light was blinking on the machine and my voice emerged. He had been free from emotional connections for exactly forty minutes! Later, he marveled at the synchronicity of endings and beginnings.

I had mixed feelings about David's realization that my call might mean more than business. On the one hand, I felt it was better that both of us entered our initial meeting with equal intent and with our eyes open. On the other hand, I felt the playing field was being loaded with land mines which created pressure for both of us. Nonetheless, I felt the time drag and drag until we could finally meet and satisfy our mutual curiosity.

COMPLETING PHASE ONE OF DNA RECODING

I drove to my HMO for my follow-up pap smear. I had made and canceled the appointment so many times, due to scheduling conflicts, that I knew I had no interest in going. Yet I felt it was necessary to place closure on the questions regarding my physical health. I entered my HMO and sat down to wait. I waited for nearly a half hour, realizing I was going to miss my second appointment if they did not see me relatively soon. I approached the front desk, asked how much longer, and was told they were just about ready to see me. I returned to my seat and waited an additional ten minutes. Finally, I decided this was not meant to be and returned to the receptionist, asking her to return my plastic membership card.

The receptionist said, "One moment please," and went to get the card which was with my medical records. When she returned, a nurse accompanied her. The nurse asked me to step into the back to speak with her for a moment. I entered an examining room and, short on patience, bluntly asked her about the reasons for the hold-up. The nurse said she was sorry for the delay but there was an error on my chart. The appointment had been scheduled for a pap smear when I really needed to have a colposcopy. I said, "No, there is no mistake," and explained I had changed the appointment to a pap smear because I was not receptive to someone scraping my uterus. The nurse said the pap smear would not be helpful because it would simply reveal what it had the first time. Knowing I was cleared from whatever caused the initial problem, I told the nurse I would agree to have a pap smear but not a colposcopy. We went in circles for several minutes, she insisting I needed a colposcopy and me requesting a pap smear. I finally asked her to define "questionable pap smear" since no one had bothered to do that. She said she was not "at liberty" to reveal that information.

At that point, I got fed up with the situation. I had given too much authority to medical professionals for too many years, and no one was going to tell me they could not answer my questions about my own health until they had conducted another intrusive procedure. The patient seems to rarely be allowed any choices. I thanked the nurse for her time but said I had another appointment and needed to leave. As a last note, I said I would see them in March for my annual pap smear which – by the way, happened to be normal.

When I reached the lobby, I thought to myself, am I crazy? At the time, I did not know that future pap smears would be normal, although I intended for them to be. I thought, am I risking my health and my life over my feelings about my issue with power? Then, I decided it was the only path I could follow. I was not interested in surgeries, medications and nurses with half answers. I would rather die gracefully if my time had come. I called N, my next appointment, and told her the reason I would be late. She began laughing, saying, "Anne, you just graduated from DNA Recoding. You've cleared the nine segments. I see a whole room of beings cheering around you because you took back your power. Congratulations!" Sure enough, she was right. I had been too busy fuming to notice that it was uncomfortably hot around me as I felt their presence. I had done it! I was the second person who had completed this version of DNA recoding, right behind N who had finished the prior month! I told N I would be right over.

I had several questions regarding the nine segments that I wanted to clarify with Joysiah before finalizing the information for distribution. I also had several personal questions, including feedback on my upcoming meeting with Asalaine. N began channeling

Joysiah who answered my questions on the write-up. The complete version of the summary is located in the appendix of this book.

At the end of the session, I asked Joysiah to help me understand my role in DNA Recoding beyond teaching it. Joysiah said he would read a segment of my soul contract from my soul records. He said I would use portions of repatterning and soul clearing to assist others in clearing their emotional and psychic pasts. This would enable my future clients to remove blockages to their soul growth which would either prepare them for DNA Recoding or expedite their DNA Recoding progress. I would use my psychic ability to provide information for repatternings and soul clearings, but I would not specialize in psychic readings.

He also said it was never meant for me to be a full-time repatterner or soul clearer, that I had learned those methods in order to support my work on DNA Recoding. Later, I would realize how accurate that information was as I tapped my repatterning and soul clearing tools to develop the plug-in process of the twelve DNA strands into the endocrine system and the polarity balancing ritual. At the time, I was pleased and not surprised by this information since I had witnessed incredible healing with repatterning and soul clearing. The negative drain that people carry around for lifetimes can be cleared instantaneously, resulting in major improvements in their current existence. I was happy to follow this path, realizing it was the path I was already on. When was I going to get it through my head that I was always exactly where I needed to be?

Finally, I asked about Asalaine. I thanked them for bringing him to me. They said, "Dear one, you drew him to you. We simply helped you clear the blocks." I asked if I needed to know anything prior to meeting him. They said, "Just be accepting." This is good information for a person whose dominant archangel realm is Gabriel because we tend to not only be self-critical but critical of others. We are known for our perfectionism and must constantly battle it. I promised myself I would be as accepting as possible, wondering what was so unappealing that I had to be accepting. Maybe, it was his preppy style of dress since I was averse to traditional styling, adopting an eclectic style of dress after years of self-employment.

MEETING ASALAINE

Finally, it was time to meet David. I struggled with my impulse to call David to cancel the whole meeting because I was so nervous. I have never felt confident in my appearance, and on top of my own feelings of insecurity, Wendy had set the stage by telling this man I was one of her sexiest friends.

I went to our meeting place, and sat at the bar. I purposely arrived early because my legs were like jelly, and I did not trust David watching me as I entered. I ordered a cup of coffee and sat while my stomach churned. He had told me he wore his hair long, drawn back in a ponytail, so I spotted him immediately as he entered the restaurant. I was instantly drawn to his eyes. They were incredibly intense and full of passion. He was not what I pictured, yet he was more than I imagined. He was a lit light bulb. He was so filled with life, something I had missed intently when living with Jerry. Indeed, despite the long hair, he sported the conservative style of a white golf shirt and Dockers. However, the contrast of the hair and the preppy clothes was very appealing.

We sat and talked, both having plenty to say to each other. It was as if we had not talked for centuries, and now we were trying to catch up with each other. About an hour into the conversation, I wondered what David thought of me, if he was attracted to me, or what was going on in his mind? I was a nervous wreck, hoping if I kept talking that he would not have to leave. The level of energy flowing between us was extremely intense, and my stomach felt like it was clenched in a vise grip. I was unsure if I was the only one feeling the intensity, or if David felt it, too.

Abruptly, David asked me if he could touch my hair. I hesitated, then said, "Sure," wondering what he was thinking to himself. He reached over and touched my hair, and I felt a surge of energy pulse through my head. He said something about being fascinated with curly hair and wanting to touch it. Whatever! At that point, all I knew was he was elegant, charming, articulate, intelligent, passionate, generous, and full of integrity based on our conversation and my observations. I did not know how he felt about me, but I knew the way I felt. I felt with all my heart that this was my life mate! Later, David told me when he walked into the restaurant and saw me, the light was cast upon my hair, and the combined effect of my natural curls and the light made it look like I had a halo around my head. He said he was transfixed by my hair and wanted to touch it.

David began describing his house to me, telling me he wanted to show me his classroom. He taught metaphysics in a classroom on the third floor of an old home located in a historic part of Kansas City. His home sat on an energy vortex he called "the well" that shot the energy up through the core of the house, magnified by the roof which was a perfect pyramid. It was a tremendously powerful energy that David often used when he needed to access a large amount of vital force for healing or manifestation.

As he spoke, I realized a friend of mine had taken his classes and that she had once described his house to me. In fact, the energy was so powerful that she almost passed out the first time she experienced it. I told David I thought we would have met eventually since we had a mutual acquaintance. I said I would love to see his classroom but needed to pick up a book at a bookstore close to the restaurant. We decided to stop at the bookstore since we virtually passed it on the way to his home. Guess who was in the bookstore when we arrived? Our mutual acquaintance! She looked so surprised when she saw us, exclaiming "I didn't know you two knew each other?!" We just laughed at her look of surprise. Our mutual amusement already made me feel like a couple. Plus, the synchronous situation further confirmed our synergy. After chatting for awhile, we left for David's home.

David showed me around his house which was a magnificent example of old, moneyed Kansas City living. By now, my head was aching in addition to my stomach, due to the level of energy moving between us. I still had no idea what David thought of me since nothing had been said. The house and the classroom were beautiful, and I could see how powerful David was from what he had created. He asked if I wanted to sit in the well and experience the energy. I said, "yes," and sat on the bench directly above the energy source. The energy was phenomenal, so clean and pure. It tickled me as it went through me, reminding me of that feeling right before an orgasm.

I blurted, "Have you ever made love to anyone in the well? It would be fantastic!" I might as well have said "When are we going to make love in the well?" Surprisingly, he said "no," that he had never met the right person, suggesting that finally he had. After my embarrassing comment and the tour of his house, I felt that our meeting had gone well beyond the thirty minutes David said he had allotted based on his busy schedule. We had already been together for three hours. I told David I probably needed to leave since I had overstayed my visit. He said, "You're not leaving because I need to take you to dinner." No problem, although I didn't know how my stomach was going to handle eating. I assumed from his invitation to dinner that he was enjoying my company as much as I enjoyed his, which was a welcome relief based on my uncertainty about his reaction to me.

David and I went to a local restaurant. There had been no silence between us, and we had already spent three wonderful hours together. I knew I had loved him for many lifetimes and felt very comfortable with him despite my nervousness. But, I had no idea what he was thinking or feeling about me, and was afraid to ask. As we sat looking at the menus, he looked me straight in the eye and asked if I was aware of the amount of energy between us. I told him, as I looked directly back into his eyes, that I was very much aware of it. He remarked he was exceptionally nervous, but his nervousness was only surpassed by his level of excitement. Well, at least that made two of us!

David asked if I knew why there was so much energy running between the two of us. I told him that I hesitated to share information that might cause unnecessary pressure on an emerging relationship. As I paused to consider the implications of sharing more information, David said he was already overwhelmed, so I might as well tell him what I knew. I shared the information I had received from my guides about the accurate description of his age, height, profession, and love of dogs. I tried to downplay the fact that I had been working on manifesting him since early May because I did not want him to think I was some kind of stalker. I explained how we had the same grid structure, that we aligned with each other better than anyone else and that no one on the planet had the same energy frequency. Talk about shocking someone on the first date! David took the information surprisingly well, commenting that my explanation clarified the way he was feeling about me which was equally intense. I was relieved to share what I knew, but I did not feel any more reassured about him or his feelings toward me.

After dinner, we returned to his home and walked his dog, then sat on the swing on the front porch and talked. We still had not run out of things to say. It was such an odd feeling. I felt that I had known this man my entire life, but I really knew virtually nothing about him. Deep in my heart, I also realized this was everything I had ever wanted and we would be together a long time. I wondered why Joysiah had told me to be accepting since I felt very accepting of this man. There was no trepidation, only relief that I had finally found him. I wondered if he felt the same way about me.

David began talking about how he had been looking for the perfect partner his entire life. He knew exactly what he wanted in a relationship and, even during his multiple marriages, realized he had not yet attained it. He told me how he had created a list that described his perfect person, and he reviewed it every day. He had also been in the process of manifesting someone. I laughed when I realized we had both been creating each other at the same time. David also shared his feelings regarding the timing of my call with his closure with his ex-wife and how my phone call awaited him when he got home that day.

I asked to see his perfect partner list. I thought it was brave of him to agree to show it to me. It is amazing how much we are willing to reveal about ourselves to total strangers, especially after both of us had been so recently hurt after opening our hearts up to relationships that did not succeed. But after all, we were not strangers. This was Asalaine who had come into physical form to be with me. And he had been looking for me as much as I had been searching for him! David returned with his list, and I reviewed it. The list described me perfectly with one possible exception. He wanted a "sailor," and I had only sailed once on a tiny boat. I said I did not know if I was a sailor, but he said he already knew I was.

It was getting dark so we went inside. In the living room, he reached out to kiss me and it was so intense, so immediate, and so overwhelming that we both had to sit down. Then he took my hand and led me upstairs. That was the beginning of forever, and we both knew it.

SUMMARY

AUGUST DNA RECODING LESSONS

- Segment Six, Manifestation, and Segment Eight, Releasing Fear, both involve manifestation. However, Segment Six focuses on teaching us to use our own power to manifest rather than relying on requests to spirit guides. Segment Six is the recognition of our power as fully capable creators. But we are somewhat hindered in Segment Six to manifest based on the number of un-coiled DNA strands. Then Segment Seven, Removing Illusions, is experienced which enables us to test new manifestation skills in light of illusionary obstacles. At this time, we are tested in terms of letting go of fears that would materialize less than positive outcomes. Segment Seven is tough because we are the running the gauntlet to test our manifestation power.
- Once a recoder has mastered the ability to unveil illusion and allow events to work in their behalf, they are allowed to enter Segment Eight, Releasing Fear, which clears the illusions from Segment Seven and allows manifestation. Segment Eight is also when we receive at least ten of our twelve DNA strands so manifestation becomes quick and easy.
- Manifestation must align with our soul contract since all of the power from the twelve DNA strands will be focused on fulfilling those contracts. This is when we use our new power to become adept at a particular line of work. A recoder will not be using his or her new power to create youthful appearances or turn water into wine. However, when we are in flow with our soul contract, we are in a position to manifest whatever we want because we feel complete in our joy, peace, and happiness.
- In Segment Eight, Releasing Fear, all of our fear implants are removed and in Segment Nine, Freedom from Guilt, our guilt implants are removed. We are finally able to

experience life in joy and love rather than in fear and guilt, with all of the benefits afforded by that viewpoint. Fear and guilt implants were utilized to ensure we learned our lessons well on Earth since these are key components of our experience. However, they no longer serve a purpose after we complete DNA Recoding because we are motivated by positive rather than negative emotions.

- Caretakers will do a better job of "house-sitting" our body if they are given permission to read our soul records. This ensures that a caretaker will react to unplanned situations similar to the recoder they are trying to replicate. They are also more likely to align with the recoder's emotional reactions since they have full knowledge of the recoder's thoughts and feelings, although they are unable to manifest full emotional reactions because they are still replacements with limited third dimensional experience and no vested interest in any particular outcome.

- Segment Nine, Freedom from Guilt, is the creme-de-la-creme of the DNA Recoding experience. We now have twelve strands of DNA re-coiled, and all of our guilt implants have been removed. This is the first time we have experienced life on Earth without fear and guilt in our mental body. Fear will still be present as a physical response because the human body has an automatic fight or flight mechanism. However, emotionally, we are no longer motivated by fear. Imagine the full capacity of one's energy without fear and guilt! Although we still reside in a dense vehicle, our energy has lightened significantly since we are vibrating at a higher rate. This rate will continue to heighten as the Earth increases its own frequency, enabling us to manifest more quickly and easily.

- Anne underwent the nine segments of DNA Recoding quickly since the genetic engineers and the Nibiruan Council wished to learn by observing her reactions and experiences. Some will experience DNA Recoding with equal, if not greater, speed. Others will be slower since too much speed can cause pressure on the recoder and the genetic engineers if the recoder is not ready for the

HAPPILY
EVER AFTER

After undergoing DNA Recoding, I have a growing metaphysical practice, my ideal life partner, and I am living my life with greatly reduced fear and guilt. I continue to feel remnants of fear based on habit, but I simply repattern them as they arise. Often, I feel as if I am floating in bliss when I look at David. I am eternally thankful that I have the privilege to share my life with him.

When I tell people the story about how I left the majority of my fear and guilt behind or how I met David, they have one of two reactions. They decide if it can happen to me, it can happen to them, and they ask me how to go about moving in the same direction. Or they determine that I am the luckiest person in the whole world and that something like that would never happen to them. Guess which of those two types of individuals are ready for DNA Recoding?

David and I are very proud of the creation of our relationship. Everything is easy and perfect when we are together which is what Anu and Joysiah promised me from the beginning. We are totally in love and, while not co-dependent, feel a piece of us is missing when we are not in the presence of the other. Our love is powerful yet gentle, supportive without being consuming, and sharing instead of needy. We met on August 24, 1996, and we were happily married a year later on August 24, 1997. Even with seven previous marriages between us, there is no doubt that this was the one we were preparing for, the one we always wanted but had not yet found. We cherish our sacred union and thank our earlier partners who helped us become what we are for each other. We foresee many blissful incarnate years together and have pledged our union for eternity.

As we discovered soon after meeting, David was already in Segment Seven of recoding. When I shared the DNA Recoding information, he recognized the segments he had already experienced. We never discovered how he initiated DNA Recoding, but we assumed he had completed the work prior to walking in. Apparently, Asalaine is the oversoul of David, just as Lahaina is the oversoul of me, so the walk-in process was simply a transference of more of Asalaine into third dimensional form, similar to how I was becoming more and more of Lahaina. This transference began on David's birthday in February, 1996 so by the time I met him in August, he had nearly completed the transition.

David insists that he is still David rather than a transference of the Asalaine energy. However, most of his prior friends do not recognize him because he has changed so dramatically. His personality is much softer and lower key. He used to wear navy blue blazers and ascots, but now feels more comfortable in jeans and a T-shirt. When I met him, he claimed he was comfortable with his life and would never leave his home or his daily routine. By June of the following year, he had sold the traditional house he had spent years renovating a la *Colonial Home* in the historical section of Kansas City and moved into my contemporary southwestern home in the suburbs. He had also stopped practicing chiropractic in order to devote his full-time attention to nutritional counseling and traveling to different cities with me to teach metaphysical classes.

I have yet to win the lottery. However, I earn whatever money I need, and I expend less energy doing it compared to my work habits of the past. Besides, now that I have learned how to manifest the desires of my heart, I expect to win the large amount of money that I have always felt was coming to me. My guides tell me that I never won the lottery because people would claim all that I have created was handed to me on a silver platter, that I was one of the lucky ones. However, I have learned to be the captain of my ship, and my guides need to listen to me and assist me in my big win. I am in a state of joyous anticipation. I realize that I have dramatically changed my life in a very short time and have become the creator of all of my experiences. I am specifically creating my life to fulfill the desires of my heart and I am anxious to teach these valuable techniques to others. Knowing that I have learned how to link with my guidance system and use my personal skills to vibrate with the abundance of the universe, I now know that this abundance is within me!

At this point, there are many individuals who are experiencing DNA Recoding, some more assiduously than others. I have found that DNA Recoding does not resonate with everyone. There are some who find it to be the solution for which they are searching, and there are others who find it to be either of little interest or too difficult once they start. Those who have undergone DNA Recoding will attest to major shifts in their life, not only from a personal perspective which often feels like a major upheaval, but also from an enlightenment perspective. These people are operating with greatly reduced fear and guilt in their lives and have telepathic abilities which give them access to an array of information that assists themselves and others.

DISCOVERING THE
FINAL FOUR PHASES
OF DNA RECODING

I thought I had completed DNA Recoding when I finished the nine segments. However, I discovered that there were four more phases. The second phase was discovered at the end of 1996, the third phase in the spring of 1997, and the final two phases in the summer of 1999. Initially, I was disappointed because I liked feeling a sense of completion about finally retrieving my missing DNA strands. But I also understand that our soul evolution is never finished. Plus, I am sure that even if Anne were to reach completion on Earth, there are more expansive experiences for Lahaina to undergo in other dimensions.

Unfortunately, N and I needed to part ways after the nine segments of DNA Recoding. Her direction, via Anu, was significantly different from the information I was given by Laramus and Joysiah. N and Anu became almost dictatorial in their delineation of DNA Recoding, and they expected everyone to follow the exact process according to their time frame or be bumped from the project. After retrieving my power, I had no desire to join an organization that was restrictive and defined my path for me. Although I wish them the best of luck spreading their version of the DNA Recoding information, I have felt compelled to honor the information my guides sent me regarding the final four phases since they have always provided me with guidance for my highest good.

According to Joysiah and Laramus, the second phase of recoding is called the Plug-in Process. It consists of balancing the endocrine system which is the window to Divine Spirit. Once the endocrine system is balanced, the twelve DNA strands can be plugged into each of the endocrine glands, thereby connecting the energy in the astral body to the physical body. I spent the last two weeks of 1996 creating the balancing modalities in preparation for the plug-in, and

I have utilized them on many recoders. Everyone who has undergone DNA Recoding feels even more in touch with his or her power after plugging into the power via the endocrine system.

I have also received confirmation that the DNA Recoding process works, both through my own experiences and through my clients. For example, several months after I completed phase two when I plugged into the energy, I attended a spiritual workshop. One of the exercises consisted of using a pendulum to dowse for the percentage of fear, guilt, and pride in our mental body since we were working on eliminating those negative frequencies. I used my pendulum and obtained an answer of zero percent for the amount of fear and guilt residing in my mental body. I assumed these numbers to be incorrect since others in the class were obtaining percentages in the twenties to forties. I asked the teacher to check my numbers since they were apparently incorrect. Maybe my ego had overridden the results! She verified that I held no fear or guilt in my mental body and asked what I might have done to clear myself. I told her about the DNA Recoding process which was supposed to remove fear and guilt, somewhat amazed yet not amazed that what I had undergone the prior year had worked so effectively.

During that same workshop, we also conducted an exercise to balance our endocrine system since my teacher believes it will become the primary operating system in our body in preparation for the ascension process. She explained that the endocrine system was in the process of replacing the immune system as the body's key system since we could not house a "fighting" system and be balanced. In other words, the immune system uses warrior energy to combat invading germs, an energy inappropriate to the balance needed for ascension. Again, my percentages were different than the others in the class. Whereas the other students had blockages that created a sixty to ninety percent efficiency factor, I was open in all of my endocrine glands by ninety-eight percent or more. Apparently, when I balanced my endocrine system for plug-in, I had removed the majority of constrictions. This was further confirmation that the process worked.

In April, 1999, three years after I had encountered Anu, Laramus, and Joysiah and a year after I had published my first version of *The Power of Twelve*, I learned that there were more steps to completing DNA recoding. At first, I was annoyed because I felt these steps should have been revealed to me prior to the initial printing. However, as time transpired and I continued to accumulate the new information, I realized I was naïve to believe our spiritual growth would ever be complete.

By this time, I had been assisting people all over the world in removing blocks and barriers at the subconscious and superconscious level for almost two years. Often, someone would complain about their flagging enthusiasm at clearing layer after layer of issues in search of a balanced life. They wanted their plate of issues to be empty rather than full. I could certainly relate to that feeling of frustration. Sometimes, issues would immediately clear and never emerge again, a condition both my clients and I greatly preferred. Other times, I would clear an issue at one level, only to discover there were multiple levels that exposed themselves at a later date after the initial clearing. Although I wanted to clear everything at one time, it was not possible. First of all, I did not hold the insight to recognize the other levels that needed clearing at the point that I eliminated the initial blockage. I needed to have time for that insight to be revealed based on living without the blockage I had just cleared. Secondly, I needed to experience life without the initial blockage in place in order to build a repertoire of new experiences. The new experiences provided a different insight into the original issue, thereby surfacing a different set of related issues.

Ultimately, my guides gently reprimanded me about my frustration regarding the multi-levels that sometimes needed to be cleared. They reminded me that we are energy beings, and energy is constantly moving and evolving. We are so task-oriented in our society that we want to achieve our agenda and put it to rest in order to feel we have accomplished something. However, energy operates differently. It is never static. Energy is exciting because it constantly is moving and shaking, creating a rich panorama of life experiences that entertain us while moving us into new states of awareness. Our desire to be complete conflicts with the fundamental nature of energy since completion is impossible in a constantly moving energy state. Once I understood this viewpoint, I advised my clients to begin to enjoy seeing their plate as full rather than continually trying to empty the plate by eliminating their issues, recognizing that perhaps an empty plate did not signify success. Actually, an empty plate signified "death" rather than "completion" since there would no more energy circulating. I implored them to revel in the activity of addressing their issues rather than wishing them away so they could enjoy their growth experience. Otherwise, we view our clearing efforts as drudgery rather than addressing them with the elation of uncovering the illusions that interfere with our ability to live physical life from a spiritual orientation.

I became grateful for the additional information after overcoming my initial disappointment at realizing, once again, I had not finished DNA Recoding. This time, my teacher came in the form of Robert Detzler, a Unity minister who had left the ministry to work full-time on a technique called Spiritual Response Therapy (SRT). I had invited Robert to teach his technique in Kansas City in 1998, but based on his popularity, could not sponsor a workshop until 1999. As I have come to learn, despite my frustration in desiring everything "now," his timing was perfect. I was searching for a simple way to teach soul clearing techniques without necessitating the lengthy, expensive training I had experienced. By the time Robert arrived in Kansas City, I was very comfortable with soul clearing after much practice, and I was ready to incorporate new methods into my repertoire. I had also finished many of the massive marketing efforts required to sell my new book and mentally and emotionally felt ready to take on more.

Since we were providing lodging for Robert, we had the opportunity to talk to him before and after the three-day class he taught. I shared *The Power of Twelve* with him, and he conferred with his guides, or his High Self as he called them, to determine their opinion. Robert said the techniques in the book, according to his spiritual team, were extremely effective. However, based on his work with thirteen energy bodies instead of the four to which I was accustomed, he said there were ten of the thirteen energy bodies that contained DNA, and my process only covered seven of them. When I initially heard his pronouncement, I moved into denial because I did not want to re-address the process, nor did I like feeling that the readers of the original book had not received all of the information they needed. Then I reminded myself about the concept of Divine Order, a state in which we were supposedly living where everything occurs exactly as it should at the correct time. I conferred with my own guides, and they concurred that I needed to add two more phases to completely cover all of the energy bodies that utilized DNA energy.

Based on a very aggressive work schedule, I delayed addressing the additional fourth and fifth phases until August, 1999. When I had time to sit quietly and explore the missing information, I realized I had already lived through the changes myself and would have a very easy time recording them. In fact, some of the changes occurred as a result of the information I had learned in my class with Robert. Again, a Divine Order seemed to be accommodating me. Plus, the remaining phases were very simple. They would not require a lengthy process for those interested in experiencing DNA Recoding.

The fourth phase deals with opening our heart energy so we can process all incoming information and filter all of our life experiences through our heart rather than our mind. Essentially, the process reprioritizes our hearts over our minds since modern society has taught us to do more thinking than feeling. For myself, I underwent a difficult transition in meeting David and marrying him since I had managed to survive very nicely by being a thinker and doer rather than a feeler who exists in a state of being. Obviously, I was not going to alter a lifetime habit overnight so I have been challenged to address the transition on an ongoing basis during the three years we have lived together. Based on my learning experiences with opening my own heart energy, I have been able to devise some simple energy exercises that will accomplish that goal. As I have learned via soul clearing, it is the level of specificity in our requests coupled with an emotional yearning for a new state of being that moves the stale energy. Therefore, opening the heart is relatively easy. Keeping it open requires a commitment to erasing old habits that prioritize brain over heart.

The fifth and, as of today, final phase of DNA Recoding involves re-aligning your team of guides and teachers to ensure you have the optimal assistance in place after achieving the twelve-strand DNA consciousness. In addition to hiring the right players, this phase also clears you and your spiritual team through the highest levels of spiritual awareness known to us at this time. After this is accomplished, you will be able to have access to the highest level of psychism possible, on all dimensional levels, thereby expanding the quality and the quantity of the spiritual information you attain.

I work with clients who continually tell me how their lives have changed due to DNA Recoding. They enjoy the joy and peace of mind the recoding energy has brought them. Although they are actively participating in life, they feel comfortably removed from the negativity that affected them in the past. Abundance comes more easily to these recoders and, when there are stumbling blocks, there is little reaction or resistance, which makes the barriers easy to overcome. My clients who know each other also remark on how personalities have changed. Those who led more passive lifestyles are more "on," grabbing more as they move through their experiences. Those who were directive have become more easygoing as they have learned to enjoy the flow, knowing they direct their destiny by manipulating their energy rather than feeling that they need to exert control.

For each of you, I hope you decide there is magic for the taking, and your experience on this planet is the grandest experience in the universe. Live it, enjoy it, maximize it, revel in what you create. And remember, you are only here on temporary assignment. One day, you will return to your place of origin or you will move on to new worlds full of rich experiences. Feel proud knowing that your tenure on Earth was enriched by what you created while you were here. Perhaps that will include bringing the twelve strands of DNA to this planet. Perhaps it will be something else that is equally glorious. Whatever it is, it will be perfect for you.

APPENDIX A

•

PHASE ONE OF DNA RECODING

SUMMARY OF
THE NINE
SEGMENT PROCESS

DEFINITION OF DNA RECODING

DNA Recoding is a process that enables a human being who has two strands of DNA to acquire twelve strands of DNA energy. Twelve strands of DNA are characteristic of advanced civilizations, and they are a fundamental element of the parents of the *Homo sapien* two-strand system. Approximately 450,000 years ago, a group of advanced beings from the planet of Nibiru visited Earth. They decided to take up residence on the planet based on the emerging pleasantness of its habitability as the Ice Age drew to an end. They were particularly interested in the rich gold deposits on Earth, and they mined those deposits for approximately 150,000 years. Finally, these advanced beings mutinied, claiming they no longer wished to toil in the mines. Based on the need for a labor force, a new being was born, a primitive worker who was constructed by cross-breeding the genes of a gentle ape-like creature called the *Homo erectus* who was living on Earth with the genes of the Nibiruans. Hence, the "lulu" or two-strand primitive worker was born.

The primitive workers assisted the Nibiruans for many years. However, they needed to be birthed via the wombs of the Nibiruan females since they were hybrids and could not reproduce. Understandably, the women grew tired of acting as baby-producing machines, and, like the miners, they too rebelled. The Nibiruan geneticists returned to the drawing board and created an enhanced version of the lulu, one called Adapa, or the Adam we know from the Bible. This improved two-strand being could reproduce and is known to us as the *Homo sapiens*, our current body type.

Now we have reached the stage in our evolution where it is time to acquire a full twelve-strand consciousness. The reconnection of this complete circuitry enables us to have access to twelve levels of spiritual, emotional, physical, and mental awareness and information instead of the two levels afforded by two strands of DNA. Access to twelve levels results in expanded consciousness. DNA Recoding is an empowering and approachable process that allows us to function at higher skill levels and operate at full evolutionary potential, exponentially increase our psychic abilities, release debilitating emotions of fear and guilt, improve our health by balancing the endocrine system, quicken manifestations, live in path and purpose, and position ourselves for ascension. DNA Recoding is not a scientific study of evolution. It is a method of expanding human potential.

Many think they are currently experiencing DNA Recoding. However, often they are simply experiencing the pre-work. It is very important for you to have a clean, light vibration when undergoing DNA Recoding. Healing modalities like Reiki, Rolfing, acupuncture, past life regression, repatterning, and so forth increase the vibration of your energy field by removing discordant emotional patterns. Although it may feel as if you are increasing your consciousness, true DNA Recoding does not begin until you are actually working with your spirit guides or genetic engineers to re-coil the ten additional strands of DNA. Implants were put in place to de-magnetize ten of the twelve strands of DNA, thereby preventing them from coiling. De-activation of these implants has to occur in order for the twelve strands to re-coil. There are many techniques to initiate DNA Recoding, and this process is just one of them.

When you regain twelve strands of DNA, those twelve strands are initially attained energetically through the astral body since the physical body is too dense to accept the higher energy vibration created by more strands. You would not care to reside in your body if it housed twelve strands of DNA because it would be uncomfortable. It would give you more voltage than you could handle. Integrating the twelve strands into the astral body is the first step toward increasing consciousness because it establishes a higher vibration in your energy. The second step involves plugging the twelve strands of DNA into the endocrine system. The third step is comprised of attaining balance and acceptance amidst the mass consciousness of polarity (e.g., good/bad, right/wrong, left/right) by renegotiating your current polarity contracts for unification contracts. The fourth step prioritizes your heart over your mind so you lead with your feelings rather than tricking your instincts through mental gymnastics. The final step ensures you are working with the optimal spiritual committee to support your expanded consciousness, and it opens your awareness to the One level, that of the Divine Creator.

If you are reading this information, it is highly likely you have agreed through your soul contract to act as an ambassador to Earth by hosting the new, expanded energy. Although your body may not contain twelve DNA strands, access to twelve levels of information instead of the two you currently use will exponentially improve your life since you will have more data with which to work. In addition to having access to greater awareness, all fear and guilt implants are de-activated as a part of the DNA Recoding process, again a significant improvement to your current life experience in the mass consciousness that is driven by these emotions. Originally, these implants were intended to enhance our learning experiences on Earth. However, they no longer provide value because DNA Recoding is a self-empowered process that relies on positive rather than negative motivators. Imagine, a life of choices based on joy and love rather than fear and guilt. You are virtually guaranteed a better quality of life!

Once you have completed the nine segments and re-coiled your ten additional DNA strands, you will be able to funnel the energy from the additional strands toward the fulfillment of your soul contract. All the power of your twelve strands is used to fulfill your contract. It is not used to make you look young again or make you walk on water. Remember, we were not selected casually to spearhead this process. We were selected based on our commitment to establishing an enhanced life experience on Earth. In addition to seeding the twelve-strand energy, you have a very important soul contract to fulfill for the highest good of everyone. You will become "adept" at the work you were meant to perform during your lifetime as you master your particular area, be it healing, communicating, teaching, channeling, manifesting, or clearing energy. Your heart will resonate when you perform this work, affirming the correctness of your actions. This is when your financial rewards will expand and you will glow with good health because you are working in bliss, aligning your daily actions with your heart energy. All of the wonderful things that the Earth has to offer comes through the fulfillment of your soul contract.

DNA Recoding is not to be confused with ascension which allows a soul to consciously move back and forth between dimensional experiences. Ascended souls are souls with full consciousness. Unlike each new physical incarnation when we begin with lost consciousness and need to rebuild it, ascension allows us to remember every soul experience we have ever had and build upon that history. DNA Recoding ultimately guarantees that we will ascend since the twelve-strand DNA vibration is needed.

THE HOW TO'S OF DNA RECODING

There are many ways to acquire the twelve-strand vibration depending on your particular soul contract. DNA Recoding is one of many, so find the process that resonates with your heart. Bear in mind that the following process has been provided by non-physical beings who live in a dimension outside the Earth realm, specifically the Sirian/Pleiadian Council and the Nibiruan Council. The Pleiadians and Nibiruans are involved because they originally altered the DNA of the evolving *Homo erectus* on Earth, and the planetary councils are asking their assistance to help us move to our next stage of consciousness. Additionally, like the Sirians, the Pleiadians and Nibiruans are tied to our progress since they reside in our solar system. Scientists determined in 1990 that our solar system is energetically tied to the Sirian system. Apparently, we rotate around the galaxy in a spiral corkscrew path that is connected to our Sirian counterparts. I am sure we will discover one day that we are equally tied to the Pleiadian and Nibiruan systems in some way. Given that energy is interrelated and we live in a cosmic soup of interlocking blueprints and matrices, the Sirians and Pleiadians are confined in terms of their own progress until we move up the evolutionary scale.

Prior to beginning DNA Recoding, it is necessary for you to accept your soul contract which defines your purpose for incarnating on Earth. This will ensure you use your newly acquired powers to fulfill your soul contract which will be in the highest good of all. It should not be difficult for you to accept your soul contract since it is your reason for being here, and it will resonate with you. If you are not already aware of your soul contract, you will be given as much information as possible from your guides. If you are unable to communicate consciously with your guides at this time, ask a psychic counselor to help you. However, some information about your soul contract may not be shared, since it will be meaningless until you achieve greater awareness which will assist your level of comprehension. This information will be provided by your guides when it is deemed to be timely.

Once you accept your soul contract, your formal request for DNA Recoding can be made to the Sirian/Pleiadian council which signifies approval by changing your soul status in your soul records, called the Akasha or the Akashic records. These are the multi-dimensional beings who are most actively involved in helping us move to a new level of consciousness. They have sent many older souls from their societies to assist in this process, and those souls, called starseeds, live among us as fellow human beings. Many have lost consciousness of their origins because these older souls need to embrace change from an insider's point of view, from a place of compassion. However, the more you progress through the DNA Recoding experience, the more you will recall your experiences as an older soul in other dimensions.

When reading your formal request for DNA Recoding, prepare by taking a bath to which you have added one cup of baking soda and one cup of sea salt. This will cleanse your aura, the energy field that surrounds your body. Then, light a white candle and read the following request out loud:

"To the Sirian/Pleiadian council and all beloved brothers and sisters of the Universe, to Prime Creator who created all things in all people, I am requesting of my own free will access to full consciousness through the recoding of my DNA, and I am ready to begin at this moment."

You may use a pendulum or kinesiology (muscle testing) to dowse to determine if you received permission to recode from the Sirian/Pleiadian Council. If you do not know how to dowse or are not yet able to receive psychic transmissions, you can either purchase a book on dowsing or contact a psychic counselor. Or you can contact Anne Brewer at InterLink at (913) 722-5498 or *interlnk@qni.com* and she will determine if you have received acceptance. If there are blocks to DNA Recoding, we can recommend a practitioner who can assist you, either Anne or someone better aligned with your problem.

DNA Recoding will require commitment. You will need to rid yourself of discordant emotions like anger, fear, and guilt since these dense, toxic emotions do not match the pure, high vibration of the twelve-strand energy. Some have difficulty releasing old, toxic behavior patterns, and you may feel worse before you feel better as you peel back the layers of the onion to get to the source of your discordant emotions. It is important that you spend the time to eliminate toxic feelings or there will be physical discomfort during DNA Recoding. You guides wish for you to be comfortable, and they are attempting to assist you in preparation so it will be an enjoyable rather than an uncomfortable experience.

Bear in mind, you will not be approved for DNA Recoding unless you have released the majority of your negative blocks, since you would endure too much discomfort if these blocks existed in your body when recoding begins. Most of you have been working on this for years, so you will be relatively clear upon becoming aware of DNA Recoding. It is important for you to remember that the permanent release of discordant energy depends on the release of *emotional* rather than *physical* blocks. In other words, if you go to an acupuncturist who opens up blocked channels in your meridians, the channels will not remain open unless you emotionally clear the source of the problem. When emotional blocks remain present, the physical body might rid itself of anger one day but receive it back the next.

The following methods are recommended for releasing negative emotional patterns in preparation for DNA Recoding. Some recommended emotional cleansing methods are:

- Energy work like Reiki, attunement, or craniosacral therapy;

- Acupressure or acupuncture;
- Toning;
- Retinal therapy;
- Energy repatterning;
- Reflexology or massage Rolfing;
- Soda and salt baths (one part each);
- Liver and colon cleanses;
- Soul clearing;
- Chiropractic therapy;
- Stretching disciplines like yoga; and/or
- Transformational breathing.

It is beneficial to eat as little animal protein as possible in support of cleansing the body for DNA Recoding. Protein in the form of animal products creates a heavy energy in one's system when DNA Recoding is attempting to lighten the energy field. Obviously, this is counterproductive to the process. Plus, meat and fowl are filled with antibiotics and hormones and fish is filled with pollutants. These chemicals interfere with the cleansing of the body, creating a continual dosage of toxins to eliminate. When eating meat or fowl, it is best to eat the antibiotic/hormone free variety. Additionally, animals which are raised in captivity for slaughter contain negative energy based on their living situation. One ingests the negative energy from the animal that has resulted from penned breeding and raising methodologies, again creating an ongoing intake of negative emotions that must be cleared. When you are eating protein, whether during or after DNA Recoding, the food should always be blessed in order to raise the vibration of the slaughtered animal to a much higher frequency prior to your ingesting it.

If you are reading this information and it is resonating with you, you are probably an older soul. This means you may have already experienced expanded consciousness in your earlier soul experiences. For you, DNA Recoding is a process of remembering what you agreed to forget when you entered a physical body on Earth. You are simply activating codes already residing in your system that stimulate recall of past experiences. This is why you resonate so strongly with the information because you are impulsed to remember what you had been asked to leave behind when entering the Earth plane. The only new information will be how to transform the human body you are inhabiting to a higher state of consciousness since you operated in prior soul experiences in an energy body.

DNA Recoding is not a completely defined process. Your guides are learning along with you, since few human beings have moved to a more fully conscious state from their dense physical form. You will be assigned a genetic engineer during DNA Recoding to assist you. We suggest you communicate regularly with your genetic engineer since you may be undergoing changes that you might not understand. At times, you may feel like you are slightly crazy, but we assure you that you are not. As you move through Segments Three and Four (Clairaudience and Clairvoyance) in the first phase, you will be able to create your own form of communication with your genetic engineer because your telepathic channels will open. However, until that time occurs, you may want to utilize the skills of a psychic individual to keep communication open. Rest assured that your genetic engineer will love and care for you and will allow no harm to come to you. In fact, you would be impressed by the amount of protection you receive during this process, and you are promised an outcome that will bring enhancement to your life.

Although there are five phases to DNA Recoding, it is not an entirely sequential process since you might finish something from Segment Four then return to Segment One in the first phase, or you may feel impulsed to complete something in phase three or four prior to beginning phase one. The non-sequential aspect of DNA Recoding is due to the fact that the codes for altering your DNA are scattered throughout your body. During your sleep state, your astral form visits your genetic engineer for DNA Recoding work, and changes are made in your astral body. Sometimes, in the translation from astral to physical experience, something from work on a prior segment is misaligned and needs realignment, or a code located in one part of the body is opened which causes a code in another part of the body to react.

When you begin to recode, you extract yourself from the pool of mass consciousness of fear and guilt. You are part of the recoder pool of consciousness, one based in love and joy. As you expand your consciousness and continue through the five phases, your upgraded consciousness grows in strength, creating a new pool of consciousness toward which Earth's mass consciousness can strive. For this reason, you may feel some stress on your intimate relationships if these people are not experiencing DNA Recoding, because you no longer exist in the same pool of consciousness. You will particularly notice this when you finish Segments Eight and Nine, since all of your fear and guilt implants are removed at this time. How could you enjoy spending time with those filled with fear and guilt when you no longer experience those emotions?

However, it is very important to understand that you do not need to leave your intimate relationships. Your upgraded energy can be used to improve those relationships by incorporating more love and understanding, essentially enhancing the dynamics of the relationship. Sometimes, you benefit from partners who are not recoding because they act as a baseline or a grounding element while you are undergoing much change. If you truly become discontent with your partners due to the upgrade of your energy, your guides will assist you in finding more appropriate relationships, since true love and partnership magnifies the recoder collective consciousness you are manifesting.

It is hoped that all lightworkers on Earth will elect to go through DNA Recoding. Yet not everyone will complete the process. Bear in mind, whether you complete some or all of the process, that you have had the perfect experience for you since everything is in Divine Order. The speed with which you proceed through the five phases of DNA Recoding will depend on how quickly you release your fears because fear will inhibit progress. If you insist on retaining feelings of fear during DNA Recoding, it can actually undo some of the work that has been done. It is very important throughout the process to have strong faith and reduced fear until your fear implants are removed in Segment Eight. Embrace the new changes you are experiencing and, if you do not understand them, contact an intuitive counselor who can help interpret them for you. DNA Recoding is a personal experience and each of you must determine your own experiences and your own pace. Those of you who move too quickly could risk harming your energy field which obviously defeats the purpose of DNA Recoding! As DNA

Recoding progresses, your vibration will lighten and, in fact, you will begin to "glow." Ultimately, you will consist of more energy than density which will provide you with the ability to "re-create" yourself into whatever you need at any point in time.

Those of you who are currently undergoing DNA Recoding might be experiencing a variety of different sleep patterns depending on your reaction to the process. Some might have altered your typical sleep patterns, either moving from a long, hard sleep to a brief, light sleep or vice versa. Some of you may temporarily lose your ability to recall dreams. Since dreams are a window to the other side, they are sometimes blocked to prevent you from feeling an intense desire to remain with your guides. Although you cannot remember, your astral body sojourns are a joyous experience as you reunite with old friends. Eventually, you will be able to recall your experience when your guides are assured you will not wish to leave Earth to remain with them.

PHASE ONE,
THE NINE SEGMENTS

Although, as mentioned, DNA Recoding is not necessarily a sequential process, it will cover the following steps:

SEGMENT ONE – RELEASING ANGER

Anger is an ongoing challenge during the DNA Recoding process because it has the potential of causing discomfort. You are asked to release anger during the initial segment in order to eliminate negative energy prior to re-coiling your DNA strands, therefore minimizing your discomfort as the higher energy level from DNA Recoding enters your denser energy level. It is important that you are at peace with yourself as you expand in consciousness. Liver cleanses are great for moving quickly through Segment One since the majority of anger is stored in the liver. In fact, any form of cleansing to release toxins is effective during this stage.

During this time, you should make peace with those who have angered you in the past. When working to release anger from past relationships, write a list of the names of those with whom you have been involved and release them from your anger and blame. You may release them in person or at a soul level as long as you really feel the release of your anger toward them. Sometimes, it helps to envision them as vulnerable children to assist in remembering that their actions represent the best they can do based on their upbringing. Note the use of the word *"release"* rather than *"forgive,"* for this is an extremely important differentiation. Forgiveness is not part of Divine Creator Truth because it is a value that assumes someone has done something wrong while the other has done something right. The Divine Creator holds no judgment so there can be no right or wrong. In the Creator's eyes, there is simply being, learning, and calibrating.

Right and wrong results from the polarity principles operating on Earth, and it breeds judgment which separates us from each other. Polarity was meant to provide us with a robust menu of choices, but we have opted to take sides, which severs our union with each other. Separation keeps love from growing, thereby weakening you. A more appropriate value than forgiveness is *"acceptance"* because it allows everyone to exist and learn at their own rate. It acknowledges polarity and creates a neutral stance. Acceptance is a value you must embody to successfully recode since you must remain in a neutral place to allow love to be predominant in your energy.

SEGMENT TWO – MANAGING ANGER

If you stuff anger during DNA Recoding, you will place yourself in pain. Segment Two ensures that anger does not rebuild in your system after you clear it in Segment One, thus recreating the density from which you are attempting to separate. It also protects you and others since Segment Six gives you the ability to manifest your thoughts very quickly, both negative and positive, an attribute that could cause more harm than good unless you have moved through Segment Two.

Stuffing anger will cause discomfort when recoding since it recreates the toxins that have been eliminated. Do not stuff anything when facing conflicts. As you experience DNA Recoding, you will find that you will feel more neutrality toward situations rather than a completely irrational surge of anger. You will also experience greater compassion. However, do not expect to be able to remove anger completely from your repertoire. After all, we reside in a human body, and anger is an aspect of our experience. Anger actually protects you by ensuring that you explode rather than implode and harm yourself physically. In the rare events when you experience anger, you should not stuff it because you will not be communicating how you feel about a particular situation.

SEGMENT THREE – CLAIRAUDIENCE

Your telepathic channel begins to open in Segment Three. As you clear the lower emotions from your system, you become lighter. Your guides are better able to communicate with you, either through channeling, automatic writing, dowsing with a pendulum, or whichever telepathic form you wish to use. This is the point at which you can speak directly to your guides rather than getting the information via your dream state, intuition, or another individual who has psychic abilities.

If you resist what you begin to hear as your channel opens, there may be discomfort in either your right or left ear or in your third eye (central brow). There may even be some ear drainage, earaches, or headaches, but do not be alarmed since it means the channel is opening and you need to support that transition. Obviously, if these symptoms continue, explore other causes by visiting a health practitioner or healer.

During Segments Three and Four, it is useful to avoid heavy electrical environments where the current flows in a random state because it causes static in your telepathic channel and makes it difficult for your guides to communicate with you. Electricity flows randomly in locations like amusement parks, casinos, heavy computer areas like telemarketing centers, electrical plants, nuclear plants, and so forth. Less static occurs in heavy electrical environments like airplanes since the electricity moves in a single direction. Try to remove electrical devices from your sleeping environment, particularly electric blankets, heated water beds, and TVs. If you sleep near too many electrical devices, it is difficult for your telepathic channel to remain clear and, besides, it is bad for your health.

Watching TV and listening to the radio can interfere with your progress. When using cable or radio waves, be sure to eliminate the electromagnetic radiation (EMR). This can be done by purchasing one of the many items that are sold to neutralize these harmful rays. Or, simply buy a roll of blue surveyors tape since the color of the tape neutralizes EMR. You can keep the roll in a drawer in the center of your house and carry a six inch strip with you in your wallet. Although certain types of music are healing, the appliances that play the music might be detrimental due to the electrical currents. When listening to music, move the electrical equipment out of contact with the heart chakra. It is best to spend time opening and developing personal channels by getting back to nature. Moving away from electricity enables the genetic engineers to make more progress because you can hear them.

During Segments Three and Four, work is begun on re-coiling the DNA strands in your astral body. However, no memory of this work will be retained because you would want to remain in your more enjoyable energy form than deal with the transition from a two to a twelve-strand being. You may experience physical symptoms as your genetic engineer "rearranges" your DNA, although your guides will do the best they can to minimize it. Efforts on your part to stay clear via therapies like Reiki, repatterning, acupuncture, massage, chiropractic therapy, liver and colon cleanses, healthy diet, and a host of other options will reduce the amount of potential discomfort.

When your astral body is away, a "caretaker" will be left in place of you so no one will know you are elsewhere. The caretaker is a physical and mental copy of you. However, this assisting soul will need to be trained in order to do a good job since it is not an emotional or spiritual carbon copy of you. If you wish your caretaker to replicate you as best it can, you must give him or her permission to read your soul records or tapes. Your records are private and other lightworkers are not allowed to use them without permission. More information is provided about training your caretaker in Segment Five.

SEGMENT FOUR – CLAIRVOYANCE

Segment Four will open your third eye so you will be able to telepathically see your guides and other entities who reside on Earth's astral planes and in other dimensions. This may be a gradual process since your third eye has probably atrophied through lack of use. Clairvoyance may begin with the sensing of dark forms followed by lighter forms and, finally, a full color range. Some people see the forms in their everyday physical settings and others see them psychically. Most of you will see flashes of light or dark out of the corner of your eye as well, since it is easier to use peripheral rather than direct vision to catch a glimpse of a non-physical entity.

If you begin seeing etheric entities next to friends and loved ones, there may be a tendency for you to experience fear. Remember, you do not exist on the same astral plane. Plus, these entities can only harm you if you give them your power through fear. Also, fear will keep you from moving through this segment, so overcome it as quickly as possible. If you feel uncomfortable in the presence of etheric visitors, shine your white light brightly and, if they are negative beings, they will retreat from you.

SEGMENT FIVE – INTEGRATION

Segment Five is critical because it builds the foundation for the final four segments. It is a segment that some of you will choose not to clear. This is the time when you must start to implement your soul contract, and this may require some alterations in your life. These alterations will seem like natural choices to you if you are interested in continuing to grow, i.e., changing careers, going back to school to pursue new interests, shifting from a masculine to feminine orientation, doing more healing work in your spare time. This integration provides the focus you will need for your work during the final stages of DNA Recoding.

In order to create the two-strand system, implants were inserted in your astral body to prevent the ten additional strands of DNA from coiling together into five double helixes. This is why scientists are perplexed by the leftover or junk elements in our DNA. They have not been able to determine why it is there or its use. The ten additional strands are scattered throughout your energy body and, as each implant is removed, they begin to return to a coiled configuration. If your guides realigned and reconnected all ten strands at the same time, you would blow up – which would not achieve your objective! Therefore, they must proceed in a delicate and cautious manner, taking each step when it is most beneficial to you.

There may be some things that will not clear in Segments One through Four due to the method in which the strands are recoiled. During Segment Five, it will be necessary to go back and ensure that everything has been integrated. Also, sometimes it is not possible to fully complete the work during each session because it may cause discomfort. Your genetic engineers need to wait to complete the task when your body is ready.

During Segments Five through Seven, your caretakers will be left for longer intervals since your guides need your astral body for longer periods of time. You may have some unusual experiences when the caretakers reside for longer periods because they have never lived in the third dimension and do not have an affinity for the energy. If you are still carrying discordant emotions, they may resist them by pushing against them because they are unfamiliar with negativity. This is a time to increase your energy cleansing routines like Reiki, acupuncture, massage, colonics, and so forth.

It is also useful to make a "to do" list for your caretaker in order for him or her to be productive during your absence. For example, tell your caretaker that you arrive at work on time every day, that you always accomplish your job responsibilities, that you routinely exercise, or that you are on a diet and do not eat sweets. Train them to be more of a "housekeeper" than a "house sitter." If you are dissatisfied with how your caretaker manages life while you are away, request a new one. Caretakers are young souls who wish to experience life in the third dimension, and they are novices. This is a growth experience for them, too. If your caretaker prefers to lounge in bed all day rather than clean your house, you have the right to request one who complies with your wishes. Caretakers have no emotional connection to your life since they are copies and have not lived your experiences. Do not expect your caretaker to embrace the range of emotions you take for granted. Caretakers will be more neutral and passive, something that may be remarked upon by your friends and family.

Segment Five is exciting because you can begin to transfer to other dimensions, simultaneously experiencing the multiple lifetimes you may be playing at the same time that you are on Earth. During this time, recall might occur in the form of a dream or flashes of deja vu. However, you will know that it is not a dream because it is very realistic and sequential. Segment Five is also a time when you must focus on your soul contract. Some of you may not wish to move past this segment because of the additional commitment required. However, for those who wish to proceed, your guides must be assured that you are committed to your soul contract before increasing your power.

SEGMENT SIX – OWNING YOUR POWER

By the time you reach Segment Six, your guides are ninety-eight percent positive that you are firmly on your path and you will not back off your soul contract, so you begin to retrieve greater levels of power. It is the segment that enables your mind to manifest whatever it desires very quickly, bringing you what you desire (or do not desire, if you are not careful). This is a time to keep clean, positive thoughts since negative thoughts may manifest and slap you in the face.

Segment Six is tricky since you are no longer relying on your guides to manifest for you. You are finally doing it yourself. You have been taught to ask your guides for assistance and to state affirmations in present tense to realize what you want. However, do not be surprised if your guides gently remind you to "do it yourself" once you reach Segment Six since they want you to recapture your power. For example, if you desire financial abundance, experience the decisions and resulting emotions that come with unlimited wealth. If you wish to have your life mate join you at this time, view yourself as a radio frequency that can broadcast a message and send a message full of love to your future mate. Support that signal with the feelings you will have with your life mate, experiencing the emotions of sharing time or making love. The more intense the feelings that you generate during this time, the faster you will bring what you desire to you, as long as you are not holding conflicting feelings that dis-create as fast as you create.

For those of you who have read *The Tales of Alvin Maker*, you have arrived at the point where you are the *maker* rather than a passive *receiver* of what your guides can do for you. Your guides play the role of assister since your role is to create. This is a transition from the "help me" requests of your spirit guides to the recognition that you own your own power and need to begin flexing your manifestation muscles. Bear in mind, at this point less than half of your strands of DNA are connected, which limits your ability to move to complete manifestation. Use this time to increase your manifestation strength in preparation for future phases which will provide you with more power.

SEGMENT SEVEN – REMOVING ILLUSIONS

Segment Seven can be described as follows: you feel the presence of a light at the end of a long dark tunnel which symbolizes your mission, and you must traverse the tunnel to reach the light. Your personal power is the torch that you light to see as you move through the darkness toward your mission. Every time you hit an obstacle, you use your torch (or power) to shed light on the obstacle, thereby exposing the illusion that has been created.

In Segment Six, you learned how to be a *maker*. Now, in Segment Seven, you have become a *creator*. By the time you experience Segment Seven, you will probably have approximately eight strands of DNA re-coiled which will assist you in your creation efforts. Creators can manifest any reality they choose since they realize the "physical" world is based on illusion. Whenever you hit a perceived obstacle but choose to identify it as an illusion, you shift to a positive creator. Unfortunately, you also act as a creator when you hit a perceived obstacle and choose to identify it as a problem. As the creator, you can create any reality so remember to choose the positive rather than negative path.

Segment Seven is difficult because you move from the realization of yourself as the power source in Segment Six to running the gauntlet to test that power in Segment Seven. You will also probably begin to attract more attention from negative energy since it is interested in your emerging power. If you do not already have a daily routine of clearing yourself, now is the time to start. Use whatever protection method works best for you. One example might be to envision gold light in the form of mesh. Encircle yourself with the mesh and zip it up just like Cinderella sat in her pumpkin carriage and closed the door. Or envision white light and send streams of it through your body, entering at the crown chakra and exiting through the soles of your feet. Do not forget to request assistance from your guides, genetic engineer, and caretaker as well, as Spirit cannot assist without your permission since you live in a free choice/free will zone.

SEGMENT EIGHT – RELEASING FEAR

By Segment Eight, either all or most of your DNA strands are re-coiled so refinement needs to occur in how the brain handles the incoming information from additional levels of consciousness. This work proceeds quickly and your astral body will not need to spend extended time periods with the genetic engineers. Your codes, just like a computer chip, are accessed. Each code is reprogrammed, which enables the DNA to carry additional information to you. The firings or synapses of energy sequences throughout the brain will operate differently once your implants have been reconditioned, especially since the sequences are firing into additional DNA strands.

By the end of Segment Eight, all of your fear implants will be removed. These implants were placed in your system prior to your Earth incarnations in order to allow you to maximize your experience since fear is a prevalent emotion on Earth. Fear is a tremendous learning tool which allows you to be motivated by negativity: recognize it for what it is worth, and determine whether or not you choose to return to a positive form of creating. This may sound masochistic to you, but these implants serve as a tremendous learning tool as well as a protective device since many of you came from worlds that held no fear. You would have been completely vulnerable on Earth without fear which is a handy emotion to have when living on a planet filled with violence. After becoming street smart, you can lose that fear and still survive. In fact, you excel at survival because you bring a more developed consciousness of life without fear to the planet.

Whereas Segment Six, Owning Your Power, was a time to take back your power and begin feeling the importance of your role as a maker, Segment Eight provides you with the juice to manifest immediately. This is when you reap the rewards of learning how to harness your own energy rather than being on automatic pilot while your guides manage the manifestation energy. Segment Eight also helps you clear the illusions from Segment Seven since you will not react in fear when life seemingly does not respond to your liking. Segment Seven enables you to completely manifest whatever you choose as long as you use your own power.

SEGMENT NINE – FREEDOM FROM GUILT

You now have your twelve re-coiled strands of DNA. It should feel like pure pleasure to you since all of your guilt implants will now be removed in addition to the fear implants removed during

Segment Eight. This is a new experience – you can make decisions that are not based on fear and guilt. Imagine the full capacity of your energy without fear and guilt! Enjoy every minute of this experience: you are one of the few who no longer holds fear and guilt in your mental body.

Although you still reside in a dense vehicle, your energy has lightened significantly because you are vibrating at a higher rate. This rate will continue to heighten as the Earth increases its own frequency, enabling you to move energy more quickly and easily. Energetically, spend time exploring the twelve levels of awareness to which you now have access. Remember, you are privy to an expanded experience based on your commitment to the DNA Recoding process. In the beginning you may be frustrated; while you can view the total picture, yet your energy is still contained in a human body. However, this frustration will dissipate with time as the energy continues to lighten on Earth, allowing you to experience more and more benefits from your twelve strands. Expect for others to notice you since you will project an outer glow from your increased vibration. You have the ability to be the life of the party, and you can easily attract those who need to be with you or work with you."

Appendix B

Phase Two of DNA Recoding

PLUG-IN PROCESS

The following information was communicated by Joysiah in late December 1996. It includes the plug in information needed to connect the twelve DNA strands from the astral body to the physical body through the endocrine system. The endocrine system is in the process of replacing the immune system as the primary system in the human body. The immune system is a defense system which operates on the premise of fighting foreign material that enters the body. However, you cannot be balanced while undergoing resistance. The endocrine system is a support system that operates on the principle of balance. It provides the path to return to Divine Union. The endocrine system must replace resistance with balance in order for us to move to our next stage of evolution.

After you have completed your work in the first phase and have acquired your twelve strands of DNA in your astral body, it is necessary to connect the twelve strands into your endocrine system. This is called the Plug-in Process. Plug-in occurs after your completion of the first phase because it requires a lighter vibration to be present. Bringing the twelve strands of DNA into your energy field significantly increases the rate at which you vibrate. Think of it as a mainframe computer compared to a personal computer. The mainframe computer uses more power, and it can hold more data and process faster than the PC. You have evolved from a PC to a mainframe capacity which enables you to run more data through your system.

The power from the additional DNA strands is connected through your endocrine system because it is a "liquid" system, and the liquid acts as an insulator for the additional power. There are also some sacred geometry principles present in the liquid that utilize molecules with pyramidal structures to translate the incoming energy into a language your body will understand. This pyramidal structure helps to "hold" the energy frequency as well because that particular molecular shape is receiving an energetic "hook up" from a more evolved vibration. Essentially, you are grounding that energy frequency on the planet through your agreement to complete this process. Once critical mass is reached when enough of us carry the frequency, newborns will be able to carry the twelve strands physically in their body.

As you progressed through the first phase of DNA Recoding, you performed a general emotional housecleaning. You removed old blockages and negative energy from your system, becoming as emotionally balanced as possible by removing the negative, denser energy in order to reduce the discomfort you might have experienced from a high vibration meeting the resistance of a low vibration. Upon completing the first phase, you are free of much of your "old stuff," minus some residual negative energy that exists in the cell structure of your physical vehicle that takes longer to clear. However, there is still some tweaking that needs to occur to bring your endocrine system into perfect balance for the plug-in. Essentially, you need to completely balance your endocrine system in order to accept the twelve-strand energy.

I have a website that provides information on DNA Recoding. I received an interesting e-mail from a fertility specialist on the East Coast who had seen my site. She asked if she could use my endocrine balancing modalities on her clients since she had discovered the endocrine system needed to be balanced in order for a woman to conceive. She said she had experienced over a ninety-five percent success rate and felt the balancing of the endocrine system was a key element. I welcomed her use of the balancing modalities, struck at the time by our orientation to balancing our chakras and meridians based on our knowledge of Chinese medicine but ignoring our endocrine system.

The charts on pages 220-221, *The 12-Strand & Endocrine System Balance Sheet*, has been developed to help you focus on the areas that need balancing in your endocrine system. Once balance occurs, you can experience the plug-in process by enabling your guides to work on your system over a three-day and three-night time period. This is conducted remotely. It does not require the presence of your astral body which eliminates, fortunately, the need to use a caretaker.

The chart is divided into the first six and the last six strands of DNA. Each chart depicts the DNA strands across the top. Each strand relates to a specific emotional aspect of our experience, showing the balanced state as well as the unbalanced extremes. For example, strand one represents "courage" when it is completely balanced. The outlying emotions that cause the optimal state of courage to move out of balance are listed below the balanced state. In the case of courage, a person is out of balance when they are too courageous (i.e., warrior) as well as when they are not courageous enough (i.e., victim).

The endocrine glands are listed on the left side of the chart. Each of the endocrine glands relates to a life stage. For example, the hypothalamus corresponds to pre-birth, that time prior to entering the fetal body which was used in preparation for this lifetime. The heart is separated from the other endocrine glands because some classify it as an endocrine gland and some do not. However, the heart is our doorway to Divinity since it houses our Godspark. Our Godspark must connect with the Godsource in order for us to experience pure, positive perfection.

It is recommended that you dowse using a pendulum or muscle check using kinesiology to determine the boxes in which you have already achieved balance. If you do not know how to use a pendulum, we sell a fifteen-page booklet with simple instructions for dowsing. You can also buy a book on dowsing from a local book store or the American Society of Dowsers in Vermont. If you do not wish to know how to use a pendulum or muscle check, you can either ask a dowser to complete the chart for you or simply do all of the steps leading up to the balancing modalities as well as all of the balancing modalities to ensure you are completely balanced. It will not hurt you to rebalance what is already balanced. It will just take you more time.

When you dowse, ask the following question: "On the (ENDOCRINE SYSTEM), is the (NUMBER STRAND) balanced?" In the case of courage, you would ask, "On the *hypothalamus*, is the *1.1* strand balanced?" If you receive a "yes" on the pendulum, circle the number 1.1 in the chart to signify balance. Continue asking this question for each DNA strand and for each endocrine gland until you have dowsed both charts.

After you have determined which strands are balanced and circled those numbers, your chart will depict a series of circles that will create some interesting patterns. Looking across the page horizontally, you may notice that there are entire life stages that contain no check marks. Looking down the page vertically, you may notice entire emotional dimensions that are blank. This gives you some clues as to what you need to bring into balance for plug-in, both from this lifetime and past lifetimes.

Once you know where you experience imbalance, you need to do some pre-work prior to completing the balancing modalities. As you move through each of the following stages, return to *The 12-Strand & Endocrine System Balance Sheet* and dowse which areas have balanced. That way, you will not be conducting balancing modalities that are no longer necessary.

Set the intent to have everything in balance within a certain time frame. Ask your guides and teachers to assist you in this endeavor.

Determine if you need a soul clearing to expedite matters by asking your spirit guides, dowsing with a pendulum, or muscle checking through kinesiology, asking "Is it necessary to have a soul clearing in order to proceed expeditiously and easily through the plug-in process?" If a soul clearing is advantageous, set up an appointment with someone you know who does that type of work. Or, if you do not know someone who performs this type of work, call the InterLink office and we will recommend someone to you. A soul clearing not only clears the Akashic records of any past life experiences that are causing you to carry discordant energy at a soul level, but it also ensures that you can ultimately leave the Earth plane if you desire. You may have picked up negative programs that cause you to keep reincarnating in order to resolve them when you can readily complete them through soul clearing.

At this point, you will need to have finished the work on the first phase of DNA Recoding. Check to ensure you have completed and cleared all nine segments. If you have not, determine your blocks and complete and clear those segments. Unfortunately, *you cannot plug-in unless you have finished the first phase* since it would create discomfort. Please pay attention to this advice as some have experienced discomfort when attempting to connect the higher twelve-strand vibration before they have adequately lightened their vibration.

Open yourself at least ninety-five percent to the seven primary archangel realms. The seven primary realms are aligned with our seven primary chakras. Chakras are spinning disks that act as inflow and outflow points of energy to and from our body. If we wish to lead a balanced life, we need to be balanced in our seven primary energy centers, and this occurs when we are open to the teaching of the seven archangel realms. There is a simple exercise, *Openness to Archangel Realms*, which will assist you in this process on page 223. If you run into blocks in a particular realm, ask a soul clearing or energy practitioner for assistance.

Rescind all past life vows that are blocking your emotional balance. In past lives, you may have made vows that are interfering with your ability to be self-empowered in this life. There are three parts to the soul, the subconscious, conscious, and superconscious, and the memory of all soul experiences sits at the subconscious and superconscious level. When you wish to be empowered consciously, but your soul holds, for example, a subconscious memory of a vow of submission, you are holding conflicting agendas. This conflict in agendas affects your ability to move forward with your conscious agenda. There are two parts of vows to clear as follows:

Part One is a "generic" vow clearing that covers commitments to conditions like poverty or chastity, i.e., vows possibly made as a priest or nun in past lifetimes that no longer serve you. Level I also clears vows of obedience that were made to false messiahs or false belief systems (e.g., Mayan priests who performed ritualistic rape and sacrifice for bountiful harvests) that are obviously no longer pertinent to your experience and conflict with your ability to be self-empowered.

Part Two clears vows that you made based on misperceptions of prior life experiences. For example, you may have desired to have a life experience as a healer but were burned at the stake for witchcraft, crying out during your death that you would "never speak your truth again." This vow of "protection" no longer serves a purpose and may even interfere with your soul growth.

Please note that it may also be necessary to conduct some past life regression work with a trained hypnotherapist or psychic counselor if you have difficulty recalling your past lives. The exercise for vow disavowal is located on pages 224-225.

At this point, pause and re-dowse to determine which of the strands are balanced and which remain unbalanced on *The 12-Strand & Endocrine System Balance Sheet*. You do not need to do the balancing modalities if a strand is already balanced. When you balance a strand, if may affect other strands since they are interrelated. For example, you may need to complete all of the balancing modalities in an entire column prior to achieving balance in a single box, i.e., one box's balance is contingent upon another box's balance. Or you may clear several in one column and find that others in the same or a different column also have balanced. This means you will need to re-confirm which of your boxes are balanced while you are working on this matrix since you may balance one without being aware you have done so. Balance as many boxes as you can through the balancing modalities, dowsing to determine balance. You can have *no more than six boxes empty* when requesting the plug-in, or the plug-in will not be successful.

When all but six of your strands are balanced, you may request the plug-in. Dowse with a pendulum and ask, "Is this *12-Strand & Endocrine System Balance Sheet* sufficiently balanced for the plug-in to take place?" To initiate the plug-in, draw a bath of one part sea salt and one part baking soda, e.g., one cup each. Light twelve white candles (you can purchase the small votives or a package of tea candles) and place them around your bath tub. As you light the candles, say the following prayer request:

- (SAY THREE TIMES EACH:) "Divine Creator, Sirian/Pleiadian Council, Akashic Record Division, My Guides and Teachers, All Seven Archangels Loyal to the Divine Creator, My Superconscious Self, My Subconscious Self."
- (SAY ONCE:) "Please assist me in balancing my energy field for the plug-in of my twelve strands of DNA in my astral body into my endocrine system. Bless these candles as beacons of energy that represent my twelve DNA strands,

connecting the energy to my balanced endocrine system in order for me to meet my soul destiny contract of carrying the twelve-strand energy on Earth during its time of transition. I lay myself before you in this water to symbolize the liquidity of my endocrine system, asking you to proceed with this sacred ceremony."

- Lie in your sea salt and baking soda bath. Visualize the following colors to balance your chakras at each of the chakra locations:

  - RED: root chakra (base of spine);
  - ORANGE: pelvic chakra (below navel);
  - YELLOW: solar plexus chakra (midriff);
  - GREEN: heart chakra (heart);
  - BLUE: throat chakra (throat);
  - INDIGO: brow chakra (forehead); and
  - VIOLET: crown chakra (top of head).

- Then envelop yourself in white light. Lie very still. You will feel the energy entering your body. When you stop feeling the energy, you can get up. The plug-in will be completed during the three days following that initiation point. If, for any reason, you begin to experience discomfort, contact a healing practitioner for assistance.

PLUG-IN PROCESS
12-STRAND & ENDOCRINE SYSTEM BALANCE SHEET
(STRANDS 1 THROUGH 6)

ENDOCRINE SYSTEM	1: COURAGE Warrior Victim	2: CONCENTRATION Compulsive Inattentive	3: CREATION Greedy Self Sacrificing	4: WELL-BEING Strong Weak	5: JOY Hedonist Martyr	6: TRUTH Manipulating Pleasing
HYPOTHALAMUS Pre-birth	1.1	2.1	3.1	4.1	5.1	6.1
PINEAL Soul Entry	1.2	2.2	3.2	4.2	5.2	6.2
ADRENALS Instinct	1.3	2.3	3.3	4.3	5.3	6.3
THYROID The Soul	1.4	2.4	3.4	4.4	5.4	6.4
GONADS Youth	1.5	2.5	3.5	4.5	5.5	6.5
THYMUS Independence/Interdependence	1.6	2.6	3.6	4.6	5.6	6.6
PITUITARY Growth	1.7	2.7	3.7	4.7	5.7	6.7
HEART Maturity	1.M	2.M	3.M	4.M	5.M	6.M

PLUG-IN PROCESS

12-STRAND & ENDOCRINE SYSTEM BALANCE SHEET
(STRANDS 7 THROUGH 12)

ENDOCRINE SYSTEM	7: BALANCE Over Under	8: POWER Controlling Enslaved	9: COMMUNION Solitary Communal	10: COHESIVENESS Independent Dependent	11: SEXUALITY Male Female	12: LOVE Aggressive Servile
HYPOTHALAMUS Pre-birth	7.1	8.1	9.1	10.1	11.1	12.1
PINEAL Soul Entry	7.2	8.2	9.2	10.2	11.2	12.2
ADRENALS Instinct	7.3	8.3	9.3	10.3	11.3	12.3
THYROID The Soul	7.4	8.4	9.4	10.4	11.4	12.4
GONADS Youth	7.5	8.5	9.5	10.5	11.5	12.5
THYMUS Independence/ Interdependence	7.6	8.6	9.6	10.6	11.6	12.6
PITUITARY Growth	7.7	8.7	9.7	10.7	11.7	12.7
HEART Maturity	7.M	8.M	9.M	10.M	11.M	12.M

RELEASING BLOCKAGES
TO ARCHANGEL REALMS

The seven primary archangels provide you with a specific energy, teaching, and aspect of love, light, and truth. However, sometimes past/present life issues, traumas, or subconscious programming may have created blockages between you and the teachings/energy of the seven realms. This exercise is designed to create at least ninety-five percent receptivity to all of the seven primary archangel realms.

The seven primary realms are aligned with our seven primary chakras. Chakras are spinning disks that act as inflow and outflow points of energy to and from our body. If we wish to lead a balanced life, we need to be balanced in our seven primary energy centers, and this occurs when we are open to the teaching of the seven archangel realms.

Use the chart on the next page and a pendulum to dowse, asking "What percentage am I open to the realm of (archangel)? Am I more than fifty percent, more than sixty percent, etc.," until you have determined the percentage. Enter the percentage you are open in the corresponding box. You will discover that you will be one hundred percent open in some realms and blocked in others. Again, if you do not wish to learn how to use a pendulum, do the exercise for every archangel realm since you will not know which are blocked and which are not.

To release blockages:
- Light a white candle for each archangel realm you wish to have one hundred percent available to you.
- As you light each candle, speak the archangel's name three times and request a full release of your blockage and a Divine reconnection with the energy and teaching of that specific realm. For example: "Archangel Zadkiel, Zadkiel, Zadkiel … I request a full release of my blockage

to your realm of creative visualization and manifesting into the physical and material world. I request a Divine reconnection with the energy and teaching of your realm, knowing it to be an aspect of my self and aspect of Creator."

* Allow the candles to burn as you experience the energies shift within you. When you feel complete, blow each candle out and close the ceremony by saying "Thank you" three times.

RELEASING BLOCKAGES TO ARCHANGEL REALMS
OPENNESS TO ARCHANGEL REALMS

CORRESPONDING ARCHANGEL	CHAKRA (COLOR)	PERCENT OPEN
ARCHANGEL AURIEL Nature, Compassion	Root (Red)	
ARCHANGEL ZADKIEL Materialization, Creative Visualization	Sexual (Orange)	
ARCHANGEL ZOPHKIEL Art, Beauty, Perfection, Balance	Solar Plexus (Yellow)	
ARCHANGEL RAPHAEL Healing, Love	Heart (Green)	
ARCHANGEL GABRIEL Sound, Vibration, Communication	Throat (Blue)	
ARCHANGEL MICHAEL Protection, Truth	Brow (Indigo)	
ARCHANGEL KAMIEL Light, Power, Energy	Crown (Violet)	

(Teachings of Venessa Rahlston)

DISAVOWING VOWS

Rescind all past life vows that are blocking your emotional balance. In past lives, you may have made vows that are interfering with your ability to be self-empowered in this life. There are three parts to the soul, the subconscious, conscious, and superconscious, and the memory of all soul experiences sits at the subconscious and superconscious level. When you wish to be empowered consciously, but your soul holds, for example, a subconscious memory of a vow of submission, you are holding conflicting agendas. This conflict in agendas affects your ability to move forward with your conscious agenda.

PART ONE

To rescind vows:
* Light a white candle.
* (SAY THREE TIMES EACH:) "Divine Creator, Sirian/Pleiadian Council, Akashic Record Division, My Guides and Teachers, All Seven Archangels Loyal to the Divine Creator, My Superconscious Self, My Subconscious Self."
* Connect with Divine Creator energy by tapping on your thymus gland (located several inches below the base of your of neck on the flat part of your chest) and intone the following syllables three times each: "Ahh, Ooo, Umm."
* (SAY:) "I wish to disavow all vows I have ever made in ignorance or in truth to any false messiah, any brotherhood or sisterhood, any other entity, or to you as the Creator that are no longer assisting my higher good. I particularly wish to disavow all vows I have ever made that are blocking my ability to balance and reconnect my twelve strands of DNA into my endocrine system. Please assist me in disavowing these vows so that they are no longer limiting me. I ask that all restrictions be lifted and

eliminated so that I can expand and align with my path and purpose. In the highest good of all, thank you, thank you, thank you."

* Blow out your white candle and say: "So let it be."

PART TWO

To rescind vows:

* Darken the room.
* Light two white candles and place one on either side of you.
* (SAY THREE TIMES EACH:) "Divine Creator, Sirian/Pleiadian Council, Akashic Record Division, My Guides and Teachers, All Seven Archangels Loyal to the Divine Creator, My Superconscious Self, My Subconscious Self."
* (SAY:) "I, of my own free will, wish to bring to the surface all lifetimes in which I have made vows that now need to be rescinded because they conflict with the twelve-strand DNA energy and my ability to experience health, wealth, and happiness. So be it."
* Look directly into your eyes in a mirror for fifteen minutes. Set a kitchen timer if you need to do so.
* Sit patiently and allow your mind to bring forward visions of past lives in which you made vows that no longer serve you. As you view these situations, thank yourself for the protection these vows gave you in the past. Explain to yourself that you no longer need to make vows in fear because you are motivated by love.
* After fifteen minutes, say: "Thank you, thank you, thank you. So let it be."

ENDOCRINE SYSTEM BALANCING MODALITIES

The following ninety-six modalities have been developed to assist you in balancing your endocrine system in order to undergo the plug-in process. The endocrine system has to be balanced in order to connect the twelve strand energy frequency without causing stress on you physically. Please note that the following items should typically be completed prior to using the balancing modalities since the modalities will not override and clear any incomplete work from these steps: 1) the nine segments from phase one of DNA Recoding; 2) elimination of blockages in the seven Archangel realms; 3) disavowal of vows. These items have been discussed in detail on pages 199-225.

At this point, you should be aware of which strands on your *12-Strand & Endocrine System Balance Sheet* remain unbalanced. It is now time to utilize the balancing modalities for any remaining unbalanced areas. Sometimes, you only need to conduct the balancing modality on one endocrine gland of one strand for the rest of the column to clear since there is a domino effect. Sometimes, you need to balance the entire column. You do not need to proceed in any particular order. Pick and choose the boxes that you most wish to balance.

Reference your *12-Strand & Endocrine System Balance Sheet*. Let us say, for example, that strand three (creation energy) is not balanced for the thyroid gland (soul lifestage). This is reflected by the absence of a circle around the number "3.4" in the box in column three, row four. Turn to pages 239-242 for the balancing modalities on strand three. Locate "3.4: The Soul" and complete the balancing modality described for it. After you have completed the modality, your box will be balanced when you ask the question "On the thyroid gland, is the number three strand (3.4) balanced?"

Each balancing modality contains the following information: a color that corresponds to the endocrine gland, the meridian affected by the lack of balance, an affirmation that represents the balanced state in physical form, and the modality for bringing that condition into balance. Please note that three charts have been provided in addition to a verbal description of the location of the meridian to assist you in finding it. Sometimes, you will need to utilize the color, the meridian, and the affirmation to bring the strand into balance. Sometimes you will only need to use one of the three items.

The balancing modalities have specifically been developed to be as simple as possible in order for everyone to have access to the materials needed. Frequently, you will use color and breath to clear. Sometimes, you will need to purchase a candle or a pitch pipe to complete the work, if you do not own a musical instrument. Do not be fooled by the simplicity of the modalities. Many people have used them, and they work!

Remember, you can conduct the plug-in ritual described on pages 218-219 as soon as you have balanced all but six boxes. The remainder can be balanced without any stress to your physical body.

ENDOCRINE SYSTEM BALANCING MODALITIES
CHART ONE

Right

Left

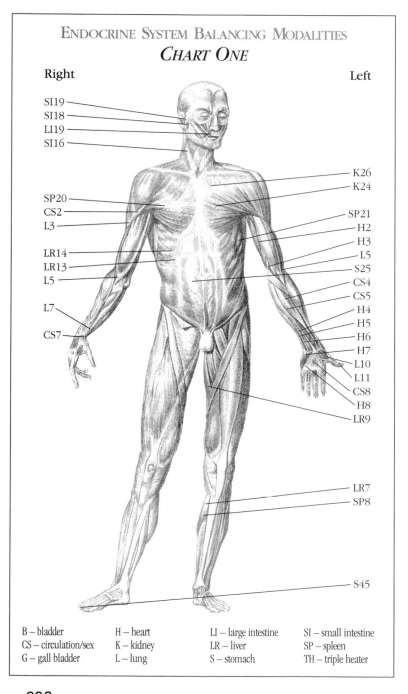

SI19
SI18
LI19
SI16

K26
K24

SP20
CS2
L3

SP21
H2
H3
L5
S25
CS4
CS5
H4
H5
H6
H7
L10
L11
CS8
H8
LR9

LR14
LR13
L5

L7

CS7

LR7
SP8

S45

B – bladder	H – heart	LI – large intestine	SI – small intestine
CS – circulation/sex	K – kidney	LR – liver	SP – spleen
G – gall bladder	L – lung	S – stomach	TH – triple heater

ENDOCRINE SYSTEM BALANCING MODALITIES
CHART TWO

Left   Right

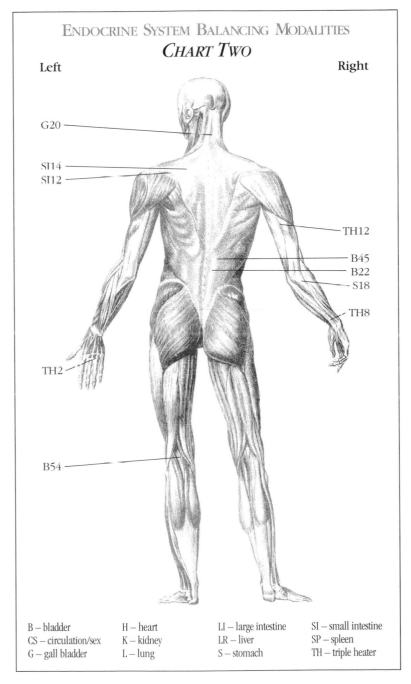

G20

SI14
SI12

TH12

B45
B22
S18

TH8

TH2

B54

B – bladder	H – heart	LI – large intestine	SI – small intestine
CS – circulation/sex	K – kidney	LR – liver	SP – spleen
G – gall bladder	L – lung	S – stomach	TH – triple heater

ENDOCRINE SYSTEM BALANCING MODALITIES
CHART THREE

Right

Left

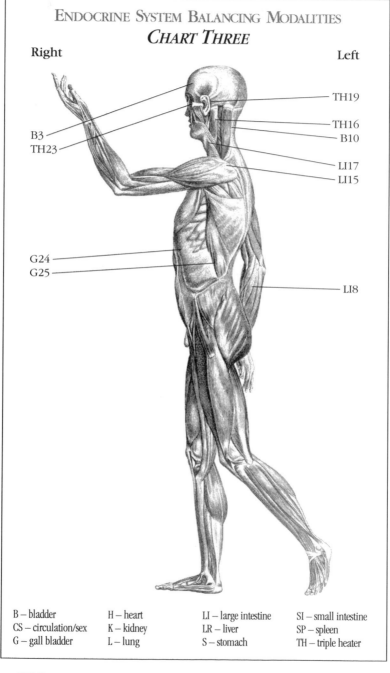

TH19

TH16
B10

B3
TH23

LI17
LI15

G24
G25

LI8

B – bladder	H – heart	LI – large intestine	SI – small intestine
CS – circulation/sex	K – kidney	LR – liver	SP – spleen
G – gall bladder	L – lung	S – stomach	TH – triple heater

STRAND #1
COURAGE

1.1: PRE-BIRTH

Color Magenta

Meridian Small intestines, point #16, located behind the right sternocleidomastoid muscle (on side of neck) on level with the Adam's apple. (Chart 1)

Affirmation I am courteous.

Balancing Modality Suck air quickly in through your mouth and hold it while you pump your abdominal muscles out 7 times. Exhale with 7 breaths through your mouth, pushing out the abdominal muscle with each exhalation. Visualize the color magenta being inhaled into your body on the inhalation breath. Repeat this sequence 7 times. Then, hold your right hand over your right point #16 small intestines meridian and say 7 times aloud, "I am courteous."

1.2: SOUL ENTRY

Color Violet

Meridian Heart, point #7, located on pinkie side of left hand at point where the hand meets the wrist. (Chart 1)

Affirmation I delegate according to an individual's best talents and gifts.

Balancing Modality Inhale through your nose and exhale with your tongue touching the roof of your mouth, making a long "Sssss" sound like a snake. Repeat this 20 times. Then, exhale all of your air and hold your breath, relax deeply, and imagine you are breathing internally for as long as you comfortably can. Hold your right hand over your left point #7 heart meridian and say 2 times aloud, "I delegate

according to an individual's best talents and gifts."
Visualize the color violet glowing and expanding
in the left point #7 heart meridian until you feel it
has "taken hold."

1.3: INSTINCT

Color Orange

Meridian Heart, point #7, located on pinkie side of left hand
at point where the hand meets the wrist. (Chart 1)

Affirmation I know my purpose in life which supports my
"true" way.

Balancing Let your jaw hang down loosely with your tongue
Modality resting on the floor of your mouth, and gently
pant in and out through your mouth like a dog.
Your body should feel loose and relaxed. Breathe
this way for about 2 minutes. Say 4 times aloud,
"I know my purpose in life which supports my
"true" way." Visualize the color orange glowing
and expanding in the left point #7 heart meridian
until you feel it has "taken hold."

1.4: THE SOUL

Color Blue

Meridian Gall bladder, point #24, located approximately 5"
below left nipple in line with the nipple. (Chart 3)

Affirmation I embody integrity in every thought that I have.

Balancing Place your right thumb on the side of your right
Modality nostril to block the air flow. Exhale and inhale
through your left nostril. Then, place your right
forefinger on the left nostril. Exhale and inhale
through your right nostril. Alternate nostrils 4
times, completing 2 cycles of breathing. Place
your left hand on the left point #24 gall bladder
meridian and say 4 times aloud, "I embody
integrity in every thought that I have." Visualize
the color blue and bring it into your heart, feeling
the color merge with the feeling of peace you
have in your heart when you live in integrity.

1.5: YOUTH

Color Red

Meridian Small intestines, point #16, located behind the right sternocleidomastoid muscle (on side of neck) on level with the Adam's apple. (Chart 1)

Affirmation I am courteous.

Balancing Modality Place your right thumb on the side of your right nostril to block the air flow. Exhale and inhale through your left nostril. Then, place your right forefinger on the left nostril. Exhale and inhale through your right nostril. Alternate nostrils 4 times, completing 2 cycles of breathing. Visualize the color red expanding through your entire body, entering through your crown chakra. After you have established this color throughout your body, say 2 times aloud, "I am courteous." See the color red flowing from your body at the right point #16 small intestines meridian, letting it in through the crown chakra and out through the right point #16.

1.6: INDEPENDENCE/INTERDEPENDENCE

Color Green

Meridian Liver, point #14, located about 4 inches under right nipple in line with right nipple. (Chart 1)

Affirmation I envision all possibilities.

Balancing Modality Inhale through your nose. Exhale through your mouth. Now wait for the body to determine when it needs to repeat the inhale. While waiting, relax and let go, repeating the affirmation "I envision all possibilities." Visualize the color green exiting your body at the location of the right point #14 liver meridian as you exhale. Repeat this sequence 3 times.

1.7: GROWTH

Color Indigo

Meridian Gall bladder, point #20, located at the back of the neck where the hairline meets the spine. (Chart 2)

Affirmation I move forward with purpose and make the changes that are needed, and I have clear vision as I move forward.

Balancing Modality Say 2 times aloud, "I move forward with purpose and make the changes that are needed." Touch the color indigo (use a swatch of fabric or a candle) as you are stating the first affirmation. Say 2 times aloud, "I have clear vision as I move forward" while covering the point #20 gall bladder meridian with your left hand.

1.M: MATURITY

Color White

Meridian Heart, point #7, located on pinkie side of left hand at point where the hand meets the wrist. (Chart 1)

Affirmation I am open to every experience.

Balancing Modality Hold your left hand over the point #7 heart meridian. Visualize an earlier experience when you were not open to what you were receiving from that experience. Envision a different ending, one that would have occurred had you been in flow with the process. See the entire setting bathed in the white light of Divine Creator energy, feeling the purposefulness of the experience and how, when you are open, the entire situation aligns with your true purpose. Lift your left hand up to the heavens and feel the freedom that surges.

STRAND #2
CONCENTRATION

2.1: PRE-BIRTH

Color Magenta

Meridian Lung, point #3, located on the right biceps even with the nipple line. (Chart 1)

Affirmation I take in all that is wise and inspiring.

Balancing *Modality* Light a magenta candle. Say 2 times aloud, "I take in all that is wise and inspiring." Breathe in and out through your nose, drawing in the color magenta from the candle as it burns. When you exhale, radiate the color magenta around your entire body, lighting up your body. Repeat this breath 2 times. Hold your left palm over the right point #3 lung meridian using your left hand. Keep the meridian covered for 1 minute. After completing this balancing modality, let the candle burn without extinguishing it.

2.2: SOUL ENTRY

Color Violet

Meridian Large intestines, point #8, located on the left forearm, just below the elbow on the outside of the arm. (Chart 3)

Affirmation I accept myself.

Balancing *Modality* Inhale deeply through your nose and exhale with your tongue against the roof of your mouth, making a long "Sssss" sound like a snake. Repeat this 3 times. Next, balance your point #8 large intestines meridian by doing the following meridian massage. Lightly stoke up the outside of your right arm with your left hand 3 times, starting at the tips of your fingers and brushing up over your shoulders and up your neck and the side of your face. Repeat this using your right hand and brushing up your left arm. Say 4 times aloud, "I accept myself."

2.3: INSTINCT

Color Orange

Meridian Heart, point # 3, located on the inside of the left arm, just above the elbow. (Chart 1)

Affirmation I am impartial, and I know my purpose in life which supports my true way.

Balancing Visualize the color orange. Say 2 times aloud,
Modality "I am impartial." Then, say 3 times aloud, "I know my purpose in life which supports my true way."

2.4: THE SOUL

Color Blue

Meridian Liver, point #7, located on the inside of the left leg, just below the knee. (Chart 1)

Affirmation I explore and am receptive to new ideas, methods, and opportunities.

Balancing Cover the left point #7 liver meridian with the
Modality right hand and say 2 times aloud, "I explore and am receptive to new ideas, methods, and opportunities. Visualize the color blue expanding from the left point #7 liver meridian throughout the entire body. Think of a time in the past when you were not receptive to new ideas, methods, and opportunities. Visualize a positive outcome to that experience by opening yourself to new possibilities. Surround the new outcome in the color blue.

2.5: YOUTH

Color Red

Meridian Large intestines, point #15, located on the left shoulder where the arm meets the shoulder. (Chart 3)

Affirmation I am perfect.

Balancing Modality Tone the note of F# 9 times, sending the note out of your body through the point #15 large intestines meridian. You will probably need to use a pitch pipe or musical instrument to assist you in locating the note. Say 4 times aloud, "I am perfect." Feel that sense of perfection enter your body through the left point #15 and spread throughout your body.

2.6: INDEPENDENCE/INTERDEPENDENCE

Color Green

Meridian Bladder, point #45, in middle of back, just above waist line on right side of spine. (Chart 2)

Affirmation I have deep, reflective thoughts.

Balancing Modality Hold your right hand over the right point #45 bladder meridian. Say 4 times aloud, "I have deep, reflective thoughts."

2.7: GROWTH

Color Indigo

Meridian Large intestines, point #15, located on the left shoulder where the arm meets the shoulder. (Chart 3)

Affirmation I share my values without imposing them on others.

Balancing Modality Breathe in deeply through your nose, filling your body. Breathe out through your mouth, making a long "Haaaaa" sighing sound. Repeat this breath twice again.

2.M: MATURITY

Color White

Meridian Spleen, point #20, located at the end of the collar bone where the right arm adjoins to the shoulder. (Chart 1)

Affirmation I clearly see where I am going.

Balancing Modality Place your right hand over the left point #20 spleen meridian. Breathe in deeply through your nose, filling your body. Breathe out through your mouth, making a long "Haaaaa" sighing sound. As you release this breath, push the color white through the left point #20 spleen meridian. Repeat this procedure once again.

STRAND #3
CREATION

Color Magenta

Meridian Heart, point #3, located on the inside of the left arm, just above the elbow. (Chart 1)

Affirmation I encompass all discordant elements when creating so that each can contribute to the end result according to its nature.

Balancing Modality Place your right thumb on the side of your right nostril to block the air flow. Exhale and inhale through your left nostril. Then, place your right forefinger on the left nostril. Exhale and inhale through your right nostril. Alternate nostrils 4 times, completing 2 cycles of breathing.

3.2: SOUL ENTRY

Color Violet

Meridian Circulation-sex, point #2, located on the right biceps, slightly higher than the nipple. (Chart 1)

Affirmation I am in touch with my own feelings.

Balancing Modality Say aloud 3 times, "I am in touch with my own feelings." Complete 1 breath as follows: Let the lower abdomen move inward as you inhale. Hold your breath, soften your eyes, and bring your head back, then turn your head to the right, then turn your head to the left, and finally breathe out half of the air you are holding through your nose while facing left. Now exhale the remainder of the air you are holding through your mouth, blowing out in a gust of wind. Visualize the color violet expanding in the #2 pelvic chakra (below the navel and above the pubic bone), your creation/sexual chakra. Hold the visualization until you feel a surge of creative energy emitting from the area.

3.3: INSTINCT

Color Orange

Meridian Spleen, point #8, on the inside of the left calf about four inches below the knee. (Chart 1)

Affirmation I am self-assured.

Balancing Modality Say aloud 4 times, "I am self-assured." Visualize the color orange going into the left point #8 spleen meridian. Place your right thumb on the side of your right nostril to block the air flow. Exhale and inhale through your left nostril. Then, place your right forefinger on the left nostril. Exhale and inhale through your right nostril. Alternate nostrils 8 times, completing 4 cycles of breathing.

3.4: THE SOUL

Color Blue

Meridian Lung, point #3, located on the right biceps even with the nipple line. (Chart 1)

Affirmation My mind is precise.

Balancing Modality Say aloud 2 times, "My mind is precise." Visualize the color blue going into the right point #3 lung meridian and traveling through your body to the #2 pelvic chakra (below the navel and above the pubic bone), your creation/sexual chakra. Stir the energy of that area by stimulating it with the color blue.

3.5: YOUTH

Color Red

Meridian Kidney, point #24, on the left side of the sternum (upper chest), approximately a hand's width down and directly underneath the beginning of your collar bone. (Chart 1)

Affirmation I regulate and direct the flow of my creativity.

Balancing Hold your right hand over your right mu point
Modality for the liver (located under the ribs in line with
the right nipple). Say aloud two times, "I regulate
and direct the flow of my creativity."

3.6: INDEPENDENCE/INTERDEPENDENCE

Color Green

Meridian Large intestines, point #17, located just above the
left collarbone at the base of the neck. (Chart 3)

Affirmation I release worn-out beliefs.

Balancing Do the following meridian massage: Lightly stoke
Modality up the outside of your right arm with your left
hand 3 times, starting at the tips of your fingers
and brushing up over your shoulders and up your
neck and the side of your face. Repeat this using
your right hand and brushing up your left arm.
Visualize your old beliefs in the form of a green
mass. Pack those old beliefs with their limitations
into a hard ball and pitch that ball into the
heavens and watch it disappear. Say aloud 4
times, "I release worn out beliefs."

3.7: GROWTH

Color Indigo

Meridian Bladder, point #3, located above the left eye at the
top of the forehead where the forehead meets the
hairline. (Chart 3)

Affirmation I have energy reserves that I share and contain
appropriately.

Balancing Breathe in deeply through your nose, filling your
Modality body. Breathe out through your mouth, making a
long "Haaaaa" sighing sound. Repeat this breath
twice again. Place your left hand over the left
point #3 bladder meridian. Say 2 times aloud,
"I have energy reserves that I share and contain
appropriately." Again, breathe in deeply through
your nose, filling your body. Breathe out through

your mouth, making a long "Haaaaa" sighing
sound. Repeat this breath 2 more times.

3.M: MATURITY

Color White

Meridian Liver, point #9, located on the inside of the left
leg, slightly higher than midway between the knee
and the crotch. (Chart 1)

Affirmation I welcome transformation in myself and others.

Balancing Say aloud 9 times, "I welcome transformation in
Modality myself and others." Place your right hand over
your heart. Then place your left hand over your
right hand. Blink slowly 10 times.

Strand #4
WELL-BEING

4.1: PRE-BIRTH

Color Magenta

Meridian Heart, point #5, located on the pinkie side of the left hand, 3 fingers above the wrist bone. (Chart 1)

Affirmation I am open to everybody and every situation.

Balancing Modality Place the right hand over the left point #5 heart meridian. Say 4 times aloud, "I am open to everybody and every situation." Hold your right hand over your right mu point for the liver (located under the ribs in line with the right nipple). Visualize the color magenta entering that mu point. As the color enters, feel yourself be receptive to every person and situation. Hold that feeling as you tone the "ore" sound, hollowing your mouth as if you have a small ball at the back of your throat to create resonance and touching your tongue to the roof of your mouth. Inhale deeply through your nose and exhale with your tongue touching the roof of your mouth, making a "Sssss" sound like a snake. Repeat 4 times.

4.2: SOUL ENTRY

Color Violet

Meridian Triple heater, point #2, located at the back (outside) of the left ring finger just above where the finger meets the palm. (Chart 2)

Affirmation I bring harmony and balance to relationships.

Balancing Modality Say 9 times aloud, "I bring harmony and balance to relationships." Complete 3 breaths as follows:

Let the lower abdomen move inward as you inhale. Hold your breath, soften your eyes, and bring your head back, then turn your head to the right, then turn your head to the left, and finally breathe out half of the air you are holding through your nose while facing left. Now exhale the remainder of the air you are holding through your mouth, blowing out in a gust of wind. Look straight ahead as you repeat this breath two more times.

4.3: INSTINCT

Color Orange

Meridian Heart, point #7, located on pinkie side of left hand at point where the hand meets the wrist. (Chart 1)

Affirmation I have clear insight which allows me to integrate all differences.

Balancing Modality Inhale through your nose. Exhale through your mouth. Now wait for the body to determine when it needs to inhale. While waiting, relax and repeat the affirmation "I have clear insight which allows me to integrate all differences." Visualize the color orange entering the left heart point #7. As it enters, send it through your body to the root chakra (located at the base of your spine). Let the color accumulate in the root chakra area until you feel as if you are sitting in a pool of orange. Feel your integration with all things as you visualize a web of longitude and latitude lines protruding from your body, linking with the universe above and the Earth around you.

4.4: THE SOUL

Color Blue

Meridian Triple heater, point #19, located on the left side of the head, directly behind the upper part of the ear, in line with your left eye. (Chart 3)

Affirmation I create the right atmosphere for any activity.

Balancing Complete 4 breaths as follows: Let the lower
Modality abdomen move inward as you inhale. Hold your
breath, soften your eyes, and bring your head
back, then turn your head to the right, then turn
your head to the left, and finally breathe out half
of the air you are holding through your nose
while facing left. Exhale the remainder of the air
you are holding through your mouth, blowing out
in a gust of wind. Look straight ahead as you
repeat this breath 3 times. Say once aloud, "I
create the right atmosphere for any activity."

4.5: YOUTH

Color Red

Meridian Lung, point #5, located just above the crook of the
left arm below the biceps. (Chart 1)

Affirmation I inspire others.

Balancing Say 2 times aloud, "I inspire others." Place your
Modality right hand over the left point #5 lung meridian
Say 2 times aloud again, "I inspire others."
Complete 2 breaths as follows: Let the lower
abdomen move inward as you inhale. Hold your
breath, soften your eyes, and bring your head
back, then turn your head to the right, then turn
your head to the left, and finally breathe out half
of the air you are holding through your nose
while facing left. Now exhale the remainder of the
air you are holding through your mouth, blowing
out in a gust of wind. Look straight ahead as you
repeat this breath once again.

4.6: INDEPENDENCE/INTERDEPENDENCE

Color Green

Meridian Triple heater, point #23, located on the left temple,
just beyond the eyebrow and slightly above the
eye. (Chart 3)

Affirmation I am loving.

Balancing Say 2 times aloud, "I am loving." Place your left
Modality hand over the left point #23 triple heater meridian.
Say 2 times aloud again, "I am loving."

4.7: GROWTH

Color Indigo

Meridian Heart, point #6, located on the pinkie side of the
left hand, 2 fingers above the wrist bone. (Chart 1)

Affirmation I treat everyone with love and understanding.

Balancing Complete 2 breaths as follows: Let the lower
Modality abdomen move inward as you inhale. Hold your
breath, soften your eyes, and bring your head
back, then turn your head to the right, then turn
your head to the left, and finally breathe out half
of the air you are holding through your nose while
facing left. Now exhale the remainder of the air
you are holding through your mouth, blowing out
in a gust of wind. Look straight ahead as you
repeat this breath again. Say 2 times aloud, "I treat
everyone with love and understanding." Place your
thumbs on your temples. Feel a sense of love
coming into your temples from the Divine Creator.
Extend that feeling to all others in your life.

4.M: MATURITY

Color White

Meridian Gallbladder, point #25, located on the left side
of the abdomen at waist level, in line with the
armpit. (Chart 3)

Affirmation I know who I am and where I stand.

Balancing Visualize the color white entering the left
Modality gallbladder point #25 while saying 1 time aloud
"I know who I am and where I stand." Feel the
certainty that comes with that knowing.

Strand #5
JOY

5.1: Pre-birth

Color   Magenta

Meridian   Small intestines, point #8, located directly underneath the right elbow. (Chart 2)

Affirmation   I am courteous.

Balancing Modality   Do the following meridian massage: Lightly stroke down the inside of your right arm with your left hand 3 times from the armpit to the fingertips. Repeat this using your right hand and brushing down your left arm. Lightly stroke up the outside of the right arm with your left hand 3 times, starting at the tips of your fingers and brushing up over your shoulders and up your neck and the side of your face. Repeat this using your right hand and brushing up your left arm. Now, place your hands over your eye with fingers spread wide and brush your hands over your head, down the back of your neck as far as you can reach, then pick it up where you left off and stroke down your back and buttocks. Continue stroking down the outside of your legs, rounding the outside of your feet to your little, then big, toes. Finish by stroking up the inside of your feet and legs, over the genitals and up the center of your body to your armpits. Say once aloud, "I am courteous." Breathe in deeply through your nose, filling your body. Breathe out through your mouth, making a long "Haaaaa" sighing sound. Repeat this breath 3 more times.

5.2: SOUL ENTRY

Color Violet

Meridian Triple heater, point #12, located midway between the armpit and the elbow on the back of the right arm. (Chart 2)

Affirmation I maintain the right temperature for the optimal flow of any activity.

Balancing Modality Say 2 times aloud, "I maintain the right temperature for the optimal flow of any activity." Inhale deeply through your nose and exhale with your tongue against the roof of your mouth, making a long "Sssss" sound like a snake. Repeat this 5 times. Place your left hand over the right point #12 triple heater meridian. Begin a continuous breath, inhaling and exhaling without pausing at the bottom of the exhale or the top of the inhale. Repeat this continuous breath for 10 cycles.

5.3: INSTINCT

Color Orange

Meridian Circulation-sex, point #4, located on the left inside forearm, midway between the crook of the arm and the wrist, somewhat closer to the wrist. (Chart 1)

Affirmation I appropriately confide in others.

Balancing Modality Place your right hand over the left point #4 circulation-sex meridian, and say 2 times aloud, "I appropriately confide in others." Visualize the color orange expanding in the left point #4 circulation-sex meridian area. Allow the orange color to move into the #2 pelvic chakra (below the navel and above the pubic bone), your creation/sexual chakra. Complete 1 breath as follows: exhale with a "Ha" sound, then inhale. Exhale with a "Whoo" sound, then inhale. Exhale with a "Hee" sound, then inhale. Exhale with a "Tsu" sound, then inhale. Exhale with a "Sssss" sound, then inhale.

5.4: The Soul

Color Blue

Meridian Spleen, point #20, located at the end of the collar bone where the right arm adjoins to the shoulder. (Chart 1)

Affirmation I live in a state of peace and joy.

Balancing Modality Say 1 time aloud, "I live in a state of peace and joy." Allow yourself to remember an earlier time, prior to coming to Earth, when you lived in a constant state of peace and joy. Feel that ever-present feeling of freedom that is derived from continual peace and joy. Allow that feeling to merge with the color blue and disperse it to the atmosphere through your right point #20 spleen meridian.

5.5: Youth

Color Red

Meridian Lung, point #10, located on the left hand where the thumb meets the back of the hand. (Chart 1)

Affirmation I inspire others through example.

Balancing Modality Breathe in deeply through your nose, filling your body. Breathe out through your mouth, making a long "Haaaaa" sighing sound. Repeat this breath 5 times. Say 1 time aloud, "I inspire others through example."

5.6: Independence/Interdependence

Color Green

Meridian Bladder, point #54, located at the back of the right knee in the bend of the leg. (Chart 2)

Affirmation I have deep reserves of energy that I share and contain appropriately.

Balancing Modality Inhale deeply through your nose and exhale with your tongue against the roof of your mouth, making a long "Sssss" sound like a snake. Repeat this breath 7 times. Place your right hand over the right point #54 bladder meridian. Say 4 times out loud, "I have deep reserves of energy that I share and contain appropriately." Visualize the color green holding those deep reserves of energy. Place that green bubble of energy in your heart chakra.

5.7: GROWTH

Color Indigo

Meridian Spleen, point #21, located on the left side of the chest near the armpit on level with the sixth rib from the top. (Chart 1)

Affirmation I am at peace.

Balancing Modality Place your right hand over the left point #21 spleen meridian. Say 19 times aloud, "I am at peace." Feel the peace as you state your intention. Visualize that peaceful feeling in the form of the color indigo, and let it disperse throughout your body.

5.M: MATURITY

Color White

Meridian Small intestines, point #19, located on the right side of the face at the top of and behind the cheekbone in front of the ear. (Chart 1)

Affirmation I extract what is pure in any situation.

Balancing Modality Inhale deeply through your nose and exhale with your tongue against the roof of your mouth, making a long "Sssss" sound like a snake. Repeat this breath 8 times. Say 2 times aloud, "I extract what is pure in any situation." Visualize the color white enveloping your heart as you experience this purity.

Strand #6
Truth

Color Magenta

Meridian Small intestines, point #12, touch left shoulder midway between neck and arm and slide hand down over the top portion of the back. You will be covering point #12. (Chart 2)

Affirmation My humor is warm and loving.

Balancing Modality Say 3 times aloud, "My humor is warm and loving." Visualize the color magenta surrounding your body. Bring the color into your body through the heart chakra.

6.2: Soul Entry

Color Violet

Meridian Small intestines, point #12, touch left shoulder midway between neck and arm and slide hand down over the top portion of the back. You will be covering point #12. (Chart 2)

Affirmation I enjoy sexual intimacy based on truth for the bonding it brings.

Balancing Modality Complete 3 breaths as follows: Let the lower abdomen move inward as you inhale. Hold your breath, soften your eyes, and bring your head back, then turn your head to the right, then turn your head to the left, and finally breathe out half of the air you are holding through your nose while facing left. Now exhale the remainder of the air you are holding through your mouth, blowing out in a gust of wind. Look straight ahead as you repeat this breath 2 more times. Then, say 2 times aloud, "I enjoy sexual intimacy based on truth for the bonding it brings."

6.3: INSTINCT

Color Orange

Meridian Small intestines, point #12, touch left shoulder midway between neck and arm and slide hand down over the top portion of the back. You will be covering point #12. (Chart 2)

Affirmation I sort out what is best and resolve all splits between approaches.

Balancing Place your right thumb on the side of your right
Modality nostril to block the air flow. Exhale and inhale through your left nostril. Then, place your right forefinger on the left nostril. Exhale and inhale through your right nostril. Alternate nostrils 8 times, completing 4 cycles of breathing. Visualize the color orange entering the left point #12 small intestines meridian. As it enters, say 2 times aloud, "I sort out what is best and resolve all splits between approaches."

6.4: THE SOUL

Color Blue

Meridian Heart, point #3, located on the inside of the left arm, just above the elbow. (Chart 1)

Affirmation I have a strong heart.

Balancing Say 4 times aloud, "I have a strong heart." Release
Modality the fear of being yourself by formulating the feeling, then dispersing it as you move your eyes diagonally from the upper left to the lower right until all of that feeling is released. Place your right hand over the left point #3 heart meridian. Visualize the color blue expanding in this area.

6.5: YOUTH

Color Red

Meridian Circulation-sex, point #5, located on the left inside forearm, approximately a hand's width from the wrist. (Chart 1)

Affirmation I have intimate heart-to-heart connections.

Balancing Modality Say 3 times aloud, "I have intimate heart-to-heart connections." Visualize the color red at the alpha chakra (located in the middle thigh area).

6.6: INDEPENDENCE/INTERDEPENDENCE

Color Green

Meridian Bladder, point #22, located on the right side of the spinal cord, just above the waist.

Affirmation I am reflective.

Balancing Modality Place your right thumb on the side of your right nostril to block the air flow. Exhale and inhale through your left nostril. Then, place your right forefinger on the left nostril. Exhale and inhale through your right nostril. Alternate nostrils 4 times, completing 2 cycles of breathing. Say 2 times aloud, "I am reflective." Visualize the color green expanding in the throat chakra area.

6.7: GROWTH

Color Indigo

Meridian Lung, point #7, located on the right arm in line with the thumb, just above the wrist. (Chart 1)

Affirmation I have pride in my family.

Balancing Modality Bend over and position the palms of your hands a foot away but facing your body. Imagine a blue light as you sweep your hands slowly up your body, stopping at the heart chakra. Let the blue light fill your heart. Sweep your hands over your head and down the back of your body and legs. Now, imagine an indigo light as you sweep your hands slowly up your body, stopping at the brow chakra (located in the middle of your forehead at your third eye). Let the indigo light fill your brow chakra. Sweep your hands over your head and down the back of your body and legs.

6.M: MATURITY

Color White

Meridian Spleen, point #20, located at the end of the collar bone where the right arm adjoins the shoulder. (Chart 1)

Affirmation I am vital.

Balancing Modality Say 2 times aloud, "I am vital." Place your left hand over your right point #20 spleen meridian. Tone the note of C# 10 times, sending the note "out" of your body through the right point #20 spleen meridian. You will probably need to use a pitch pipe or musical instrument to assist you in locating the note. Breathe in deeply through your nose, filling your body. Breathe out through your mouth, making a long "Haaaaa" sighing sound. Repeat this breath 6 times.

Strand #7
Balance

7.1: Pre-birth

Color Magenta

Meridian Heart, point #7, located on pinkie side of left hand at point where the hand meets the wrist. (Chart 1)

Affirmation I eliminate the resistance between my heart and the hearts of others.

Balancing Modality Inhale deeply through your nose and exhale with your tongue against the roof of your mouth, making a long "Sssss" sound like a snake. Repeat this breath 5 times. Say 2 times aloud, "I eliminate the resistance between my heart and the hearts of others."

7.2: Soul Entry

Color Violet

Meridian Stomach, point #45, at the end of the right middle toe. (Chart 1)

Affirmation I am content and at peace.

Balancing Modality Say 4 times aloud, "I am content and at peace." Visualize a violet pool of water in which you are floating effortlessly on the top. The violet represents contentment and peace. Feel the contentment and peace seep through you as you float on top of it.

7.3: Instinct

Color Orange

Meridian Triple heater, point #16, located on the back of the neck behind the left sternocleidomastoid muscle (on side of neck), midway between the hairline and the shoulders. (Chart 3)

Affirmation All relationships are important to me.

Balancing Modality Say 4 times aloud, "All relationships are important to me." Inhale fully and, without pausing, exhale. Then exhale fully and, without pausing, inhale. Continue inhaling and exhaling without pausing for several minutes.

7.4: THE SOUL

Color Blue

Meridian Spleen, point #21, located on the left side of the chest near the armpit on level with the sixth rib from the top. (Chart 1)

Affirmation I act responsibly.

Balancing Modality Say aloud 7 times, "I act responsibly." Place your right hand over the left point #21 spleen meridian. Tap your thymus (located in the middle of your chest, midway between the collar bone and the breasts) 30 times.

7.5: YOUTH

Color Red

Meridian Circulation-sex, point #8, located in the middle of the left palm. (Chart 1)

Affirmation I circulate love.

Balancing Modality Inhale through your nose. Exhale through your mouth. Now wait for the body to determine when it needs to repeat the inhale. While waiting, relax and let go, repeating the affirmation "I circulate love."

7.6: INDEPENDENCE/INTERDEPENDENCE

Color Green

Meridian Large intestines, point #19, above upper right lip. (Chart 1)

Affirmation I am aware of my self-righteousness, and I do something about it.

Balancing Say 10 times aloud, "I am aware of my self-
Modality righteousness, and I do something about it." Take in the feeling of humility, knowing that you are Divine but that you are also humble in relationship to the Divine Creator who is all-knowing. Complete 1 breath as follows: exhale with a "Haa" sound, then inhale. Exhale with a "Whoo" sound, then inhale. Exhale with a "Hee" sound, then inhale. Exhale with a "Tsu" sound, then inhale. Exhale with a "Sssss" sound, then inhale.

7.7: GROWTH

Color Indigo

Meridian Liver, point #14, located about 4 inches under right nipple in line with right nipple. (Chart 1)

Affirmation I envision my spiritual ideal and do those actions that support my ideal.

Balancing Remember when you were a child and had ideas
Modality about what you wanted to be when you grew up. You were sure you could become a prima ballerina or a concert pianist or a famous baseball player. It never occurred to you that you could not be something you wanted. Hold that feeling of realization of your goals as you place your left hand over the right point #14 liver meridian. Say twice aloud, "I envision my spiritual ideal and do those actions that support my ideal."

7.M: MATURITY

Color White

Meridian Heart, point #8, located on pinkie side of left hand, midway between the wrist and the base of the pinkie. (Chart 1)

Affirmation I project a positive influence.

Balancing Modality Inhale deeply through your nose and hold your breath. Push air gently into your lower abdomen. While holding the air in your abdomen, squeeze and release your sphincter muscle 2 times. Then exhale through your nose.

STRAND #8
POWER

Color   Magenta

Meridian   Liver, point #13, located under rib under right nipple in line with right nipple midway between the waist line and the nipple. (Chart 1)

Affirmation   I create the strategies for manifesting my plans and goals.

Balancing Modality   Say 3 times aloud, "I create the strategies for manifesting my plans and goals." Breathe in through your nose, drawing in a feeling of creativity. Exhale and let go of any blocks to creativity.

Color   Violet

Meridian   Heart, point #7, located on pinkie side of left hand at point where the hand meets the wrist. (Chart 1)

Affirmation   I know all aspects of myself, both light and dark, and fully appreciate who I am.

Balancing Modality   Say 7 times aloud, "I know all aspects of myself, both light and dark, and fully appreciate who I am." Place your right hand over the left point #7 heart meridian. Then cover your heart chakra with your left hand while your right hand is still in place. Look up, right, down, and left with your eyes. Repeat this eye movement sequence 2 times.

8.3: INSTINCT

Color   Orange

Meridian   Liver, point #13, located under rib under right nipple in line with right nipple midway between the waistline and the nipple. (Chart 1)

Affirmation   I envision my spiritual ideal and do those actions that support that ideal.

Balancing   Say 3 times aloud, "I envision my spiritual ideal
Modality   and do those actions that support that ideal." Make a cross with your eyes by looking up, down, left, and right. Focus ahead and visualize the color orange glowing in the distance, as the sun would rise on the horizon. See your spiritual ideals coming to fruition as the orange explodes over the horizon.

8.4: THE SOUL

Color   Blue

Meridian   Triple heater, point #16, located on the back of the neck behind the left sternocleidomastoid muscle (on side of neck), midway between the hairline and the shoulders. (Chart 3)

Affirmation   I keep things in proportion and see the big picture.

Balancing   Exhale strongly through your nose, squeezing
Modality   your stomach in. Inhale deeply through your nose. Repeat this sequence 4 times. Visualize the color blue entering the left point #16 triple heater meridian.

8.5: YOUTH

Color   Red

Meridian   Small intestines, point #19, located on the right side of the face at the top of and behind the cheekbone in front of the ear. (Chart 1)

Affirmation   I allow for the development of the finer qualities of myself.

Balancing Visualize a rainbow extending over you. This
Modality rainbow is composed of all of your finer qualities.
Watch as people cluster around you to admire the
rainbow, knowing they are viewing the best that
you have to offer. Say once aloud, "I allow for the
development of the finer qualities of myself."
Watch as the rainbow grows and expands until it
encircles your neighborhood, city, state, continent,
world, and, finally, the universe.

8.6: INDEPENDENCE/INTERDEPENDENCE

Color Green

Meridian Gall bladder, point #20, located at the back of the
neck where the hairline meets the spine. (Chart 2)

Affirmation I come from integrity.

Balancing Inhale through your nose. Exhale through your
Modality mouth. Now wait for the body to determine
when it needs to repeat the inhale. Repeat this
sequence 4 more times. Say 2 times aloud,
"I come from integrity."

8.7: GROWTH

Color Indigo

Meridian Small intestines, point #19, located on the right
side of the face at the top of and behind the
cheekbone in front of the ear. (Chart 1)

Affirmation I enjoy sexual intimacy for the bonding and joy
it brings.

Balancing Place your left hand over the right point #19 small
Modality intestines meridian. Visualize making love with the
perfect life mate, one who brings great joy to you
through the heart connection that binds you. Say
3 times aloud, "I enjoy sexual intimacy for the
bonding and joy it brings."

8.M: MATURITY

Color White

Meridian Lung, point #11, located at the tip of the left thumb. (Chart 1)

Affirmation I take pride in my family for each is acting according to his Divine plan.

Balancing Modality Focus on something near to you. Then focus on something far away. Repeat this sequence 2 more times. Say 2 times aloud, "I take pride in my family for each is acting according to his Divine plan." Make a cross with your eyes by looking up, down, left, and right.

STRAND #9
COMMUNION

Color Magenta

Meridian Small intestines, point #16, located behind the right sternocleidomastoid muscle (on side of neck) on level with the Adam's apple. (Chart 1)

Affirmation I resolve all splits between me and my partner.

Balancing Modality Say 8 times aloud, "I resolve all splits between me and my partner." Visualize the color magenta entering the right point #16 small intestines meridian. Allow the color to fill your entire body. Tone the note of D, 5 times. You will probably need to use a pitch pipe or musical instrument to assist you in locating the note.

Color Violet

Meridian Small intestines, point #16, located behind the right sternocleidomastoid muscle (on side of neck) on level with the Adam's apple. (Chart 1)

Affirmation My humor is warm and loving.

Balancing Modality Breathe in deeply through your nose, filling your body. Breathe out through your mouth, making a long "Haaaaa" sighing sound. Repeat this breath 4 times. Say 2 times aloud, "My humor is warm and loving." Place your right hand over the right point #16 small intestines meridian. Visualize the joyful response of others when you use your humor lovingly rather than at the expense of others.

9.3: INSTINCT

Color Orange

Meridian Triple heater, point #19, located on the left side of the head, directly behind the upper part of the ear, in line with your left eye. (Chart 3)

Affirmation All relationships are important to me.

Balancing Modality Place your right hand over the left point #19 triple heater meridian. Tone the note of C, 2 times. You will probably need to use a pitch pipe or musical instrument to assist you in locating the note.

9.4: THE SOUL

Color Blue

Meridian Circulation-sex, point #7, located on the inside of the right arm where the hand meets the wrist. (Chart 1)

Affirmation I circulate love.

Balancing Modality Say 2 times aloud, "I circulate love." Visualize the color blue surrounding your entire body as you circulate your love, sending the blue out in waves to everyone and everything in the universe.

9.5: YOUTH

Color Red

Meridian Spleen, point #20, located at the end of the collar bone where the right arm adjoins to the shoulder. (Chart 1)

Affirmation I know where I am going.

Balancing Modality Say 2 times aloud, "I know where I am going." Inhale deeply through your nose and exhale with your tongue against the roof of your mouth, making a long "Sssss" sound like a snake. Repeat this breath 3 times. Visualize the color red encircling your head like a ring around your forehead. Feel the energy circulating clockwise around the ring, feeling a sense of certainty being grounded regarding your confidence in where you are going.

9.6: INDEPENDENCE/INTERDEPENDENCE

Color Green

Meridian Circulation-sex, point #8, located in the middle of the left palm. (Chart 1)

Affirmation I have the capacity for a lifelong love commitment.

Balancing Modality Place your right hand over the left point #8 circulation-sex meridian. Say 2 times aloud, "I have the capacity for a lifelong love commitment. Place your right thumb on the side of your right nostril to block the air flow. Exhale and inhale through your left nostril. Then, place your right forefinger on the left nostril. Exhale and inhale through your right nostril. Alternate nostrils 6 times, completing 3 cycles of breathing.

9.7: GROWTH

Color Indigo

Meridian Spleen, point #21, located on the left side of the chest near the armpit on level with the sixth rib from the top. (Chart 1)

Affirmation I am at peace.

Balancing Modality Place your left hand over your left point #21 spleen meridian. Inhale fully and, without pausing, exhale. Then exhale fully and, without pausing, inhale. Continue inhaling and exhaling without pausing for several minutes. Then say 3 times aloud, "I am at peace."

9.M: MATURITY

Color White

Meridian Kidney, point #26, located under the neck, just below the left collarbone. (Chart 1)

Affirmation I easily accept changes in direction.

Balancing Modality Say 5 times aloud, "I easily accept changes in direction." Visualize the color white descending from above and entering your crown chakra. Imagine all of the changes that will be required of you in the future, changes that will be easy to accommodate by your acceptance of them. Feel at peace with yourself, knowing you have the ability to move with these changes by not resisting them.

STRAND #10
COHESIVENESS

Color   Magenta

Meridian   Lung, point #7, located on right arm in line with the thumb, just above the wrist. (Chart 1)

Affirmation   I take pride in my family.

Balancing Modality   Say 4 times aloud, "I take pride in my family." Complete 1 breath as follows: exhale with a "Ha" sound, then inhale. Exhale with a "Whoo" sound, then inhale. Exhale with a "Hee" sound, then inhale. Exhale with a "Tsu" sound, then inhale. Exhale with a "Sssss" sound, then inhale. Repeat this breath. Visualize that you are standing in a pool of the color magenta. Feel its cooling refreshment as you splash through the colored pool.

Color   Violet

Meridian   Gall bladder, point #24, located approximately 5" below left nipple in line with the nipple. (Chart 3)

Affirmation   I move forward with vision and make the necessary changes that are needed.

Balancing Modality   Cover the left point #24 gall bladder meridian with the right hand. Visualize the color violet entering this meridian point and descending to the feet, exiting the soles of your feet and entering the Earth. Now sense yourself moving forward with vision and making the necessary changes that are needed while you are grounded by the violet threads of light. Exhale all the air from your lungs and relax deeply. Without breathing, imagine that you are breathing internally, obtaining your oxygen from within. Envision a life made easy by your readiness to make the necessary changes along your path.

10.3: INSTINCT

Color Orange

Meridian Liver, point #14, located about 4 inches under right nipple in line with right nipple. (Chart 1)

Affirmation My vision and creativity allow my ideas to flow.

Balancing Modality Say 4 times aloud, "My vision and creativity allow my ideas to flow." Visualize the color orange as a cloud of color that holds all of your creative ideas. See the cloud grow and expand as you add more and more ideas.

10.4: THE SOUL

Color Blue

Meridian Small intestines, point #14, touch left shoulder midway between neck and arm and slide hand down over the top portion of the back. You will be covering point #14. (Chart 2)

Affirmation My language is clean and strengthening.

Balancing Modality Say 3 times aloud, "My language is clean and strengthening." Surround yourself in red light and breath in and out several times. Then surround yourself in orange light and breathe in and out several times. Repeat this with yellow, green, blue, indigo, violet, and white light. Complete 1 breath as follows: exhale with a "Ha" sound, then inhale. Exhale with a "Whoo" sound, then inhale. Exhale with a "Hee" sound, then inhale. Exhale with a "Tsu" sound, then inhale. Exhale with a "Sssss" sound, then inhale.

10.5: YOUTH

Color Red

Meridian Small intestines, point #19, located on the right side of the face at the top of and behind the cheekbone in front of the ear. (Chart 1)

Affirmation I take the riches out of life for the full blossoming of my being.

Balancing Modality Say 3 times aloud, "I take the riches out of life for the full blossoming of my being." Visualize the color red surrounding your entire body, as if you are sitting inside a red egg. Complete 1 breath as follows: exhale with a "Ha" sound, then inhale. Exhale with a "Whoo" sound, then inhale. Exhale with a "Hee" sound, then inhale. Exhale with a "Tsu" sound, then inhale. Exhale with a "Sssss" sound, then inhale. Complete a second Five Elements breath.

10.6: INDEPENDENCE/INTERDEPENDENCE

Color Green

Meridian Stomach, point #45, at the end of the right middle toe. (Chart 1)

Affirmation I am clear headed.

Balancing Modality Inhale deeply through your nose and hold your breath. Push air gently into your lower abdomen. While holding the air in your abdomen, squeeze and release your sphincter muscle 3 times. Then exhale through your nose. Repeat this breath 2 times. Cover your right point #45 stomach meridian with your right hand. Say 3 times aloud, "I am clear headed."

10.7: GROWTH

Color Indigo

Meridian Heart, point #7, located on pinkie side of left hand at point where the hand meets the wrist. (Chart 1)

Affirmation I understand each person's needs.

Balancing Say 3 times aloud, "I understand each person's
Modality needs." Think back to a time in your life when you put your own needs in front of another person's needs because you did not understand what they desired. Visualize a different outcome based on hindsight which has given you greater understanding in terms of what the other needed at the time. Remind yourself that you always have the capacity to view a situation from another's perspective.

10.M: MATURITY

Color White

Meridian Spleen, point #20, located at the end of the collar bone where the right arm adjoins the shoulder. (Chart 1)

Affirmation I am responsible.

Balancing Say 3 times aloud, "I am responsible." Cover
Modality the right point #20 spleen meridian with your left hand. Inhale deeply through your nose and hold your breath. Push air gently into your lower abdomen. While holding the air in your abdomen, squeeze and release your sphincter muscle 5 times. Then exhale through your nose. Repeat this breath 4 times. Visualize the color white throughout your entire body. Feel it purifying you.

Strand #11
SEXUALITY

Color Magenta

Meridian Heart, point #4, located on the pinkie side of the left hand, 4 finger widths above the wrist bone. (Chart 1)

Affirmation I transcend all differences to give fully as appropriate.

Balancing Modality Breathe in deeply through your nose, filling your body. Breathe out through your mouth, making a long, "Haaaaa" signing sound. Repeat this breath once again. Hold your right hand over left point #4 heart meridian and say 4 times aloud, "I transcend all differences to give fully as appropriate."

Color Violet

Meridian Small intestines, point #18, located directly on the right cheekbone. (Chart 1)

Affirmation I determine what is in the highest good of all concerned and resolve conflict between approaches.

Balancing Modality Say 2 times aloud, "I determine what is in the highest good of all concerned and resolve conflict between approaches." Visualize the color violet entering the right point #18 small intestines meridian as you feel your creativity enhanced rather than limited by situations involving conflicting points of view.

11.3: INSTINCT

Color Orange

Meridian Lung, point #5, located on the right inner arm, just above the crook of the arm. (Chart 1)

Affirmation I have pride in my family.

Balancing Modality Hold your left hand over the right point #5 lung meridian. Inhale sharply through your nose, puffing out your chest and hold the breath. Exhale with force through your mouth, imagining that you are pushing the air out through your legs. Repeat this breath once more. Say once aloud, "I have pride in my family."

11.4: THE SOUL

Color Blue

Meridian Spleen, point #21, located on the left side of the chest near the armpit on level with the sixth rib from the top. (Chart 1)

Affirmation I am at peace.

Balancing Modality Say once aloud, "I am at peace." Tone the "aahh" sound 5 times, hollowing your mouth as if a golf ball was sitting on your tongue to create resonance and placing the tip of your tongue on the roof of your mouth. Visualize the color blue seeping throughout your entire body, coming in through the crown and oozing out through the feet.

11.5: YOUTH

Color Red

Meridian Lung, point #3, located on the right biceps even with the nipple line. (Chart 1)

Affirmation I allow myself to experience my grief.

Balancing Modality Hold your left hand over the right point #3 lung meridian. Breathe the feeling of grief into your body through point #3. As you feel grief, say once aloud, "I allow myself to experience my grief." Complete 2 breaths as follows: Let the lower abdomen move inward as you inhale. Hold your breath, soften your eyes, and bring your head back, then turn your head to the right, then turn your head to the left, and finally breathe out half of the air you are holding through your nose while facing left. Now exhale the remainder of the air you are holding through your mouth, blowing out in a gust of wind. Look straight ahead as you repeat this sequence.

11.6: INDEPENDENCE/INTERDEPENDENCE

Color Green

Meridian Liver, point #13, located under rib under right nipple in line with right nipple midway between the waist line and the nipple. (Chart 1)

Affirmation I am receptive to new ideas.

Balancing Modality Place your right thumb on the side of your right nostril to block the air flow. Exhale and inhale through your left nostril. Then, place your right forefinger on the left nostril. Exhale and inhale through your right nostril. Alternate nostrils 4 times, completing 2 cycles of breathing.

11.7: GROWTH

Color Indigo

Meridian Heart, point # 2, located on the inside of the left arm, midway between the crook of the arm and the armpit, slightly closer to the crook of the arm. (Chart 1)

Affirmation I have clear insight which allows me to integrate all differences.

Balancing Modality Say twice aloud, "I have clear insight which allows me to integrate all differences." This is all that is necessary to balance this box.

11.M: MATURITY

Color White

Meridian Bladder, point #10, at the base of the hairline on the left side of the neck. (Chart 3)

Affirmation I have ideas and creativity and put them into action.

Balancing Modality Lie down. Do not use a pillow to support your head. Visualize the color white entering the left point #10 bladder meridian until your entire head is filled with white light. Say once aloud, "I have ideas and creativity and put them into action."

Strand #12
LOVE

12.1: Pre-birth

Color Magenta

Meridian Small intestines, point #16, located behind the right sternocleidomastoid muscle (on side of neck) on level with the Adam's apple. (Chart 1)

Affirmation I am intellectually alive which results in my emotional well-being.

Balancing Modality Hold your left hand over the right point #16 small intestines meridian. Examine one of the action plans you have devised in the past to increase your intellectual abilities. Trace those intellectual abilities to a situation that resulted in your emotional well-being. Feel the satisfaction that occurred. Feel the color magenta entering into point #16 small intestines meridian as you say 4 times aloud "I am intellectually alive which results in my emotional well-being."

12.2: Soul Entry

Color Violet

Meridian Heart, point #3, located on the inside of the left arm, just above the elbow. (Chart 1)

Affirmation I eliminate the resistance from one heart to another.

Balancing Modality Think of someone you love, either alive or dead, and feel the heart connection, represented by a violet cord that extends from your heart to theirs. Next, place your right hand over the left point #3 heart meridian and say 4 times aloud, "I eliminate the resistance from one heart to another." Now, extend that feeling of openness to everyone in your life. Feel the inter-relatedness of all beings who are here in your life at this time. Extend that feeling to your town, to your state, to your country, and to the entire planet.

12.3: INSTINCT

Color Orange

Meridian Stomach, point #25, located about 1/12 inches above and to the right of the navel. (Chart 1)

Affirmation I appreciate and love others.

Balancing Modality Tone the note of D# 4 times, sending the note out of your body through the right point #25 stomach meridian. You will probably need to use a pitch pipe or musical instrument to assist you in locating the note.

12.4: THE SOUL

Color Blue

Meridian Large intestines, point #15, located on the left shoulder where the arm meets the shoulder. (Chart 3)

Affirmation I have a clear, sharp mind.

Balancing Modality Let the color blue wash through your entire body as if it is being cleansed by the color. Say once aloud "I have a clear, sharp mind." Complete 10 breaths as follows: Let the lower abdomen move inward as you inhale. Hold your breath, soften your eyes, and bring your head back, then turn your head to the right, then turn your head to the left, and finally breathe out half of the air you are holding through your nose while facing left. Now exhale the remainder of the air you are holding through your mouth, blowing it out in a gust of wind. Look straight ahead as you repeat this breath 9 more times.

12.5: YOUTH

Color Red

Meridian Large intestines, point #15, located on the left shoulder where the arm meets the shoulder. (Chart 3)

Affirmation I am aware of my self-righteousness, and do something about it.

Balancing Modality Feel that feeling of self-righteousness when you are experiencing a situation when you are convinced you are right and someone else is wrong. See your self righteousness as the color red. Watch the red dissipate as you recognize there is no right or wrong, only different experiences which create differing points of view. Feel the weight dissipate from your shoulders as you release the feeling of needing to be right. Say once aloud, "I am aware of my self-righteousness, and do something about it."

12.6: INDEPENDENCE/INTERDEPENDENCE

Color Green

Meridian Triple heater, point #8, located on the back of the right forearm approximately one-fourth of the way above where the back of the hand meets the arm. (Chart 2)

Affirmation All relationships are important to me.

Balancing Modality Place your right thumb on the side of your right nostril to block the air flow. Exhale and inhale through your left nostril. Then, place your right forefinger on the left nostril. Exhale and inhale through your right nostril. Alternate nostrils 4 times, completing 2 cycles of breathing. Say 10 times aloud, "All relationships are important to me." Exhale all of the air out of your lungs and visualize the color green filling your lungs as you relax deeply. Without breathing, imagine that you are breathing internally, obtaining your oxygen from the color green. Repeat this breath once again.

12.7: GROWTH

Color Indigo

Meridian Small intestines, point #12, touch left shoulder midway between neck and arm and slide hand down over the top portion of the back. You will be covering point #12. (Chart 2)

Affirmation I am able to absorb what is valuable out of any situation.

Balancing Modality Say aloud 10 times, "I am able to absorb what is valuable out of any situation." Place your right hand over the left point #12 small intestines meridian. Exhale all of the air out of your lungs and visualize the color indigo filling your lungs as you relax deeply. Without breathing, imagine that you are breathing internally, obtaining your oxygen from the color indigo.

12.M: MATURITY

Color White

Meridian Triple heater, point #16, located on the left side of the neck approximately one inch behind and below the ear. (Chart 3)

Affirmation I manifest an atmosphere around me so others feel like they fit.

Balancing Modality Place your right thumb on the side of your right nostril to block the air flow. Exhale and inhale through your left nostril. Then, place your right forefinger on the left nostril. Exhale and inhale through your right nostril. Alternate nostrils 10 times, completing 5 cycles of breathing. Visualize the color white filling your entire body, oozing from your body so you are surrounded in a cloud of white light. Say aloud 3 times, "I manifest an atmosphere around me so others feel like they fit."

APPENDIX C

•

PHASE THREE OF DNA RECODING

DISCOVERING
PHASE THREE

BALANCING POLARITY

Almost one year after I finished phase one and two of the DNA Recoding process, I encountered a juncture that felt significantly different from the preceding peaceful year when I had established my union with David and evolved into a spiritual healer with a growing metaphysical practice. Prior to hitting this juncture, I had settled into a mind-set that was very comfortable. I knew who I was, I recognized my talents, I understood my soul path and purpose, and I awoke each day with an innate knowing of what I needed to accomplish. Suddenly, those feelings flew by the wayside. I lived for two months with an unsettled feeling of discomfort. Although I had not changed my lifestyle, I felt "off path and purpose" and stopped seeing clients, feeling as if I had nothing to offer. I seemed to lose a part of myself, repeating constantly to David that I did not know who I was anymore. This was very disturbing since, after previous years of questioning, I had grown very sure once I completed DNA Recoding. I could not reconcile this disconnected feeling with the supreme knowing I had enjoyed as a result of DNA recoding.

Additionally, I kept attracting negative situations into my life. Having mastered the basics of manifestation, I could not understand how I was responsible for the negative situations. I knew I had a lesson to learn, but I could not determine what it was. All I knew was the more loving I became, the more I seemed to attract unloving people into my life. The more generous I became, the more money difficulties I seemed to encounter. I knew the rubber band effect of bouncing back and forth between opposites was an attempt to communicate something when I received an unexpected tax return of $2,500 and discovered, shortly thereafter, that we had termites under our deck, promptly needing to spend the amount. On the one hand, I could have admired by creation energy by being even in terms of nothing lost, nothing gained. However, I hold a profit mentality that says I should always net something.

Finally, through a conversation with my mentor Venessa and subsequent channelings with my guides, I determined that I was being hampered in my path toward unification by soul contracts that were based on the premise of polarity. The more I achieved unification, the step beyond balance when resistance is nil, the more the mass consciousness of polarity attempted to impose balance by bringing the opposite situation.

The following information was provided by Joysiah and a group energy of seventy-six guides named Geremyia who had begun channeling to me after I completed the DNA Recoding process. Their channeled material was published in my second book, *Breaking Free to Health, Wealth and Happiness, 100's of Ways to Release Limiting Beliefs.* It explains what happens when we move into the state of unification but continue to hold soul commitments based on the Earth's blueprint of polarity. It also provides the rituals needed to remove the conflict so we can be immersed in unification in spite of the state of duality that our society upholds.

Please note that you will undergo a period of adjustment after completing the disavowing of polarity contracts. Apparently, once polarity disappears in our soul matrix, we can finally tap into the twelve levels of awareness and information that the multiple DNA strands provide because we have attained unification. During this time period, you are reviewing information from all of your past lives, retrieving what you currently need, and discarding what you no longer use. It is almost like a computer program that takes all of the information residing on the hard drive and compresses it by removing spaces to create more streamlined and efficient processing. Needless to say, as you review this massive amount of information, some upheaval is introduced into your life. The less you resist the discomfort by accepting it and moving on, the faster you will complete your compression program. The more you resist it because it feels uncomfortable which is foreign to your experiences by this time, the longer it will take to complete this phase. However, once you have completed this process, you will experience greater bliss. It also creates a state of bliss which is difficult to describe since we are more familiar with the upheaval our increasingly hectic lives seem to bring. Suffice it to say, the blissful feelings are well worth the rocky road one must pass to reach the destination.

TRANSCENDING EARTH'S POLARITY BLUEPRINT MESSAGE FROM GEREMYIA

Earth is a planet that operates on the premise of polarity. You see it everywhere. It exists in nature in the form of tranquil lakes versus violent earthquakes. It exists in the annual cycles in the fruitfulness of summer versus the dormancy of winter. It exists in male and female qualities where the male is characterized as the aggressor or doer while the female is the nurturer or receiver. When your soul decided to enter the polarity library of Earth to learn from its resources, it came with a dual purpose. One objective was to live in the midst of duality and learn to overcome it by discovering Divine Union or unification within this seemingly contradictory framework. Souls are often overzealous in the learning experiences they choose, and discovering unification on a planet of duality probably seemed like a good challenge. Most of you have discovered via your frustration with attaining unification in a polar world that this objective was somewhat ambitious! You have spent multiple lifetimes dealing with conflicts resulting from dual perspectives like good and bad or right and wrong. Finally, you are emerging from this yin/yang pull on your perspective into a mode of acceptance rather than judgment. And, now that you are realizing your objective of "balanced" or "neutral" living amidst polarity, you are ready to accomplish your second objective, which is to represent the principles of Divine Union to other souls. You accomplish this by living through example.

The road toward attaining Divine Union in your own soul path has been fraught with frustration and continues to hold many challenges. This is mostly due to the fact that the blueprint for Earth contains polarity which firmly entrenches the concept in the mass consciousness. You are faced with the dilemma of rising above the mass consciousness, which means you must overcome the strong pull on your mental process in order to discover unification. This means you must eliminate certain concepts from your thoughts.

For example, there is a best-selling book entitled *Men are from Mars, Women are from Venus*. This book revels in the differences between males and females. Instead of assisting people in discovering methods for bringing male and female energy into balance or unification, it drives a stake between the genders by upholding the differences. To achieve balance, you must *honor* the differences in order to live in harmony rather than to *bridge* the differences. Honoring the differences means bringing the male and female energy into balance in each individual. It is the balancing of these polar energies that allow couples to join in Divine Union. Unification will never occur by *tolerating* differences, even if toleration results in living without conflict. Divine Union only occurs by *honoring* differences.

There is another influence beyond the mass consciousness that drives you to separation, whether it is between you and a partner or a friend or a work peer. It exists in the form of your soul contracts or vows. Prior to reincarnating on Earth, your soul agreed to fulfill certain contracts in order to evolve. These contracts were based on the premise of polarity because that is the operating mode of your planet. In order to successfully complete your contracts which were developed among soul groups who honored unification, the contracts had to match the values of the planet on which you incarnated. Therefore, you were given contracts that were based on polarity since a unified concept would not be appropriate for Earth.

But, at this point in your evolution, some of you have moved beyond the concept of polarity, understanding that harmony results from honoring differences as well as similarities. You strive to balance differences through acceptance and love rather than increasing differences through tolerance and separation. You try to uphold the value of unification in your daily existence, be it getting along with your spouse or your neighbor or your boss. Unfortunately, despite your orientation toward union, you are continually being pulled by separation since your soul contracts were based on the principle of polarity rather than unity.

Once you rise above the mass consciousness of polarity and choose the path of unification, your prior soul contracts oppose rather than assist your new reality. You no longer honor the *Men are from Mars, Women are from Venus* mentality because you manifest based on unification. You recognize the common denominators in everyone. There are no divisions.

You must rescind your prior vows or you will be working against yourself. This can become quite uncomfortable at times because the more you move toward unification, the more you experience the opposite extreme based on the polarity premise of your prior vows. For example, a couple who honors the masculine/feminine balance in both parties, instead basing their relationship on the more traditional viewpoint which honors the differences between men and women, will still feel conflict. The more each individual moves toward Divine Union by acknowledging and accepting differences, the more separation is attracted because of the violation of prior soul agreements. This can be very confusing since the couple understands and implements unification, yet they are randomly torn by feelings of separation. It is almost as if they are dealing with a force that is stronger than their desire for unity. Their heart desires to be whole, while their actions defy it. Those who have experienced this dichotomy think they are going crazy since they constantly feel like they are working against their desires.

The following ritual was developed to break contracts based on polarity in order to align your soul vows with the principles of unification. It can be done by individuals or couples. This ritual should only be done if you have already minimized polarity thinking and create your reality based on the premise of unification rather than separation. Otherwise, you will be breaking vows that can still be accomplished under the premise of polarity thinking, which will interfere with your intended soul experiences for this lifetime. Also, please conduct the following ritual for breaking the vows either outdoors on a patio or indoors on a protected surface. This is a very powerful ritual, and some who have conducted it have discovered that the flames from the fire are quite expansive, or the intense heat burns through the bottom of trivets and pot holders.

Ritual for Breaking and Rescinding Polarity Vows

* Line a Pyrex bowl or deep pot with aluminum foil and place a blue candle in the bottom. If you are indoors, play music which uplifts you spiritually. If you are outside, you can ring chimes, listen to the birds sing, or feel the wind in your face to capture that feeling of upliftment.
* Light a blue candle.
* You will need to photocopy the following request since you will be burning it in the Pyrex bowl or pot.
* (IF BREAKING VOWS ALONE:) Sign the following request at the bottom and cut it horizontally in half. Read the first half aloud, then lay it aside. Read the second half aloud. Light the first half with the flame from the blue candle and burn it in the bowl. Light the second half with the same candle and burn it, too. Do not be surprised if your candle disappears before your eyes. Often, the power of the words consumes the wax of the candle.
* (IF BREAKING VOWS WITH A PARTNER:) Both partners sign the following request at the bottom and cut it horizontally in half. Both partners will be sharing this paper when performing the ritual as follows: Partner #1 reads the first half aloud while Partner #2 holds the remainder. Partner #1 hands the first half to Partner #2, then takes the remainder and reads it aloud. Next, Partner #2 reads the first half aloud while Partner #1 holds the remainder. Partner #2 hands the first half to Partner #1, then takes the remainder and reads it aloud. Partner #1 lights the first half with the blue candle flame and burns it in the bowl. Partner #2 lights the remaining half with the blue candle flame and burns it in the bowl.
* Let the candle burn completely. Discard the waste. If only ashes remain, you may want to discard them outside.

PRAYER REQUEST
TO RESCIND POLARITY

- (SAY THREE TIMES:) "Creator of All Beings, My Personal Guides and Teachers, My Superconscious Self, My Subconscious Self."
- (SAY:) "I call on my Superconscious Self to envelop me in white light. I call on my special guides and teachers to surround me with their love and protection. I call on the Planetary Councils that support the movement of Earth away from polarity and toward simplicity and unification to assist me. I ask to be protected and shielded from those who support polarity as I break and rescind all vows and agreements I have made that support the notion of polarity, both those that were intended in my higher good and those which were made, intentionally or unintentionally, with any Dark Forces, as they no longer serve me in my quest for Divine Love. I formally rescind each and every vow and agreement intended to be implemented under the laws of polarity that I have ever made in this life or any other life, in both my physical and subtle bodies, and in this time or any other concept of time including those concepts of time that exist beyond my comprehension. This includes both positive and negative contracts since neither will support the concepts of simplicity and unification. These contracts are to be replaced with contracts that support simplicity and unification that will lead to advancement and greater knowledge. Therefore, I break and rescind each and every vow and agreement I have ever made that supports polarity. I ask for my Superconscious Self to be surrounded with white light and that I be provided with new pictures of reality based on the principles of unification and integration. I claim my wholeness, both individually and as a part of the greater whole. I ask my Superconscious Self to manifest the highest possibilities of me integrating all I have requested

so that the power of that can be fully manifested in my experience. I thank my Superconscious Self, my guides and teachers, and the Planetary Councils for assisting me in the healing I have received."

- (SAY THREE TIMES:) "Thank you. So let it be!"

Signature:

_____

RITUAL FOR FUSING VOWS OF UNIFICATION WITH A PARTNER

There is a final step for those who have conducted the rescinding of polarity vows *with a partner*. In order to be aligned with your purpose and complete the work you and your life partner have contracted to do on Earth, you must re-fuse or meld your vows based on the premise of unification.

- Each person cuts a small piece of hair and places it in a bowl. Thoroughly mix the hair together.
- Both partners sign the following request at the bottom. Partner #1 reads the request aloud and hands it to Partner #2. Partner #2 reads the request aloud. Then, cut the request in half. Place each half in a Pyrex bowl or pot with the hair. Each partner takes a white candle and lights it with a match or lighter. They use the white candle to ignite their half of the request. Be sure the entire contents burn thoroughly, re-igniting the paper or the hair if it burns out.
- You will need to photocopy the following request since you will be burning it in the Pyrex bowl or pot.

Prayer Request
to Fuse Vows of
Unification

- (Say Three Times:) "Creator of All Beings, Archangel Zophkiel from the Realm of Balance, My Personal Guides and Teachers, My Superconscious Self, My Subconscious Self."
- (Say:) "I call on my Superconscious Self to envelop me in white light. I call on my special guides and teachers to surround me with their love and protection. I call on the Planetary Councils that support the movement of Earth away from polarity and toward simplicity and unification to assist me. I request a re-fusion of my contract with my life partner, based on the principles of unification and integration. I claim my individuality and my wholeness through this union. I am one with the universe."
- (Say Three Times:) "Thank you. So let it be!"

Signatures:

_____

_____

Appendix D

Phase Four of DNA Recoding

OPENING THE HEART ENERGY

HUMAN BEINGS VERSUS HUMAN DOINGS

Are you a human being or a human doing? Although many people would immediately state, "I am a human being," a further examination of your characteristics might prove otherwise. A human being lives in heartwholeness, balancing both the left brain aspects of analysis and thinking with the right brain aspects of intuition and creativity to conceive a rich life. Human beings experience balance in their lives because they integrate their mind with their heart. On the other hand, a human doing is a human being who has lost touch with heartwholeness due to the pressures of modern living. A human doing is trying to accommodate the stringent demands of today's living by prioritizing head over heart. Human doings use their mental energy to attempt to achieve balance and harmony in a world characterized by a frenetic pace, a decomposing family structure, and environmental decay. Human beings live in harmony with their surroundings, whereas human doings are focused on survival in a tumultuous environment.

Most of us have shifted some of our human being aspects to those of a human doing. This shift in style seems necessary in light of the rapid momentum of life. Take some time to review the following list to determine where you might have deviated from a human being to a human doing. It is important to be honest with yourself in order to assess your status. Nobody wants to admit they are less than complete. However, the first step toward completely opening your heart energy is to acknowledge your current state.

HUMAN BEINGS	VERSUS	HUMAN DOINGS
1 Uses an intertwined mental and emotional process of thoughts and feelings to respond to situations, i.e., gives equal emphasis to the rational and the intuitive.		1 Primarily uses a mental process to respond to situations, i.e., prioritizes the rational over the intuitive.
2 Emphasizes living in the moment but has an eye open toward the future.		2 Focuses primarily on the future, viewing today's events as stepping stones rather than destinations.
3 Derives satisfaction through an interactive experience with people, places, and things.		3 Derives satisfaction through the accomplishment of material goals and objectives.
4 Holds the perception that there is always enough time for the important things in life.		4 Holds the perception that there is never enough time for the important things in life.
5 Views life as a repetitive process that establishes rich traditions.		5 Views life as a repetitive process that establishes tedious routines.
6 Feels comfortably aligned with personal ideals.		6 Constantly strives for perfection without feeling perfection has been achieved.
7 Is motivated internally by the heart's desires.		7 Is motivated externally by the pressures of modern day living.
8 Feels equally comfortable either giving or taking direction.		8 Feels vulnerable when relinquishing control.
9 Achieves union with others through trust and love.		9 Establishes union with others through activities.

DNA RECODING AND HEART ENERGY

In order to fully utilize the twelve-strand DNA energy, you must have an orientation as a human being rather than a human doing. Otherwise, the additional DNA loses its potency because it filters through the linear thinking of your mind which contains your judgment. When you are in a state of judgment, you cannot expand. You must be in an intuitive, feeling state to allow the heightened twelve strand DNA energy with its expanded knowledge to infiltrate your awareness.

Have you ever tried to meditate, but you failed because you could not quiet the judge inside your head? This judge might have reminded you that you were not really meditating, bringing comparisons to others who probably achieved a meditative state that was superior to yours. Or you judged yourself because you could not seem to clear your head of random thoughts to achieve a state of meditation, remembering that you needed to pick up cheese at the supermarket or you needed to call your mother, then judging yourself for allowing your mind to wander. If you allow your mind to act as the primary filter through which you obtain information, delegating your heart to instances when you want to feel rather than think, you will not be able to effectively tap into your complete intuitive side. Your intuitive side does not judge. It is a receptor that accommodates all incoming pieces of information. Later, you can rely on your discernment to determine usefulness or fancifulness.

In order to maximize the information that is available to you via DNA Recoding, you must table your linear thinking. You will need to allow your heart to absorb information that is sometimes seemingly nonsensical, probably because it is not a part of mainstream thinking. Do not expect the information you receive via the twelve-strand energy to resemble mainstream thinking since it is drawn from a different echelon. Your heart will allow this information to enter. Your mind will shut it out.

Additionally, it is important to ensure that the additional manifestation power you derive from the twelve-strand energy be based on heart rather than mind energy. You will easily manifest with the additional boost in DNA. However, you want to channel your manifestation energy through the circuitry of the heart since the heart is your hook-up to Divine Love. When manifesting, you will improve both your own condition and the condition of the Earth's energy when you focus on what you want via your heart. Your heart will never betray you since it connects you to the Divine Creator.

The heart is the connection between your finite, or physical self, and your infinite, or God self. The Hindus and Egyptians understood this concept as depicted in their myths about the Divine Ka. According to ancient legend, one day a lotus flower appeared out of the primordial sea of energy. In the Egyptian version, a tiny mound about the size of a thumbnail was situated on the lotus flower. In the Hindu or Vedic version, the object was egg-like. The egg communicated with the ultimate God, or the superior consciousness of the Creator God, who was also birthed from the primordial sea of energy. The first word uttered in a fearful, apprehensive manner was Ka, meaning "Who?" The Ultimate God's answer reassured the egg by establishing a point of context, explaining it was a derivative of the Source of All. The Ka ceased to fear and began to create since it was a fragment of Source and contained Source's creation energy. Since everything is derived from the Divine Ka, you are in the Divine Ka and the Divine Ka is in you. Therefore, the Divine Ka exists inside you as well as outside you. According to the Hindus and Egyptians, you bridge the spiritual (external) to the physical (internal) via a gold cord that connects your external God-self, or superconscious, to your internal God-spark. The gold cord runs from the God-self situated outside you to your solar plexus and up to the heart where your internal God-spark is located.

Thus, every human heart contains a God-spark or a Divine Ka that serves as the fulcrum for that individual's soul. As you nourish your Divine Ka with uplifting emotions like love instead of starving it with toxic emotions like fear, it grows in size and strength. There is a healthy exchange between your God-self and your God-spark, and you thrive in this state of cosmic awareness. When the Divine Ka achieves spiritual enlightenment, where fear and judgment are replaced with unconditional love and acceptance, it sings the song of Divine Love. In other words, the "heart sings."

Awakening the Divine Ka within your heart is an important step toward expanded consciousness. When you recognize your God-spark within, you realize the Divine Essence is no longer found outside yourself at a distance. When you pray, you no longer relinquish your power to an external Divine Essence. Rather, you partner with the Divine, the aspect of Divinity inside your own God-spark with the Divine Essence from when you were created. In other words, God is experienced both far and near. You are co-creating rather than praying for mercy or salvation.

RE-PRIORITIZING HEART OVER MIND

The first step to re-prioritizing heart energy over mind energy is to determine consciously that the heart is more important in your soul growth than the mind. However, even after taking this conscious step, you must erase the memories that sit at a subconscious level. Often, we try to transition to a new way of being based on newly embraced attitudes. However, our habits formed from the old way of thinking seem to get in the way, no matter how hard we try to change. This is because the habits are reinforced by subconscious memories that have not been repatterned to the new way of thinking.

Several years ago, I encountered this problem with some of my soul clearing clients. I would clear someone of soul blockages from past life programs that interfered with their current life's agenda. Yet, they were so habituated to the old methods of thinking that their behavior did not change after the soul clearing. My spiritual team provided me with a twenty-one day prayer request format. They explained that my client's behavior did not shift despite the alteration in soul level programming because the blueprint in the physical body's cellular memory had not been altered. In order to alter the cellular memory which was firmly entrenched at a physical level, the person's neurological programming had to be shifted. In other words, they were cleared at the soul level, but they kept reinforcing the cellular memory, never allowing it to dissipate, because they were in a continuous loop of creating the same thoughts that maintained the cellular memory that fed the same thoughts that supported the cellular memory, ad infinitum.

My spiritual team explained that the cellular memory could be reprogrammed to shift after twenty-one days. Based on Deepak Chopra's popularity, it has become common knowledge that we are continually incorporating new cells in our system and discarding old ones. In a matter of weeks, we have a new heart, new lungs, new surface skin, and so forth. Therefore, if we program the new cells entering our system with a new idea, eventually we will have more new cells holding the new program than old cells with the old program. Once new cells constitute the majority, critical mass is reached and the entire cellular memory of the system shifts to the new programming.

After my guides had provided this information, I received multiple confirmations on the importance of twenty-one days. I had shared this information with my friend, Dr. Tom Rodman, who responded by saying, "Did you know it takes twenty-one days for the under layer of skin to reach the surface based on the rate of surface cell loss?" I thought that fact was interesting given the concept of needing to reach critical mass by having more new than old cells present. When I shared the twenty-one day process with a client in New York, she immediately referenced Dr. Gerald Epstein with whom she had worked, stating that Dr. Epstein's research indicates it takes twenty-one days to alter neurological programs. Other clients told me that Unity Church bases many of its prayers on a twenty-one day cycle, and Dr. Stephen Covey feels it takes twenty-one days to establish a new habit. I was impressed by the number of people confirming the effectiveness of twenty-one days.

I call my twenty-one day process a "transmutation of old patterns" because that is exactly what it does at a cellular level. You call forward the following facilitators to assist you and read the prayer request for twenty-one sequential days in order to shift your cellular memory from a mind to a heart orientation. *If you miss a day, you must begin at the beginning in order for the cellular shift to be effective.* I always tell people to place the prayer request where they are most likely to see it. For me, I leave it next to my toothbrush since I am absolutely sure that I will use my toothbrush every day. If I travel, I place it on the top of the contents of my luggage, and when I unpack, I put it next to my toothbrush. In order to make it easier to keep track of your progress, I have included boxes for you to check after reading the prayer request each day. I suggest you put the day of the week that you read the prayer request in each box so you can ensure you do not unwittingly skip a day. At the end of twenty-one days, your cellular memory will be repatterned to prioritize heart over mind energy.

TRANSMUTATION OF MIND PATTERN TO HEART PATTERN

- (SAY NAMES THREE TIMES EACH:) "Divine Creator, My Super-conscious Self, My Subconscious Self."
- (SAY:) "Please locate the origin of my habit of prioritizing the absorption and interpretation of emotional, mental, and spiritual information through my mind. Clear any discordant programs that my subconscious is running that support these habits via my thoughts, behavior, and emotional responses. Review my soul records in this and all other concepts of time, on this and all other dimensional and interdimensional levels, and update those soul records to reflect my release of this mode of being. Fill me with Divine Love, Light, and Truth, enabling me to hold correct perceptions. I accept and release every person, place and circumstance that led to my discordant habits. With total acceptance and unconditional love, I permanently release the old into the universal essence. In its place, I place the habit of prioritizing the absorption and interpretation of emotional, mental, and spiritual information through my heart. I allow every physical, emotional, mental, and spiritual problem and inappropriate behavior based on the old feeling to transmute into the new. I live in the energy of human being rather than human doing."
- (Say 3 Times:) "Thank you."

DAY 1	DAY 2	DAY 3	DAY 4	DAY 5	DAY 6	DAY 7
DAY 8	DAY 9	DAY 10	DAY 11	DAY 12	DAY 13	DAY 14
DAY 15	DAY 16	DAY 17	DAY 18	DAY 19	DAY 20	DAY 21

• • • • • • • • • • • •

Phase Five of DNA Recoding

RESTRUCTURING YOUR SPIRITUAL COMMITTEE

OPENING TO THE "ONE" LEVEL OF AWARENESS

YOUR PHYSICAL VERSUS SPIRITUAL ASPECT

Because our souls occupy a physical body, we often confuse who we are at a spiritual level with who we are at a physical level. We tend to judge ourselves harshly because the good intentions we set for ourselves are often compromised as we try to integrate our lofty intentions into our physical life. How many times have you said, "I will not sweat the small stuff. I will live each day fully and joyfully rather than allowing each and every bothersome situation to knock me off balance." Then you walk into your office and discover the hard drive on your computer has crashed, and your extreme dismay drives your spirits to such a low point that your day is ruined. Instead of responding as you intended, shrugging off the computer problem and enjoying the thought of reorganizing your complete files in spite of a difficult situation, you plunge into depression as you contemplate the days it will take you to rebuild your files.

Our list of supposed failures can be long. We do not fulfill our New Year's resolutions. We fight with our parents or our children when we intend to get along, despite our differences. We get angry at the blue-haired lady who is driving at fifteen miles per hour when we are trying to get to the airport on time. We promise to exercise or diet but cannot seem to stick to any regime. No matter how much we resolve to live a life that represents joy, peace, and love, we find there are numerous loopholes into which we fall as we make our way through each day.

However, our physical behavioral frailties may not be representative of our spiritual capacity. Anyone in physical form lives in a mass consciousness that affects the entire population. We may wish to represent joy, peace, and love, and we may frequently succeed. But we must project joy, peace, and love amidst a cosmic soup that represents all of the emotions and behaviors available to every human being. When you move into the upgraded energy of DNA Recoding after breaking polarity contracts in phase three of DNA Recoding, it certainly lessens the pull that you feel from the negativity that surrounds you. However, you still exist in a human energy that incorporates all possibilities on the Earth realm, both positive and negative.

In the instances when our human element overcomes our positive intentions, we are not necessarily less spiritual. We are simply acting out our physical drama that we signed up to play when we incarnated. There are certain limitations that are part of our physical make-up. However, these should not be misconstrued to represent our spiritual side. On the spiritual side, we have the capability to far exceed our human behavior. For example, all of us play more than the single role we know of ourselves in this incarnation. Just as I discovered the Lahaina aspect of myself, each of you has an oversoul that represents your spiritual essence. Each incarnation, of which you may have many occurring at the same time, is simply a small expression of the larger aspect of you. Therefore, you cannot gauge the extent of your spiritual side through the limited viewpoint you currently hold based on your physical life.

YOUR SPIRITUAL TEAM

You have the ability to tap into the full extent of your spiritual side through your superconscious or high self. Meditation and channeling are two methodologies that some people employ to create this hook-up to the superconscious, although there are many processes that enable superconscious connectivity. The method of hook-up is unique and personal to each of us. I had a client who could retrieve information from her superconscious on a waterbed and another who entered an altered state during her network chiropractic sessions, so do not limit yourself to thinking you need to meditate or channel to gain access to your superconscious.

Your superconscious is composed of many elements. First, it is composed of all of the experiences you have ever had, including past lives on the Earth plane, past lives in other dimensions, lifetimes in physical form, lifetimes in etheric form, and even lifetimes in forms unfamiliar to us on the Earth plane. You have a tremendous wealth of information comprised of all of these experiences that you personally encountered. Second, your superconscious consists of a team of non-physical beings who support you via their own experiences. This team is made up of guides, teachers, angels, masters, members of mystical soul societies like the Great White Brotherhood or the House of the Goddess, planetary councils, saviors, and so forth. All of you work with a spiritual team through your superconscious. This team is not static. It begins prior to birth with a rudimentary group and grows as you increase in spiritual awareness and require more information. Sometimes you even outgrow your spiritual counselors, and new ones join your group while the old ones work with less advanced souls.

After DNA Recoding, it is very important to ensure that you are working with the correct spiritual team. You will want to have the optimal number of players as well as the optimal players on your team. For example, if you have too much counsel, you may feel unfocused and unable to make a decision about where to take your life. If you are working with too few who do not represent areas in which you need information that you have not experienced yourself, you might need more counselors. Or if you have evolved past the point where the experience of certain members on your spiritual team can be helpful, you may need replacements.

HOW TO
RESTRUCTURE YOUR
SPIRITUAL TEAM

In order to create the optimal spiritual committee, you can make the following prayer request:

- (SAY THREE TIMES EACH:) "Divine Creator, My Superconscious Self, My Spiritual Committee."
- (SAY:) "I am formally requesting that you survey my current state of being with my recently acquired twelve-strand DNA energy and determine if I am working with the optimal spiritual committee. I ask that the following items be completed in support of this objective:
  - All additions to my spiritual team must be entities who work in the Light and are representative of the pure, positive energy embodied by the Divine Creator.
  - My spiritual committee is to be composed of the optimal number of members for the most efficient and effective operating.
  - Additions are to be made to my spiritual team of those who can assist me in obtaining my spiritual goals during this incarnation as well as during the process of ascension. I ask that the optimal match be made in accordance with my own energy and my spiritual objectives. I request that all new members always operate in concert with me, holding my intentions as their own.
  - Any member who is currently not in my highest good or unable to assist me at my newly evolved level is to be released now to work with someone better aligned with their energy.
  - A trigger mechanism is to be put in place that allows my spiritual committee to be altered as necessary, either because I have outgrown certain relationships,

the dynamics of the group energy is no longer efficient, or for any other reasons that might hinder my spiritual growth."
* (Say Three Times:) "Thank you."

If you use a pendulum, you might dowse to determine how many members of your spiritual team worked with you prior to requesting the restructuring. You can then check to determine how many members are on your team after the prayer request. I have counted anywhere from twenty to two hundred members when I have shared soul clearing information with my clients. If you are curious, you can also dowse to request the number of entities on your team by "group," for example, how many guides, archangels, masters, saviors, and so forth, are on your team. If you are familiar with specific names, e.g., Christ, Mohammed, Archangel Michael, Thoth, House of Ra, you can dowse to determine who is represented.

CLEARING YOU AND YOUR SPIRITUAL TEAM THROUGH THE ONE LEVEL

Now that you have requested the optimal team to support you in your spiritual endeavors, it is important that you clear your superconscious self and the consciousness of every member on your spiritual team through the highest conceivable level of awareness. Otherwise, you will be limited in terms of the information you can obtain. There are many different levels of psychism, some more evolved than others, and you want to ensure you are working with the most evolved. You also want to ensure your own spiritual capacity reaches to the furthest extent that it can.

There are many people who channel information from a host of non-physical beings because they assume that anyone in non-physical form will have access to more information than they do. Unfortunately, this is not true since, once you are cleared through the One level, you have access to all available information. When you invite non-physical entities to send you information, you open the door to any entity that wants to talk to you. These entities can be benign yet uninformed, for example your Uncle

Joe who recently died. Uncle Joe may have been a nice guy, but he really did not have many answers for his own life when he was alive, and he may not be a source of highly evolved information. These entities can also be malicious and evil, such as a demon who presents itself as a helper to gain confidence, then begins to provide advice that undermines the success in your life.

I have made it a practice to work only through my own superconscious and my own spiritual committee. Otherwise, I am opening the door to any entity that wishes to talk to me. When someone asks me to channel their guides, even if they are a positive soul, I tell them I will be happy to gain information by having "my guys" talk to "their guys." This way, I am always assured of remaining clear and accessing the highest levels of information possible.

To ensure you are operating at peak spiritual performance, you will want to clear yourself and your spiritual committee through the One level. The One level represents all that there is on every dimension, in every aspect of creation, and in every concept of time. When you clear yourself to access the One level, you are obtaining information at the source of the Divine Creator. It cannot get much better than that!

OPENING TO
THE ONE LEVEL
OF AWARENESS

In order to open yourself and your spiritual committee through the One level, you can make the following prayer request. You can also repeat the prayer request each day if you wish to ensure that you and your spiritual team remain clear and continue to have access to the One level.

- (SAY THREE TIMES EACH:) "Divine Creator, My Superconscious Self, My Spiritual Committee."
- (SAY:) "Please clear me and my spiritual committee through the One level so that we may have access to the highest conceivable level of spiritual thought. Clear all barriers and blockages that I and my spiritual committee have ever created that obstruct access to the One Level. Place me in full alignment to pure positive perfection and Divine Union."
- (SAY THREE TIMES:) "Thank you."

ABOUT
THE AUTHOR

ANNE BREWER writes and teaches about identifying and removing barriers to personal growth. Through her company, InterLink, Anne works with people from around the world who wish to experience more health, wealth, and happiness. She also continues to act as President of her marketing consulting company, working with a variety of Fortune 500 corporations on consumer-related sales and marketing strategies. When she is not traveling on business, she enjoys her life in Prairie Village, Kansas, with her loving mate, David (Beaulieu), and her son, Drew.

Anne's channeled articles frequently appear in such metaphysical publications as *The Sedona Journal of Emergence*, *Pathfinder*, and *The Edge*. Her first book, *The Power of Twelve, Achieving 12-Strand DNA Consciousness*, was completed in 1996 and rewritten in 1999, and it provides instruction on how to increase personal power through expanded consciousness. Her second book, *Breaking Free To Health, Wealth and Happiness, 100s of Powerful Ways to Release Limiting Beliefs*, was published in 1999. She has been honored to apprentice with nationally reputed healers and continues to expand her knowledge through ongoing education with metaphysical teachers and her own guides.

To contact Anne Brewer for a personal appointment or to schedule a workshop:

INTERLINK
5252 W. 67th Street
Prairie Village, KS 66208
913/722-5498 (voice)
913/722-5498 (fax)
www.annebrewer.com
interlnk@qni.com

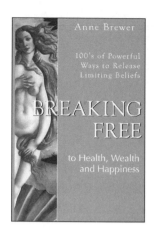

BREAKING FREE TO HEALTH, WEALTH AND HAPPINESS

100's OF POWERFUL WAYS TO RELEASE LIMITING BELIEFS

by Anne Brewer

Publisher: Sunstar Publishing Ltd.
ISBN 1-887472-59-2
Price: $15.95

Chock full of powerful suggestions, meditations, and healing practices, this book contributes profoundly to bringing joy into our experience.

Breaking Free to Health, Wealth and Happiness is a collection of healing modalities designed to help quickly heal serious issues at the soul level so you can break free to create your dreams. Anne Brewer skillfully identifies common life issues and presents ways to repattern your responses in order to connect with the outcomes you truly want. Her solid background as a corporate business-woman gives her work a well-grounded and practical outlook that is rare in metaphysical teachings. The book contains adventures in imagery, aromatherapy, creativity building, energy exchanging and clearing, and sensuality to identify limiting beliefs and transform them into positive realities. It covers the areas of well-being, relationships, purpose, wealth, spirituality, and new age insights.

INTERLINK PRODUCTS

HOW TO USE A PENDULUM, A SIMPLE COURSE IN DOWSING

If you wish to enhance your telepathic skills, you can begin the process by learning to dowse with a pendulum. Skilled dowsers can obtain a wide range of information, for example which vitamin and mineral supplements are necessary for good health and what is the optimal dose, the location of missing house keys, and information from spirit guides.
(15 pages, spiral bound)
$10.00 + $1.95 shipping

BRASS PENDULUM

Handmade pendulums by Joe Smith of the Kansas City Dowsing Society. Joe's pendulums are well-balanced due to a combination of his craft and the love he infuses into his pendulums.
(Glass pendulums are also available for $10.00)
$20.00 + $1.95 shipping

INCREASING ABUNDANCE

Does abundance elude you? Do you utilize positive affirmations in an attempt to get what you want but encounter very little success? Do you wonder why other people have the perfect job, a great mate, a terrific family, and good health while you struggle to feel satisfied with your life? When you align your expectations to anticipate abundance and come up empty, there are usually blocks at the subconscious and superconscious levels that create barriers to physical plenitude, be it health, wealth, or happiness. Those blocks can come from previous lifetimes where you made soul commitments to poverty or chastity, harsh life lessons in past

lives that cause you to undermine your abundance due to guilt or shame, or programs in the collective unconscious that make you feel undeserving on a subconscious level. Learn what blocks exist and how to clear them.
(4 hours of taped information plus written materials)
$40.00 + $4.95 shipping

FIND YOUR PERFECT MATE

Are you still searching for your partner? You may have barriers that inhibit your ability to meet him or her. For example, did you know most people only resonate at 60% (or less) conviction that their true love exists? How can you expect to find your mate without total belief in their existence? Plus, there are many additional barriers that might be preventing you from connecting. Learn your blockages toward finding your true love and clear them. Anne Brewer has based this course on her true life story in which she found her perfect mate and husband, David, in a three-month time period without leaving home. Human beings were not intended to live in solitary situations since we are innately communal beings. There really is another person with whom you were intended to share your life. You simply need to learn the techniques for finding them.
(5 hours of taped information plus written materials)
$50.00 + $4.95 shipping

HARMONIOUS RELATIONSHIPS

How many times did you observe the friction between your parents and say, "That won't happen to me when I get married." Yet, after you found your true love and lived together awhile, disharmony started to develop. Or maybe, after experiencing an unsuccessful relationship, you have decided it's not worth the effort to get involved again. Or perhaps you have never entered a relationship because you believe all relationships sour with time. Relationships can be joyful, harmonious, and uplifting as long as the energy between two people is mutually compatible. Learn about the types of energy patterns that disrupt relationships and how to clear them. Clear soul level barriers that interfere with experiencing resonance with a partner. It is much easier to maintain a positive intimate alliance when the energy supports it. This course is recommended for both singles and couples who desire a harmonious relationship.
(5 hours of taped information plus written materials)
$50.00 + $4.95 shipping

Releasing Soul Barriers to Health, Wealth and Happiness, Level One Soul Clearing

Are you continually stuck in a particular mind-set that doesn't do a thing for you? The following notions are examples of beliefs held by so many people that we no longer question them: "It's hard to make ends meet" or "A good relationship is difficult to find." If any of these sound familiar to you, join Anne to discover how she removes barriers that are blocking your ability to live a rich, full life. Many people focus on healing their emotional, mental, and physical problems but overlook commit ments made at the soul level. Soul contracts and experiences from this and/or prior lifetimes may conflict with your current life plan. Understand how experiences in this life or past lives can inhibit you from health, wealth, and happiness. Learn how to use a pendulum and some clearing techniques that you can use. If you are in a continuous cycle of unpleasant lessons, this class is a must.

(7 hours of taped information plus written materials; 2-hour introductory tape available for $15.00 + $2.95 shipping)
$75.00 + $4.95 shipping

The Power of Twelve, A New Approach to Personal Empowerment

Anne Brewer's remarkable true story of her DNA Recoding is of great assistance to all who desire to achieve full evolutionary potential. This tape series accompanies her book, expanding upon the Niburian's involvement in the *Homo sapiens* speedy development and adding personal information about Anne's life and her experiences with DNA Recoding that occurred subsequent to publishing *The Power of Twelve*. The first step-by-step process of its kind, Anne outlines the empowering and approachable process of DNA Recording. You follow her exponential growth as she embraces her new capacity for high level functioning, including greatly psychic abilities. As she releases debilitating emotions of fear and guilt and learns to manifest her desired financial goals, her report becomes a love story where she finds and meets her perfect mate. This is a story of fulfillment of soul purpose that all of you can partake.

(6 hours of taped information plus written materials)
$50.00 + $4.95 shipping

BREAKING FREE TO HEALTH, WEALTH AND HAPPINESS

A collection of healing modalities designed to help quickly heal serious issues at the soul level so you can break free to create your dreams. Anne skillfully identifies common life issues and presents ways to repattern your responses in order to connect with the outcomes you truly want. Contains adventures in imagery, aromatherapy, creativity building, energy exchanging and clearing, and sensuality to identify limiting beliefs and transform them into positive realities. Covers the areas of well-being, relationships, purpose, wealth, spirituality, and new age insights.

(243 pages, paperback; also available at book stores)
$15.95 + $3.95 shipping